Nuclear Reactions

A VOLUME IN THE SERIES

Cornell Studies in Security Affairs

Edited by Robert J. Art, Robert Jervis, and Stephen M. Walt

A list of titles in this series is available at cornellpress.cornell.edu.

Nuclear Reactions

How Nuclear-Armed States Behave

Mark S. Bell

Cornell University Press

Ithaca and London

First published 2021 by Cornell University Press

Library of Congress Cataloging-in-Publication Data

Names: Bell, Mark (Researcher), author.
Title: Nuclear reactions : how nuclear-armed states behave /
    Mark S. Bell.
Description: Ithaca [New York] : Cornell University Press, 2021. |
    Series: Cornell studies in security affairs | Includes bibliographical
    references and index.
Identifiers: LCCN 2020036416 (print) | LCCN 2020036417 (ebook) |
    ISBN 9781501754166 (paperback) | ISBN 9781501754173 (pdf) |
    ISBN 9781501754180 (epub)
Subjects: LCSH: Nuclear weapons—Political aspects. | International
    relations. | World politics. | Balance of power.
Classification: LCC JZ5665 .B44 2021 (print) | LCC JZ5665 (ebook) |
    DDC 327.1/12—dc23
LC record available at https://lccn.loc.gov/2020036416
LC ebook record available at https://lccn.loc.gov/2020036417

For Rowan

Contents

Illustrations

Acknowledgments

This book would not have been started, let alone finished, without a great many people.

While I was an undergraduate at Oxford, Nigel Bowles and Paul Martin encouraged my interest in the academic study of politics. I would not have considered pursuing graduate studies in political science (let alone actually done so) without their influence or advice. At Harvard Kennedy School, where I spent two years getting a masters in public policy while also coming to the conclusion that I wanted a career in academia rather than in policy, Matt Bunn inspired the interest in nuclear issues that motivated me to pursue a PhD and that sustained this entire project.

At MIT, I could not have asked for better advisers. Barry Posen engaged with every nut and bolt of the argument in this book and offered line-by-line comments on multiple iterations of the work. The quality and impact of his scholarship is a model that I will only ever aspire to meet; his demand that scholars tackle important questions is one I will continue to seek to live up to. Vipin Narang's mentorship and advice were critical, and he continues to be a first port of call for advice on negotiating academia. Taylor Fravel's suggestions substantially increased the clarity of the argument and writing throughout, and his questions and comments have consistently cut to core theoretical and empirical issues. Last but not least, the intellectual influence of Frank Gavin runs throughout this book. His commitment to bringing historians and political scientists together has had a profound influence on my own work. Collectively, these individuals provided a level of expertise on nuclear issues that would have been impossible to assemble at almost any other institution, but the personal support and advice they provided at every turn have perhaps been even more valuable.

Similarly, the tight-knit community of graduate students and the predoctoral and postdoctoral fellows at MIT provided intellectual stimulation, encouragement, and friendship. Among many others, Dan Altman, Noel Anderson, Paul Avey, Chris Clary, James Conran, Fiona Cunningham, Gene Gerzhoy, Brendan Rittenhouse Green, Brian Haggerty, Peter Krause, Julia Macdonald, Tim McDonnell, Nicholas Miller, Rohan Mukherjee, Reid Pauly, Josh Shifrinson, Peter Swartz, Joseph Torigian, Rachel Whitlark, Alec Worsnop, and Yiqing Xu deserve particular thanks.

Many other scholars generously gave their time, advice, and comments at various stages in the process. They include William Boettscher, Hal Brands, Målfrid Braut-Hegghammer, Matthew Bunn, James Cameron, Andrew Coe, Alex Downes, Peter Feaver, Matthew Fuhrmann, Charlie Glaser, Ryan Grauer, Kelly Greenhill, David Holloway, Jacques Hymans, Peter Katzenstein, Peter Krause, Matthew Kroenig, Keir Lieber, Sean Lynn-Jones, Marty Malin, Rupal Mehta, Alex Montgomery, Steve Miller, Rich Nielsen, Benoît Pelopidas, Evan Perkoski, Mike Poznansky, Brad Roberts, Sebastian Rosato, Joshua Rovner, Scott Sagan, Rob Schub, Todd Sechser, Keith Shimko, Etel Solingen, Caitlin Talmadge, Nina Tannenwald, Monica Toft, Stephen Van Evera, Anna-Mart Van Wyk, Jane Vaynman, Stephen Walt, Nicholas Wheeler, and Cat Worsnop.

This book was completed at the University of Minnesota, which has proved to be a wonderfully supportive intellectual home. I have benefited hugely from the insights, advice, friendship, and support of many colleagues, including Cosette Creamer, Bud Duvall, Paul Goren, James Hollyer, Tanisha Fazal, John Freeman, Helen Kinsella, Ron Krebs, Howie Lavine, Dan Myers, Rob Nichols, Kathryn Pearson, Michelle Phelps, David Samuels, Jane Sumner, and Josef Woldense. The Political Science Department provided the resources that enabled me to host a book workshop in November 2017, at which Hal Brands, Scott Sagan, Etel Solingen, and Nina Tannenwald, along with Bud, Ron, and Nisha, both took the book apart and provided a path forward to put it back together. Jen Spindel took notes throughout, and her forty-page summary of all the suggestions made was enormously helpful as I reconstructed and redrafted the manuscript. Thanks are also due to two undergraduate students, Cheyenne Tretter, who provided exceptional research and editorial assistance at several different stages, and Josh Mohling, who copyedited the entire manuscript.

In addition to the MIT Political Science Department and Security Studies Program, and the University of Minnesota's Political Science Department and College of Liberal Arts, generous financial support for this project was provided by the Harvard Belfer Center's International Security Program and Project on Managing the Atom, the Smith Richardson Foundation, and the Tobin Project. The staff at all these institutions, including, among others, Susan Twarog, Joli Divon Saraf, Casey Johnson, Diana Gallagher, Josh Anderson, Susan Lynch, Alexis Cuttance, Tia Phan, Kyle Edwards, and Sara

Flannery, provided administrative support that was a model of efficiency and allowed me to focus on research.

At Cornell University Press, Roger Haydon has diligently and patiently handled my queries throughout the review and publication process, and I also thank the reviewers and editors of the Security Affairs series for their thoughtful and incisive comments on the manuscript. Amron Gravett compiled the index and Mike Bechthold produced the map in chapter 3. Portions of this book draw on previously published articles in *International Security* and *Journal of Strategic Studies*.[1] I thank MIT Press and Taylor and Francis for the permission to reprint this content.

My deepest debts are those nearest to home. My family has been encouraging, inspiring, caring, and loving. My brother and sister have supported me even though I have been mostly absent and have seen them far less than I would want over the past few years. My parents have encouraged me unconditionally at every turn despite my being so far from home. They inspired my love of learning and intellectual curiosity about the world and are models of parenting. I am more grateful than they know for everything they have done for me, and I will keep trying to make them proud. It seems deeply inadequate that I can only offer them my gratitude.

Sarah's love, commitment, and support have been unyielding. I could not ask for a better partner. Her loyalty, compassion, and understanding have made me a better person. Our daughter Rowan arrived with impeccable timing the day after I submitted the manuscript to Cornell for review, and she has transformed and enriched our lives in more ways than I can describe. This book is dedicated to her.

Abbreviations

AIOC	Anglo-Iranian Oil Company
ANC	African National Congress
ANZUS	Australia, New Zealand, United States Security Treaty
APOC	Anglo-Persian Oil Company
ARAMCO	Arabian American Oil Company
ASEAN	Association of Southeast Asian Nations
BDEE	British Documents on the End of Empire
CENTO	Central Treaty Organization
CHUR	Churchill Archives, Cambridge, United Kingdom
CIA	Central Intelligence Agency
CIAA	US Central Intelligence Agency Archives
CINC	Composite Index of National Capabilities
DIRCO	South Africa Department of International Relations and Co-operation Archives, Pretoria, South Africa
DNSA	Digital National Security Archive
FAPLA	People's Armed Forces for the Liberation of Angola
FRUS	Foreign Relations of the United States
GDP	gross domestic product
GNP	gross national product
HEU	highly enriched uranium
ICBM	intercontinental ballistic missile
IMF	International Monetary Fund
IRBM	intermediate range ballistic missile
JCS	Joint Chiefs of Staff
MID	militarized interstate dispute
MK	Umkhonte we Sizwe

MOD	United Kingdom Ministry of Defence
MPLA	Popular Movement for the Liberation of Angola
NATO	North Atlantic Treaty Organization
NATOSD	NATO Strategy Documents
NIC	National Identity Conception
NPT	Treaty on the Nonproliferation of Nuclear Weapons
NSA	National Security Archive
NSC	National Security Council
OAU	Organisation of African Unity
OPC	Office of Policy Coordination
PLAN	People's Liberation Army of Namibia
PPPUS	Public Papers of the Presidents of the United States
PRC	People's Republic of China
RAF	Royal Air Force
REAG	Reagan Presidential Library, Simi Valley, California
SADF	South African Defence Force
SEATO	South East Asia Treaty Organization
SWAPO	South West African People's Organization
TRUM	Truman Presidential Library, Independence, Missouri
UKHoP	Records of the United Kingdom Houses of Parliament (Hansard)
UKNA	United Kingdom National Archives, Kew, United Kingdom
UN	United Nations
UNITA	National Union for the Total Independence of Angola
USSR	Union of Soviet Socialist Republics
WWCDA	Woodrow Wilson Center Digital Archive

Nuclear Reactions

Introduction

How Do New Nuclear States Behave?

In 1963, a US National Intelligence Estimate attempted to assess how China's foreign policy would change if it acquired nuclear weapons.[1] One paragraph offered a sanguine assessment, arguing that it was unlikely that "the acquisition of a limited nuclear weapons capability would produce major changes in Communist China's foreign policy." The very next paragraph, however, argued that nuclear weapons would affect Chinese foreign policy in important ways, stating that "the Chinese would feel very much stronger [if they acquired nuclear weapons] and this mood would doubtless be reflected in their approach to conflicts on their periphery. . . . The tone of Chinese policy would probably become more assertive." This contradiction did not go unnoticed: a footnote inserted by the acting director of intelligence and research declared that these two statements were "somewhat inconsistent" with each other. Today, policymakers engage in similar debates about newly nuclear states and other states that may acquire nuclear weapons in the future. How do North Korea's nuclear weapons influence its foreign policy today? How might Iran behave if it were to acquire nuclear weapons? How about Saudi Arabia? If US allies such as South Korea or Japan were to acquire nuclear weapons in the future, how would their foreign policy toward the United States change?

The answers to these questions matter greatly. Devising policies or strategies to deal with new nuclear-armed states hinges on understanding how they are likely to behave after acquiring nuclear weapons. A state that is likely to use nuclear weapons to engage in aggression demands different political and military strategies from the United States and the international community than if nuclear acquisition is likely to make the state more peaceful. More broadly, determining the political, economic, or military costs that countries should be prepared to pay to prevent nuclear proliferation hinges on assessing how nuclear weapons affect the behavior of the states that acquire them and how dangerous those effects are. If states typically expand

1

their interests in world politics or act more belligerently after acquiring nuclear weapons, preventing nuclear acquisition should be a higher priority than if nuclear weapons do not much affect the foreign policies of the states that acquire them.

This book seeks to answer these questions. Despite their importance, there is little consensus among scholars or analysts about the answers to them. For example, how would Iran's foreign policies change if it acquired nuclear weapons? Some argue that nuclear weapons would embolden Iran to increase its support for proxy or terrorist groups and that it would use nuclear weapons to coerce and intimidate other states in the region.[2] Others are more relaxed, arguing that Iran's power within the Middle East would remain largely unchanged if it acquired nuclear weapons, and that Iranian efforts at nuclear coercion would be unlikely to work.[3] Indeed, disagreements about these questions are unsurprising given the variety of ways that states have historically used nuclear weapons to pursue their political goals. For example, consider the case of Pakistan. By threatening the early use of nuclear weapons in any conflict, Pakistan has used nuclear weapons as a shield to deter Indian retaliation, enabling Pakistan to pursue low-level aggression and subversion against India with the goal of achieving long-standing revisionist goals in Kashmir and elsewhere.[4] By contrast, the United Kingdom used nuclear weapons very differently when it acquired them in the 1950s. As I discuss in detail in chapter 3, instead of engaging in aggression, Britain used nuclear weapons to try to hold on to what it had: to reassure allies that were increasingly skeptical of Britain's ability to come to their aid, to resist challenges to its position, and to act more independently of the United States. Or consider the United States. In the aftermath of World War II, with the international system in profound flux, a newly nuclear United States put in place a globe-spanning network of alliances and military bases wholly at odds with its prior history of avoiding entangling alliances and staying out of European conflicts. Nuclear weapons allowed the United States to expand its commitments while simultaneously demobilizing its armed forces after World War II. With its nuclear arsenal, the United States could maintain (and take on) alliance commitments around the world without deploying the conventional military forces that would previously have been needed to make such commitments credible. These three states, in very different strategic environments, used nuclear weapons in very different ways to advance very different foreign policy goals. Can we explain this variation in the historical record?

Existing Explanations

What do we currently know about how states change their foreign policy when they acquire nuclear weapons? Unfortunately, existing explanations do not get us very far. The most prominent and elegant account of how nuclear weapons affect international politics is the theory of the nuclear revolution. While different scholars offer somewhat different interpretations of the nuclear revolution, the core argument is that nuclear weapons and the condition of mutual assured destruction transform the nature of international politics.[5] The theory of the nuclear revolution was designed to apply to the interactions between states with secure second-strike capabilities and did not, therefore, directly seek to explain the foreign policies of nuclear-armed states more broadly. Despite this, the logic of the theory, and the mechanisms it identifies, means that the theory contains within it important insights and implications for how states should use nuclear weapons within their foreign policies.

First, theorists of the nuclear revolution argue that nuclear weapons make states more secure. The scale of destruction that nuclear weapons can inflict, the relative ease with which states can secure the ability to strike back after an initial attack (that is, achieve a second-strike capability), and the impossibility of defending against a nuclear attack mean that nuclear weapons offer a powerful deterrent against the most important security threats that states face: invasion or other major attacks.[6] Not only are they excellent tools of deterrence, but theorists of the nuclear revolution argue that nuclear weapons do not offer equivalent offensive benefits to the states that possess them. As a result, nuclear weapons tilt the advantage away from the offense and toward the defense: they "give defenders a large advantage"[7] and "created a revolution for defense advantage."[8] In short, nuclear weapons are primarily (and perhaps exclusively) defensive weapons.

However, the claim that nuclear weapons deter other states does not by itself answer how nuclear weapons affect the foreign policy of the state acquiring nuclear weapons. If nuclear weapons provide deterrent or defensive benefits, how do the states that acquire nuclear weapons respond to that additional security? Theorists of the nuclear revolution tend to make a political judgment about how states should respond to the additional security provided by the deterrent effect of nuclear weapons. Because security is the first goal of states living in an anarchic international system in which they must fend for themselves and insecurity is a core driver of the more belligerent actions that states take in international politics, nuclear weapons should make states less inclined to compete for security, power, or allies or to engage in belligerent or aggressive foreign policies.[9] Thus, although the theory of the nuclear revolution primarily seeks to explain how nuclear-armed states should engage *with each other*, rather than how nuclear-armed states should behave more broadly, the theory does imply that nuclear-armed states should be generally more peaceful because nuclear weapons solve their core security needs. States with secure second-strike capabilities simply do not need to engage in provocative or belligerent behavior to secure territory, resources, or alliances or improve the conventional balance of power. For advocates of the nuclear revolution, for example, nuclear weapons "provide [states] with security and reduce their incentives to wage war in the quest for security."[10] They "should allow the super-powers to take a more relaxed attitude toward events in third areas, including the [nonnuclear] third world," meaning that "it makes less sense to fight to control or destroy bases, territory, or military or economic resources."[11] Similarly, states with secure second-strike capabilities should not worry about competing for allies: "In the nuclear era, security is provided by second-strike capability; defections by allies are therefore less damaging," or, more bluntly, "nuclear weapons make alliances obsolete."[12]

Ultimately, the powerful conclusion of the theory of the nuclear revolution is that a nuclear-armed world is safer and more peaceful than one in which conventionally armed states must compete for security at every turn: nuclear weapons reduce or even "eliminate the security dilemma" that drives distrust among states seeking only to defend themselves;[13] "reduce the extent of the gains one can seek" in international politics;[14] make the status quo "relatively easy to maintain";[15] reduce the importance of the conventional military balance and the incentives for arms races;[16] "clear the fog of war" and "lower false optimism" about the outcomes of wars, thus reducing the possibility of miscalculation;[17] and "make states more cautious."[18]

Although it offers a powerful explanation for the absence of great power war in the nuclear era, the theory of the nuclear revolution does not get us very far in explaining how states change their foreign policies when they acquire nuclear weapons. Most importantly, the theory makes a single, powerful prediction, and it therefore implies that nuclear weapons should have the same effect on all states that possess them. However, as discussed above, when we look at the historical record, there is considerable variation in how states have changed their foreign policies after acquiring nuclear weapons. The theory of the nuclear revolution cannot explain this variation. Further, even advocates of this theory acknowledge that states have often not behaved according to its prescriptions. Robert Jervis, for example, describes US nuclear strategy as "illogical" because it "seeks to repeal the nuclear revolution rather than coming to grips with [it]," while Charles Glaser and Steve Fetter argue that US Cold War nuclear strategy "diverg[ed] significantly from the policies implied by the powerful logic of the nuclear revolution."[19]

Other theories also fail to explain the variation we see in the historical record for a different reason: they focus on explaining a single foreign policy behavior that nuclear weapons can facilitate. In particular, scholars have examined when nuclear acquisition leads to conventional military aggression. Most prominently, S. Paul Kapur argues that conventional aggression should be expected when conventionally weak states with revisionist preferences acquire nuclear weapons, because nuclear weapons provide a shield behind which revisionist states can pursue long-held territorial or other ambitions with limited fear of retaliation.[20] This work, although of great importance, focuses only on explaining aggression and therefore does not offer a full explanation of how nuclear acquisition affects a state's foreign policies. For example, Kapur does not make an explicit argument about the outcomes we should observe when conventionally powerful or status quo states acquire nuclear weapons, or whether weak, revisionist states will use nuclear weapons only to facilitate aggression.

Neither the theory of the nuclear revolution nor theories that explain when states use nuclear weapons to engage in aggression can explain the full variation we see in the historical record. The divergent ways in which states have used nuclear weapons to facilitate different foreign policy goals remain in need of an explanation.

The Argument

This book argues that nuclear weapons can facilitate a broad range of foreign policy behaviors that states may find attractive, and specifies when states are likely to use nuclear weapons to facilitate different combinations of these behaviors.

What are the foreign policy behaviors that nuclear weapons can facilitate? First, nuclear weapons can facilitate *aggression*: the more belligerent pursuit of goals in preexisting disputes or in pursuit of previously defined interests. Second, nuclear weapons can facilitate *expansion*: the *widening* of a state's goals in international politics (including the initiation of new alliance relationships or new adversarial relationships). Third, nuclear weapons can facilitate *independence*: taking actions that an ally opposes or does not support. Fourth, nuclear weapons may facilitate *bolstering*: taking actions to increase the strength of an alliance, alliance partner, or friend. Fifth, nuclear weapons can facilitate *steadfastness*: a reduced inclination to back down in disputes or in response to coercion, and an increased willingness to defend the status quo. Finally, nuclear weapons can facilitate *compromise*: accepting less in preexisting disputes. These behaviors are not mutually exclusive: a state may engage in different combinations of these behaviors and may direct distinct foreign policy behaviors toward different states. And while some behaviors do not fit easily into these categories, they provide a useful starting point to begin thinking about the varying ways that nuclear weapons can affect the foreign policies of the states that acquire them.

While nuclear weapons can facilitate each of these behaviors, different states use nuclear weapons to facilitate different combinations of these behaviors. I offer a theory that helps explain this variation: the theory of "nuclear opportunism."[21] I argue that states exist in different strategic circumstances and therefore have different political priorities. These different priorities make different behaviors more or less attractive to each state. As a result, states use nuclear weapons to facilitate different foreign policy behaviors after acquisition. For example, some states may use nuclear acquisition to facilitate aggression, while others may use nuclear weapons to bolster allies or pursue independence from an ally. According to the theory, states use nuclear weapons in an opportunistic way to improve their position in international politics and to help them achieve political goals that the state cares about. And it is the strategic situation or circumstances in which a state finds itself that determine the particular goals and behaviors a state will find attractive. Nuclear weapons, therefore, allow states to pursue their preexisting political goals with greater freedom.

The theory, shown in figure 0.1, is structured as a "decision tree" of three factors that describe the state's position in the international system and shed light on its political priorities: first, the existence of serious territorial threats or an ongoing war; second, the existence of a senior ally that provides for the state's security; third, whether a state is increasing or decreasing in relative power. This is not to suggest that other factors are of no importance—any theory is necessarily a simplification of a more complex reality. However, a simple theory makes testing the theory easier and provides a foundation that future work can build on.

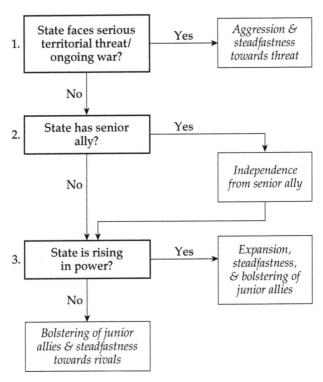

Figure 0.1. The theory of nuclear opportunism

The first variable in the tree is whether the state faces severe territorial threats or is engaged in an ongoing war. This variable comes first because it represents the most binding security environment a state can face. States in this position have little room to maneuver: their political priority must be to improve their position against the source of the threat or in the war they are engaged in, and they are likely to try to use nuclear weapons for this purpose. As a result, such states tend to use nuclear weapons to facilitate aggression and steadfastness—two behaviors that directly improve the state's position against its adversary.

For states not facing such threats, their geopolitical environment grants them greater latitude. Such states are not forced to use their nuclear weapons exclusively to improve their position vis-à-vis a primary threat and can afford to use nuclear weapons to improve their position in other ways. The second variable is whether the state has a senior ally that provides for its security. For states in this position, reducing their dependence on the senior ally is desirable, and their relative security allows them to do so. These states are likely to use nuclear weapons to facilitate independence from their senior ally.

The third variable—whether the state is rising in power—conditions the additional ways in which states in permissive security environments are likely to change their foreign policies after acquiring nuclear weapons. Secure, rising states often look to expand their influence in international politics, and so using nuclear weapons to facilitate expansion will therefore be attractive. Using nuclear weapons to stand more firmly in defense of the status quo and to bolster the state's existing allies are also likely to be attractive, as the state seeks to widen its ability to project power and influence. For states that are secure but not rising in power, expansion is less attractive. Indeed, even holding on to what the state already has may be challenging for declining states. However, nuclear weapons can help states in this position by facilitating the bolstering of allies and steadfastness in the face of challenges.

The theory of nuclear opportunism offers a different vision of nuclear weapons from that of the theory of the nuclear revolution. In particular, it makes a different judgment about how states respond to the security that nuclear weapons provide. Nuclear weapons do not cause states to worry less about their own security, reduce states' inclination to compete with each other, or cause states to stop trying to improve their position in international politics. Instead, states use nuclear weapons in service of their preexisting political goals and find nuclear weapons useful in pursuit of those goals. Nuclear weapons, in short, do not transform state preferences or international politics. Instead, they are incorporated into the practice of international politics.

To test the theory, I examine three cases: the United Kingdom, South Africa, and the United States. Each case represents a hard test for the theory and offers direct evidence about the process and mechanisms through which nuclear weapons affected each state's foreign policy. I look for changes in foreign policy behavior that occur at the point of nuclear acquisition, and then try to assess whether nuclear weapons caused the changes observed. Each case study relies on evidence drawn from multiple archives, and the South African case also draws on interviews with retired military and political elites. In each case, I test the theory both on its own merits and against alternative explanations.

Britain faced no serious territorial threats, had a senior ally that provided for its security (the United States), and was declining in relative power. As the theory of nuclear opportunism would suggest, Britain did not use its nuclear weapons to facilitate aggression, expansion, or compromise. Instead, Britain's political priorities were to maintain its position in the world and reduce its dependence on the United States. Britain, therefore, used nuclear weapons to bolster existing junior allies in Asia, the Middle East, and in Europe. Britain also became more comfortable responding more steadfastly to challenges to its position, and paying less attention to the preferences of the United States (that is, acting more independently) in doing so.

Similarly, I argue that South Africa's foreign policy changed in ways that are largely consistent with the theory of nuclear opportunism. When it acquired nuclear weapons in the late 1970s, apartheid South Africa was engaged in a war in Angola and faced potential Soviet intervention, further Cuban intervention, and Angolan forces that threatened South African territory and amplified the internal threats the regime faced. South Africa's political priority was to improve its position in the conflict, and it used nuclear weapons to become more aggressive. Nuclear weapons facilitated this behavior by giving South Africa an extra source of leverage to prevent Soviet intervention in the conflict and thus reduced the risks of engaging in aggression.

The theory of nuclear opportunism also performs well in explaining US behavior. Nuclear acquisition affected US foreign policy very differently during World War II and in its aftermath. Fighting a brutal war in Europe and the Pacific when it initiated the Manhattan Project to acquire nuclear weapons, the United States first used nuclear weapons to engage in direct aggression against the Japanese, as would be expected. However, there are also ways in which US nuclear weapons facilitated compromise and independence from the Soviet Union during the final days of the war, which diverge from the expectations of the theory. In the aftermath of World War II, the situation facing the United States changed significantly: the United States no longer faced serious threats and was rising in power. The complexity of the immediate postwar world makes evaluating the predictions of the theory challenging. Nonetheless, I argue that the United States used nuclear weapons to facilitate the bolstering of allies, as well as behaviors that combined elements of steadfastness, expansion, and aggression.

Overall, while the theory of nuclear opportunism does not perform perfectly, it offers important insights into the way in which states change their foreign policy when they acquire nuclear weapons, and outperforms existing explanations.

Nuclear Opportunism

How States Use Nuclear Weapons in International Politics

This chapter offers a theory that allows us to understand the way nuclear weapons affect the foreign policy of the states that acquire them. Foreign policy is the portion of grand strategy that deals with a state's relationships with other states. If grand strategy is the collection of means and ends with which a state attempts to achieve its goals in international politics, then foreign policy is the collection of means and ends with which a state pursues its goals with respect to a given other state.[1] Foreign policy does not therefore simply refer to the day-to-day conduct of a nation's diplomats, and is not the sole preserve of the governmental institution tasked with conducting bilateral diplomacy (for example, the British Foreign and Commonwealth Office or the US State Department). The definition of foreign policy used throughout this book includes a state's goals with respect to other states, the strategies it uses to pursue them, and the resources it dedicates to pursuing them. Importantly, foreign policy is dyadic, because a state may have very different foreign policies toward different other states. Thus, a state has a foreign policy toward a particular other state, rather than having a single foreign policy writ large. Nuclear weapons, for example, may affect China's foreign policy toward Pakistan differently from how they affect China's relationship with the United States.

The theory I offer argues that the acquisition of nuclear weapons can facilitate (that is, reduce the expected costs of) a range of foreign policy behaviors. In particular, I focus on six foreign policy behaviors that nuclear weapons can facilitate: independence, bolstering, aggression, expansion, steadfastness, and compromise. However, not all states use nuclear weapons to facilitate all of these behaviors. The crux of the theory is that different states find different combinations of these behaviors attractive depending on the strategic circumstances in which the state finds itself. In particular, the nature of the threats the state faces, its position within its alliances, and whether it is increasing or decreasing in relative power all affect which combinations of these behaviors the acquiring state finds attractive, and therefore which foreign policy behaviors the state will use nuclear weapons to facilitate. States incorporate nuclear weapons into the calculations they make about what they can achieve (and what they can get away with) in international politics, and direct nuclear weapons to purposes that the state considers useful. Nuclear weapons, in this view, are useful to the states that possess them, but they are not silver bullets that grant states free rein in international politics. I label my theory, and the view of nuclear weapons it implies, as "nuclear opportunism." The theory emphasizes that states seek to use their nuclear weapons to improve their position in international politics and that the circumstances in which a state finds itself determine the way in which it will use its nuclear weapons to do so.

This view of nuclear weapons is in contrast to the theory of the nuclear revolution. The theory of the nuclear revolution predicts that by resolving a state's fundamental security needs, nuclear weapons mean states have less need to compete and thus transform the nature of international politics. However, the political goals and concerns that states have do not end even if their security has been guaranteed. States have a wide range of political goals and those goals vary from state to state. Nuclear weapons may improve a state's security, but in doing so, they grant states greater freedom to pursue their goals in international politics rather than tamping down their ambitions. Nuclear weapons do not transform the preferences that states have, but grant them greater freedom to pursue their preexisting political goals.

Why Do Nuclear Weapons Affect Foreign Policy?

Why is it that nuclear weapons may affect the calculations of the states that acquire them? Nuclear weapons can affect states' calculations about foreign policy through a range of mechanisms. Some of these mechanisms reflect strategic responses to the military capabilities that nuclear weapons provide the state, while others are less rooted in rational-strategic calculations at the level of the state and reflect individual- or group-level responses to nuclear acquisition.

First, there are *direct military* mechanisms by which nuclear weapons affect calculations about foreign policy. For example, using nuclear weapons militarily to achieve a certain level of destruction may be cheaper or easier than using conventional military means to achieve the same level of military destruction: the destructive capabilities that nuclear weapons offer are unique among military technologies. Thomas Schelling was correct to say that "against defenseless people there is not much that nuclear weapons can do that cannot be done with an ice pick," but the significance of nuclear weapons in international politics is not *what* they can achieve but the speed and efficiency with which they can achieve it.[2] For example, the United States was able to destroy Hiroshima and Nagasaki far more easily with nuclear weapons than it would have been able to with conventional ordnance. Single nuclear weapons destroyed Hiroshima and Nagasaki; achieving the same results with conventional weapons would have required hundreds of bombs and planes. Of course, there are many military missions that nuclear weapons are poorly suited for, but nuclear weapons make large-scale and indiscriminate destruction easier to achieve.

Most states do not plan to use their nuclear weapons in a direct military sense, however. The second way in which nuclear weapons affect calculations about foreign policy is through *political* mechanisms. Nuclear weapons affect the calculations of states with which the nuclear state is interacting in its foreign policy. Nuclear weapons grant states an ability to escalate (or threaten to escalate) a conflict or crisis to the nuclear level. This raises the expected costs of escalation for adversaries, because nuclear use may impose costs on their territory, population, or military capabilities beyond those that can be imposed using conventional forces. The expected cost for the nuclear-armed state of engaging in foreign policy behaviors that may trigger escalatory responses is therefore reduced, because it is harder for adversaries to escalate in response. The same logic applies even in situations in which the threat of nuclear use is not credible, because nuclear weapons may nonetheless make a state better able to outbid adversaries in a competition in risk taking. As Schelling argues, states can exert coercive pressure on each other by making "threats that leave something to chance" even if deliberate nuclear use is not credible.[3] Every act of escalation is therefore costlier (in expectation) against a nuclear-armed state than it would be if the state did not have nuclear weapons. For the nuclear-armed state, therefore, foreign policy behaviors that raise the risk of escalatory responses may have their expected costs reduced by nuclear possession because nuclear weapons make it harder for adversaries to escalate.

Similarly, nuclear weapons may reduce the cost of certain foreign policy behaviors by affecting the calculations of actors not directly involved in the particular dyadic foreign policy interaction. For example, nuclear weapons may deter diplomatic or military interventions by hostile third parties, or encourage similar interventions by friendly third parties.[4] In this case, nuclear weapons may not affect the calculations of the state with which the nuclear state is interacting in a given foreign policy, but nonetheless affect the costs associated with that foreign policy by influencing the calculations of other states. For example, as I discuss in chapter 3, South Africa's nuclear weapons allowed it to reduce the risk of Soviet intervention in Angola, thus facilitating greater South African aggression in the ongoing war in Angola.

Third, there are *efficiency* mechanisms by which nuclear weapons may affect foreign policy costs by freeing up resources or rendering the nuclear-armed state less reliant on others. By reducing the costs of certain foreign policy behaviors, nuclear weapons may free up resources to engage in other foreign policy behaviors that the state would not otherwise be able to afford. Thus, even if the expected costs of these behaviors are not directly affected by nuclear weapons themselves, they may nonetheless be facilitated by nuclear acquisition. Similarly, the capabilities offered by nuclear weapons may mean that the need to secure external political or military support from a third party is less pressing, increasing the state's self-reliance and reducing the costs of foreign policy behaviors that risk jeopardizing support from allies. For example, as I discuss in chapter 2, nuclear weapons allowed Britain to act more independently of the United States.

Fourth, there are *bureaucratic* and *domestic political* mechanisms by which nuclear weapons affect foreign policy. Programs to acquire nuclear weapons are large, resource-intensive efforts that require buy-in from coalitions of scientists, bureaucrats, political leaders, and legislators.[5] For individuals and institutions that made the argument that nuclear acquisition would benefit the state and that invested political resources into the acquisition of nuclear weapons, there may be strong incentives to demonstrate that those benefits have in fact been achieved. Nuclear weapons may tempt nuclear advocates within the government to pursue certain foreign policies (or reduce the obstacles preventing such policies being pursued) precisely to demonstrate the utility of nuclear weapons. For example, it was the Pakistani military that both controlled Pakistan's nuclear program and then planned and advocated for the nuclear-enabled adventurism of the 1999 Kargil War on the basis that Pakistani nuclear weapons would inhibit any Indian response.[6]

Fifth, there are a range of *psychological* and *identity-based* mechanisms by which nuclear weapons affect international politics.[7] Relative to other weapons, nuclear weapons are imbued with unusual symbolism, mythology, and significance for those who acquire them. Similarly, nuclear weapons have often been viewed as powerful symbols of technological progress and prestige by those who have sought them. For example, as British prime minister Winston Churchill's scientific adviser told him, "It is surely vital, unless we are to become a second-class nation armed with inferior weapons, that we should be in a position to make our own bombs."[8] Indeed, the very fact that nuclear weapons are commonly classified as distinct from "conventional" weapons is indicative of their unusual status. Given that states care deeply about prestige, status, and self-identity, nuclear weapons may also affect foreign policy by changing how states and leaders conceive of themselves, what they are capable of, and their state's role in international politics.

Sixth, these mechanisms are all magnified by the *selection effects* involved in which states acquire nuclear weapons.[9] Many of the mechanisms described above could work in multiple directions; for example, there are plenty of normative or identity-based mechanisms that would constrain nuclear weapons from having a substantial effect on a state's foreign policy.[10] However, the states that ultimately acquire nuclear weapons are not a random selection of states. The states that are willing to bear the financial, diplomatic, and other costs associated with pursuing and acquiring nuclear weapons are likely to be those whose foreign policy calculations will be most affected by having them: nuclear acquisition is likely to be most attractive to those that will benefit most from nuclear acquisition. Similarly, those that acquire nuclear weapons are likely to be those that are most susceptible to the bureaucratic or identity-based mechanisms. For example, as Jacques Hymans argues, leaders who seek nuclear weapons tend to be those whose calculations about foreign policy will be most influenced by nuclear weapons: those who "develop a desire for nuclear weapons that goes beyond calculation, to self-expression."[11]

How Can Nuclear Weapons Affect Foreign Policy?

Nuclear weapons can therefore affect a state's calculations about foreign policy through a range of different mechanisms. But what foreign policy behaviors do nuclear weapons facilitate? This section distinguishes among six distinct foreign policy behaviors that nuclear weapons can facilitate: aggression, expansion, independence, bolstering, steadfastness, and compromise. Some of these effects have previously been conflated under the catch-all term "emboldenment," while others are not typically thought of as emboldening effects. I show why nuclear weapons may facilitate each of these behaviors. This does not imply that nuclear weapons make any particular behavior easy: nuclear weapons do not grant states free rein in international politics, and many foreign policy behaviors will be costly both before and after nuclear acquisition. Similarly, I do not assume that the expected costs of engaging in each of these behaviors will *always* be reduced by nuclear acquisition. Nonetheless, nuclear weapons *can* facilitate each of these behaviors.[12]

AGGRESSION

Nuclear weapons may facilitate aggression. Aggression is defined as more belligerent pursuit of goals in preexisting disputes or in pursuit of previously defined interests.

Nuclear weapons can facilitate aggression through any of the mechanisms discussed above. Nuclear weapons may reduce the expected cost of aggression because a state may use nuclear weapons directly to engage in military operations that would be more costly to undertake with conventional forces (the military mechanism). Nuclear weapons may also facilitate aggression because nuclear weapons raise the risk of escalation for the state's opponents, which must reckon with both the conventional forces the state previously possessed and its nuclear capabilities (the political mechanism). This should make it harder for states to respond to the escalation of the nuclear-armed state, which should therefore find it easier to escalate its efforts to revise the status quo. Similarly, nuclear weapons may deter third parties from intervening to prevent the aggression of the nuclear-armed state. Nuclear weapons may facilitate aggression because they can free up resources previously dedicated to other military contingencies, allowing a state to concentrate additional resources in revising a particular element of the status quo (the efficiency mechanism). And nuclear weapons may facilitate aggression because they alter individual leaders' assessments of what their country is capable of, or because bureaucratic institutions that advocated for nuclear acquisition face incentives to demonstrate that nuclear weapons allow the state to achieve long-held revisionist goals (the identity-based or bureaucratic mechanisms). Through all of these mechanisms, nuclear weapons can make opportunities to escalate a conflict or attempts to revise the status quo more attractive than they would have been before nuclear acquisition.

Aggression may be identified by a range of behaviors, including (a) the issuance of new or more demanding compellent threats in an ongoing dispute; (b) the dedication of larger conventional forces to missions associated with a particular dispute; (c) more belligerent rhetoric being used by government officials and political leaders toward a particular country; (d) the vertical escalation of a dispute through the use of new tactics, forces, military doctrines, or technologies; and (e) a greater tolerance for escalation and risk-taking behavior in an existing dispute.

As I discuss in chapter 5, Pakistan provides perhaps the clearest example of a state using nuclear weapons to facilitate aggression. Scholars largely agree that nuclear weapons have acted as a shield behind which Pakistan has been able to pursue more aggressively its foreign policy goals in Kashmir and against India more broadly, most notably during the 1999 Kargil War and in the use of subconventional attacks against Indian cities.[13] For example, C. Christine Fair argues that nuclear weapons "increase the cost of Indian action" against Pakistan, which facilitates "risk-seeking behavior as part of [Pakistan's] effort to change the status quo."[14] South Africa also provides an example of a state using nuclear weapons to facilitate aggression. As I discuss in chapter 3, fears regarding escalation placed substantial constraints on South African behavior in the frontline states (and particularly in Angola) before nuclear acquisition. South Africa acquired nuclear weapons to provide an additional tool with which to control escalation and thus reduced the risks associated with aggression. As a result, South African tolerance for escalation in the Border Wars increased significantly once South Africa had acquired nuclear weapons, and South Africa became comfortable engaging in operations that had previously been considered too risky. To take another example, had Iraq succeeded in acquiring nuclear weapons, documentary evidence suggests that Saddam Hussein had at least considered using nuclear weapons to facilitate conventional aggression against Israel.[15]

EXPANSION

Nuclear weapons can reduce the costs of expansion. While some scholars use the term "expansion" as more or less synonymous with "aggression,"[16] I distinguish between the two. Expansion is defined as the *widening* of a state's interests and ambitions in international politics, rather than the more aggressive pursuit of existing interests.

As with aggression, nuclear weapons may reduce the costs associated with expansion through many of the mechanisms discussed above. First, through the efficiency mechanism: nuclear weapons may allow states to free up conventional military resources that had previously been dedicated to certain tasks that the state can now accomplish with nuclear weapons or by relying on nuclear deterrence. These freed-up forces can be redeployed in pursuit of new interests at lower risk than would have been possible without nuclear weapons. In addition, nuclear weapons may lower the costs associated with taking on new allies by making other states less willing to escalate conflicts against those allies now that they have a nuclear-armed patron, or by increasing the risks associated with resisting a state expanding its interests (the political mechanisms). And nuclear weapons may facilitate expansion by altering individual leaders' assessments of their country's appropriate role in the world, or because bureaucratic institutions that advocated for nuclear acquisition face incentives to demonstrate that nuclear weapons allow the state to rethink and expand its ambitions and status in the world (the identity-based or bureaucratic mechanisms).

Distinguishing expansion from aggression is not always easy, because states have incentives to claim that the pursuit of new interests or the initiation of new alliances or rivalries is consistent with long-standing interests or goals.[17] Nonetheless, actions indicative of expansion may include a state (a) broadening its declared interests in world politics; (b) forming alliances with, or offering extended deterrence to, new states; (c) developing greater power projection capabilities; (d) providing support for insurgents, proxies, or rebel groups in new countries; (e) participating in disputes with states with which the state has no previous history of conflict; and (f) taking a more active role in multilateral or international institutions.

The United States provides an example of a state that was able to expand its interests in world politics in the aftermath of acquiring nuclear weapons. Nuclear weapons played a key role in the US Cold War strategy to contain the Soviet Union, facilitated a semi-permanent military presence in Europe, allowed the United States to extend nuclear deterrence to a range of new allies, and thus permitted the United States to pursue a more expansive grand strategy than it had previously considered in its history.[18] Similarly, after acquiring nuclear weapons, the Soviet Union sought to expand its interests in Asia. The Soviet Union reversed its previously cautious attitude toward the Chinese revolution, signing an alliance treaty with the People's Republic of

China (PRC) that included a commitment to assist China "by all means at its disposal," a phrase that deliberately invoked the use of nuclear weapons.[19] More dramatically, Joseph Stalin authorized the transfer of substantial military capabilities to the North Korean army and ultimately approved Kim Il Sung's attack on South Korea. More broadly, and consistent with the idea that states expand their interests after nuclear acquisition, quantitative research suggests that states possessing nuclear weapons are on average more likely to initiate military disputes with countries with whom they have no history of conflict.[20]

INDEPENDENCE

Nuclear weapons may reduce the costs associated with a state acting independently of allies. Independence is defined as taking actions that an ally either opposes or does not support the state taking.

How might nuclear weapons facilitate independence? Most obviously, through the efficiency mechanism of increasing the state's self-reliance. By providing an internal source of military power that the state previously lacked, nuclear weapons reduce a state's need to rely on external sources of military power—that is, alliances.[21] The alliance therefore becomes somewhat less valuable than it previously was.[22] As a result, the costs of acting independently of the ally, or in ways contrary to the wishes of the ally, are reduced because the ally's support is no longer required to the degree it was before nuclear acquisition. Because states with nuclear weapons have less need for an ally's protection, they should be less inclined to compromise their own goals in exchange for protection. However, nuclear weapons may also facilitate independence via the bureaucratic or identity-based mechanisms if the desire for independence was a core driver of nuclear acquisition in the eyes of the individuals and institutions that advocated for nuclear weapons.

Importantly, independence may be observed in the state's relationship with the ally from which the state is increasingly independent. However, independence may also be observed in the state's relationship with other states. Independence may go hand in hand with other behaviors identified by the typology when those other behaviors are at least partially constrained by the preferences of an ally. For example, nuclear acquisition may facilitate aggression either via the mechanisms identified above or because a state previously refrained from aggression for fear of invoking the displeasure of an ally.

Actions indicating an increased independence from an ally may include (a) an increased willingness to criticize an ally, (b) an increased willingness to cooperate with an adversary of an ally, (c) an increased willingness to take actions opposed by the ally, (d) a reduced inclination to inform an ally in advance of taking particular action, (e) an increased willingness to take military actions in the absence of support from an ally, and (f) withdrawing from an alliance.

France provides an example of a state using nuclear weapons to facilitate independence. As I discuss in chapter 5, France obtained nuclear weapons partly to reduce its dependence on the United States for its security. Upon acquiring a deliverable capability in 1964, France became more comfortable acting independently of the United States—for example, in criticizing the Bretton Woods monetary system, in pursuing détente with the Soviet Union, in recognizing China, and, most notably, by withdrawing from the command structure of the North Atlantic Treaty Organization (NATO).[23] Similarly, observers have argued that North Korean nuclear weapons have allowed Pyongyang to defy its Chinese patron at lower risk. Jonathan Pollack argues that "the desire to be answerable to no external power" was a key driver of the North Korean nuclear program, and that "North Korean leaders have concluded that its nascent nuclear weapons capabilities . . . inhibit the Chinese," both in terms of controlling North Korean behavior and in limiting its ability to jettison its ties with Pyongyang despite Chinese leaders becoming "increasingly perturbed" by North Korean behavior.[24] In chapter 2, I argue that Britain became more willing to respond to challenges to its position in the Middle East independently of the United States after acquiring nuclear weapons. Before Britain had acquired a usable nuclear capability, British responses to challenges to its position in the Middle East were characterized by dependence on the United States and a reliance on US military and diplomatic support. In the aftermath of nuclear acquisition, Britain became considerably more willing to use force unilaterally to restore or protect the status quo, including in cases where the United States either opposed or did not actively support British action.

BOLSTERING

Nuclear weapons may reduce the costs associated with bolstering. Bolstering is defined as taking actions to increase the strength of an existing alliance or alliance partner.[25] Thus, while independence involves using nuclear weapons as a substitute for an alliance, bolstering involves using nuclear weapons to augment an alliance.

Nuclear weapons can facilitate or reduce the costs associated with bolstering through several of the mechanisms identified above. First, through political mechanisms: nuclear weapons may offer a lower-cost way to defend an alliance partner by making hostile third parties less inclined to challenge the alliance partner. Similarly, nuclear-armed states possess a range of nuclear technologies that they can choose to offer to an ally—increasing the ally's strength (and capacity to acquire nuclear weapons of its own) in a way that is less costly than making an equivalent conventional commitment. For example, a state can transfer sensitive nuclear technologies to an ally as a way of strengthening it.[26] Second, by using nuclear weapons to accomplish tasks for which the state had previously relied on conventional forces, nuclear weapons may free up financial or conventional military resources that a state can use to take on deeper alliance commitments (the efficiency mechanism). Third, nuclear weapons could facilitate bolstering via the bureaucratic or identity-based mechanisms if the desire to maintain or enhance the credibility of a state's alliances was a key reason to acquire nuclear weapons for the leaders and institutions that advocated for nuclear weapons. Actions indicating bolstering may include a state (a) offering a firmer defense commitment than had previously been offered to an ally, (b) stationing forces or weapons systems on the territory of the ally, (c) institutionalizing or formalizing a previously informal cooperative relationship, and (d) providing additional resources to the state (including nuclear technologies).

A range of states have used nuclear weapons to bolster their allies. For example, China provided Pakistan with enough highly enriched uranium (HEU) to build several nuclear weapons, along with a nuclear weapon design, in order to bolster Pakistan against their common adversary, India.[27] Indeed, research suggests that sensitive nuclear assistance is often undertaken to bolster friends against common enemies.[28] Britain also provides an example of a state that used nuclear weapons to bolster its alliances. As discussed in chapter 2, upon acquiring a deliverable capability in 1955, Britain used its nuclear weapons to make commitments to allies in the Middle East, Asia, and Europe that it was increasingly unable to make credible with declining conventional forces.

STEADFASTNESS

Nuclear weapons may reduce the costs associated with steadfastness. Steadfastness is defined as a reduced inclination to back down in disputes or in response to coercion, and an increased willingness to fight to defend the status quo.

As with aggression, nuclear weapons can reduce the cost of this behavior through a range of mechanisms. Nuclear weapons facilitate steadfastness because they raise the risk of escalation for the state's opponents, which must reckon with both the conventional forces the state previously possessed and its nuclear capabilities (the political mechanism). Because other states find it harder to escalate against the nuclear-armed state, it should be easier for the nuclear-armed state to stand firm in defense of the status quo. Similarly, nuclear weapons may also deter potentially hostile third parties from joining in an attack against the nuclear-armed state, making it easier to stand up to threats it does face. Nuclear weapons may facilitate steadfastness because they may free up resources previously dedicated to other contingencies, allowing a state to concentrate additional resources in defending the status quo (the efficiency mechanism). And they may facilitate steadfastness via the bureaucratic or identity-based mechanisms as those individuals and institutions that advocated for nuclear weapons feel stronger as a result of acquiring nuclear weapons or feel compelled to demonstrate that they no longer have to acquiesce to the demands of other states. Through all of these mechanisms, nuclear weapons can allow states to stand more firmly in defense of the status quo. Actions indicating steadfastness may include a state (a) issuing more explicit deterrent threats to opponents, (b) more quickly mobilizing forces in response to aggression, (c) using more belligerent rhetoric during disputes and crises, and (d) responding to military provocations at higher rates.

Pakistan provides an example of a state that has used nuclear weapons to stand firmer in defense of the status quo. For example, Pakistani elites viewed the various India-Pakistan crises of the 1980s as "validat[ing] Zulfiqar Ali Bhutto's decision to acquire a nuclear weapons capability. . . . [A] nuclear capability ensures defense against physical external aggression and coercion from adversaries, and deters infringement of national sovereignty," as well as providing Pakistan with the ability to draw the United States in to resolve Indo-Pakistani disputes should escalation rise to an intolerable level.[29] Nuclear weapons have thus allowed Pakistan to tolerate higher levels of escalation in disputes with India and to stand more firmly in defense of what it perceived to be the status quo in the face of Indian provocations. To take another example, Britain also used nuclear weapons to facilitate steadfastness. In chapter 2, I argue that after nuclear acquisition Britain responded to challenges to its position in the Middle East more forcefully but without seeking to acquire resources or territory beyond the preexisting status quo.

COMPROMISE

Nuclear weapons may reduce the costs associated with compromise. In contrast to aggression, which is defined as seeking more in preexisting disputes, compromise is defined as accepting less in preexisting disputes.

Nuclear weapons may reduce the cost of compromising in disputes through several of the mechanisms above. First, through political mechanisms: because nuclear weapons raise the costs associated with adversaries challenging the state, nuclear weapons reduce the security risks that the state faces, and thus mean that a state may face lower risks if it makes compromises. For example, if nuclear weapons make conventional aggression against the state less likely, then they also reduce the value of strategic depth and therefore reduce the value of holding territory. The risks associated with making territorial compromises are therefore lower. Nuclear weapons may also facilitate compromise through the efficiency mechanism: nuclear weapons may free up military or financial resources that a state can use to directly mitigate the security risks—and thus reduce the costs—associated with making compromises. It is possible, though perhaps less likely, that nuclear weapons could also facilitate compromise via the bureaucratic or identity-based mechanisms if the desire to make compromises was an important rationale for nuclear acquisition in the eyes of the individuals and institutions that advocated for nuclear weapons. Compromise may be identified by a range of behaviors, including (a) the dedication of fewer or less offensively postured conventional forces to missions associated with a particular dispute, (b) less belligerent rhetoric being used by government officials and political leaders toward a particular country, (c) the initiation of negotiations or issuance of less onerous demands in a given dispute, and (d) the settling of territorial disputes through negotiation.

I argue below that we should not expect states to use nuclear weapons to facilitate compromise. And, indeed, it is unclear whether any state has ever behaved in this way in response to nuclear acquisition. One possible case is that Soviet "New Thinking," and the associated withdrawal from Eastern Europe, Afghanistan, and Africa, was the result of a belated recognition of the reduced benefits of controlling territory in the nuclear age. However, the role of nuclear weapons in this case is contested, and even advocates of this view acknowledge a wide range of other factors played into Soviet thinking.[30] However, regardless of whether states have responded to nuclear acquisition in this way, scholars have frequently argued that states *should* behave in this way. For example, Shai Feldman argues that Israel should respond to nuclear acquisition by being more willing to make territorial compromises with its neighbors.[31]

Nuclear Opportunism and the Primacy of Politics

When will states use nuclear weapons to facilitate different combinations of these behaviors? Why do some states use nuclear weapons to facilitate aggression, while others use them to bolster their allies or act more independently of allies?

I argue that states exist in different strategic circumstances and therefore have different political priorities. These different priorities lead states to use nuclear weapons to facilitate different foreign policy behaviors after acquisition. For example, some states may use nuclear acquisition to facilitate aggression, while others may use nuclear weapons to bolster allies. I label this theory, and the view of nuclear weapons that it implies, as "nuclear opportunism." According to the theory, states use nuclear weapons in an opportunistic way to improve their position in international politics and to help them achieve political goals that the state cares about. Nuclear weapons, according to the theory, do not transform international politics or necessarily ameliorate security competition among states. Nor do they grant states free rein in international politics. Instead, nuclear weapons are incorporated into the practice of international politics and used by states to help pursue their political goals.

The theory is structured as a decision tree of three simple variables that describe the state's position in the international system and thus shed light on its political priorities.[32] The first variable is the existence of serious ter-

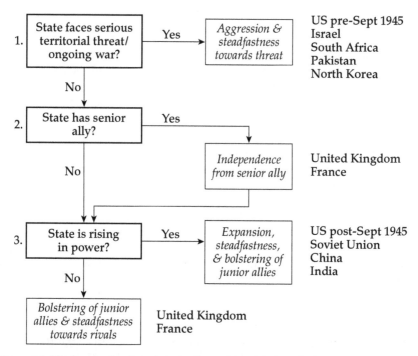

Figure 1.1. The theory of nuclear opportunism and empirical predictions

ritorial threats or an ongoing war, the second is the existence of a senior ally that provides for the state's security, and the third is whether a state is increasing or decreasing in relative power.[33]

Figure 1.1 shows the structure of the theory and the predictions made in each historical case of nuclear acquisition. Because of the structure of the theory, some states appear twice—for example, the theory predicts that the United Kingdom would use nuclear weapons to facilitate independence from its senior ally (the United States), as well as bolstering of its junior allies and steadfastness in response to threats.

VARIABLE 1: SERIOUS TERRITORIAL THREAT OR ONGOING WAR

The first variable in the sequence is whether the state faces a serious territorial threat or is engaged in an ongoing war. States in such a precarious security environment enjoy little room for maneuver. Improving their position against the source of threat or in the war they are fighting is their political priority, and such states will therefore direct their nuclear weapons to foreign policies that serve that purpose.

For states in such a precarious environment, many of the six foreign policy behaviors are relatively unattractive. For example, pursuing independence from allies is unattractive because states in dire security environments are eager to accept assistance from other states and do not wish to jeopardize their relationships with allies that may be able to help improve their security. Similarly, expansion and bolstering are generally less attractive because a state facing such threats has little latitude to engage in these behaviors. States facing serious threats do not typically seek to widen their interests in international politics or shore up the security of other states, because improving their own security must take priority.

While expansion, independence, and bolstering are less attractive, aggression and steadfastness are more attractive. States facing serious threats would generally like to more easily hold on to what they have against the threats they face, would like to take territory or other resources away from the source of threat (or be able to more credibly threaten to do so), and would like to be able to tolerate higher levels of escalation in crises. For such states, aggression and steadfastness toward the source of threat are, therefore, more attractive than the other foreign policy behaviors. Because such states find these behaviors attractive, states in this position are therefore likely to use nuclear weapons to facilitate aggression and steadfastness after nuclear acquisition, allowing them to both stand more firmly in defense of the status quo when challenged and push harder in pursuit of preexisting goals.

As shown in figure 1.2, this leads to the first prediction of the theory of nuclear opportunism: states facing severe territorial threats or involved in an ongoing war are likely to use nuclear weapons to facilitate both aggression and steadfastness against the source of the threat.[34] For example, Pakistan, facing a serious territorial threat from India, would be expected to use nuclear weapons both to pursue its offensive goals against India more belligerently (aggression) and to stand more firmly in defense of the status quo when challenged (steadfastness).

Identifying whether a state faces threats of this sort is straightforward. The threats that a state faces can be directly observed, although elite perceptions of the threat may sometimes deviate from the objective reality. This variable has several components.[35] First, the threat must be proximate—that is, it must either be on a state's borders or be able to threaten a state's borders in short order. Threats that are geographically distant, or that must pass over inhospitable terrain, do not count as severe territorial threats.[36] Second, the threat must have sufficient conventional military power (or the potential to raise such military power in short order) and a sufficiently favorable mili-

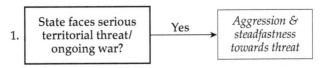

Figure 1.2. Predictions for states facing serious territorial threats or engaged in war

tary balance to threaten a substantial portion of the state's territory (that is, the threat must be able to project power offensively). Third, the threat must be perceived to have aggressive intentions. A state cannot be defined as facing a severe territorial threat if it does not feel threatened. All three of these criteria must be met for a state to face a severe territorial threat. Similarly, observing whether a state is involved in an ongoing war is straightforward.

It is worth noting that the nuclear status of the source of threat does not affect the predictions. If a state faces serious territorial threats or is involved in an ongoing war, then nuclear acquisition facilitates steadfastness and aggression *regardless* of the nuclear status of the opponent.[37] Whether or not the source of the threat possesses nuclear weapons, nuclear acquisition raises the level of escalation that the state is willing to tolerate (either in defense of the status quo or in pursuit of revisionist goals). For example, Pakistan would find improving its ability to engage in aggression and steadfastness toward India attractive, and would find that nuclear weapons facilitated those behaviors, regardless of whether India possessed nuclear weapons. In short, when facing a severe territorial threat, having nuclear weapons facilitates aggression and steadfastness, whether or not the state posing the threat itself has nuclear weapons.

VARIABLE 2: PRESENCE OF A SENIOR ALLY

States not facing serious territorial threats or engaged in an ongoing war continue down the decision tree in figure 1.1. Given the absence of severe threats or an ongoing war, the security environment faced by such states is less constricting. The second and third variables help explain how states in more permissive security environments change their foreign policies after nuclear acquisition.

The second variable in the sequence is whether the state acquiring nuclear weapons has a senior alliance partner that helps provide for the state's defense. States that reach this variable in the decision tree do not face severe threats, but states whose security is partly provided for by a senior ally are constrained if they wish to engage in behaviors that the senior ally opposes or does not support. Because the senior alliance partner plays a role in providing for the security of the junior state, the junior state must be cautious of acting in ways that may displease the senior state.[38] The support of an ally is always at least somewhat suspect, and so few states can act contrary to the interests of the senior alliance partner without at least worrying about potential reductions in support.[39] Such concerns impose constraints on the behavior of the junior partner.

The constraints imposed by dependence on a senior ally mean that states in this position are likely to be eager to increase their ability to act independently of their senior ally. As Avery Goldstein argues, "Those able to become more self-reliant often make the costly effort [to do so]. . . . Deference to a security patron is likely to be politically unattractive for the leaders of sovereign states."[40] Because these states find independence to be an attractive behavior, we should therefore expect that states in this position would use nuclear weapons to facilitate independence after acquisition. When such states acquire nuclear weapons, we should therefore expect to see them having fewer compunctions about criticizing or failing to support their senior ally, acting in ways contrary to the ally's interests, defying their senior ally, or even withdrawing from the alliance altogether.

As shown in figure 1.3, this leads to the second prediction of the theory of nuclear opportunism: states that do not face severe territorial threats and are not involved in an ongoing war, but do have a senior ally that provides for their security are likely to use nuclear weapons to facilitate independence from their senior ally. For example, the theory predicts that both Britain and France—which did not face serious territorial threats when they acquired nuclear weapons—would use nuclear weapons to become more independent from their senior ally, the United States.

Identifying whether states have allies of this sort is straightforward. Many alliances are formalized in treaties and even those that are not are typically accompanied by resource flows and diplomatic support. Identifying which party is the senior ally in the alliance is also normally straightforward. Typically, the senior state in the alliance will be the more militarily powerful state and the one contributing resources and commitments to the other state, and will be recognized as such by both partners in the alliance.[41]

VARIABLE 3: POWER TRAJECTORY

Regardless of whether a state has a senior ally that provides for its security (that is, regardless of the value that the second variable takes), states that neither face serious territorial threats on their borders nor are involved in an

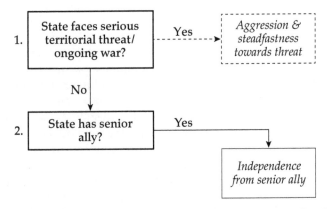

Figure 1.3. Predictions for states not facing serious threats but with senior allies. Dashed lines indicate portions of the theory not applicable in this case.

ongoing war continue down the decision tree to the third variable. This variable conditions the additional benefits they seek to gain from their nuclear weapons, and measures how a state's power position is changing over time.

Scholars have long recognized that states that are rising in power often look to expand their influence in international politics. For example, Fareed Zakaria states that "nations try to expand their political interests abroad when central decision-makers perceive a relative increase in state power," while Robert Jervis argues that "states' definition of their interests tend to expand as their power does."[42] Such states are therefore likely to find expansion attractive, and will use nuclear weapons to facilitate this behavior. For example, such states may widen their interests in international politics, initiate new rivalries, or take on new alliance commitments. Similarly, using nuclear weapons to bolster the state's existing allies and increase the power of the state's alliance networks is also likely to be attractive, as the state seeks to widen its influence. Finally, such states find steadfastness attractive—even rising states will continue to seek to safeguard what they already have.

Aggression is likely to be less attractive than expansion for states in this position. First, the threats that such states face are by definition not so immediate that they require the state's full attention (if they were, such states would have been defined as facing severe threats at the first stage of the decision tree). Rising states can afford to be patient in dealing with such threats because time is on their side: because they are increasing in power, any existing threats or rivalries will become easier to deal with over time. Second, rising states need to be careful as they increase their power not to give potential rivals too much cause to band together to oppose them.[43] Indeed, existing opponents of the state are likely to be particularly sensitive to any effort by the rising state to aggress against it. For rising states, aggression may, therefore, be more trouble than it is worth.

As shown in figure 1.4, this leads to the third prediction of the theory of nuclear opportunism: states that do not face severe territorial threats and are rising in power are likely to use nuclear weapons to facilitate expansion, steadfastness, and bolstering junior allies.

By contrast, what are the predictions for a state that reaches the third variable in the decision tree but is not increasing in relative power? Expansion and aggression are relatively unattractive for such states. Expanding a state's interests and alliances is unwise when a state does not have the ability to support such actions, and trying to acquire more in ongoing disputes is unlikely to be attractive when merely holding on to what the state already has is likely to prove sufficiently challenging as its relative power declines.

Instead, an important political priority for states in this position is to maintain the state's position. Bolstering and steadfastness are therefore attractive foreign policy behaviors. Bolstering the state's alliances is attractive because alliances help the state maintain its position in international politics even as its power declines.[44]

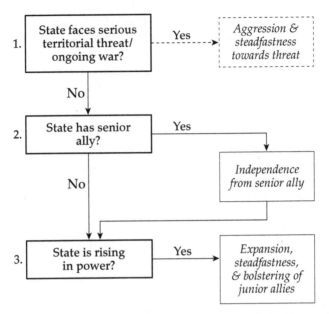

Figure 1.4. Predictions for rising states not facing serious threats. Dashed lines indicate portions of the theory not applicable in this case.

Similarly, steadfastness is attractive for states looking to maintain their position in international politics. Such states are particularly concerned with standing more firmly in defense of the status quo when challenged. Because maintaining the state's position is a priority, being able to stand more firmly in defense of the status quo is attractive, and such states are likely to use nuclear weapons to facilitate steadfastness. Overall, the theory therefore expects that when states not facing severe threats but declining in power acquire nuclear weapons, they will use them to facilitate the bolstering of existing junior allies and steadfastness in defense of the status quo.

As shown in figure 1.5, this leads to the third prediction of the theory of nuclear opportunism: states that do not face severe territorial threats and are declining in power are likely to use nuclear weapons to facilitate bolstering and steadfastness. Identifying whether a state is rising in relative power is reasonably straightforward. For example, the Correlates of War Project's Composite Index of National Capabilities (CINC) scores provide a measure of a state's share of total global power. One can, for example, examine how the CINC score has changed over the past five years, or take a moving average of a state's CINC score.[45] The variable can also be measured qualitatively by examining the speech evidence and writings of leaders and other elites in the state, because elites may have a strong belief that the state's relative power position is worsening, even if that is not in fact the case.[46]

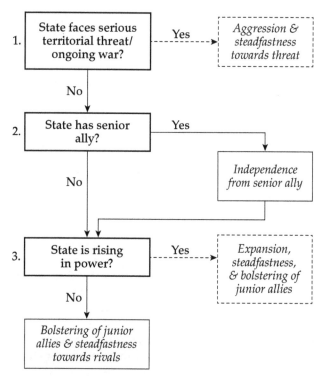

Figure 1.5. Predictions for declining states not facing serious threats. Dashed lines indicate portions of the theory not applicable in this case.

Potential Objections

There are, of course, potential objections to the theory laid out above.

First, it may be argued that while states do respond in this way to nuclear acquisition, these are brief effects that dissipate over time rather than endure. And, indeed, some scholars have argued that states experience brief periods of emboldenment or belligerence when they acquire nuclear weapons that gradually wear off as states come to realize the limited utility of their nuclear weapons.[47] Of course, even if the theory of nuclear opportunism applies to states only in the immediate aftermath of nuclear acquisition, this would still be important given that policymakers are particularly interested in the immediate effects of nuclear acquisition. For example, policymakers are likely to be more concerned about the effect that nuclear weapons would have on Iranian foreign policy immediately after acquiring nuclear weapons than they would be about what Iran might use its nuclear weapons for once it has had them for twenty years. More importantly, however, there are also strong theoretical reasons for thinking that states may only rarely reevaluate the role that nuclear weapons play in their foreign policy and, therefore, that the effects of nuclear weapons will have a highly path-dependent character, enduring over substantial periods of time. First, scholars often emphasize the importance of civilian oversight in stimulating innovation, but the high level of secrecy that often surrounds nuclear weapons should be expected to hamper this process, making reevaluating the role nuclear weapons play in a state's foreign policy harder.[48] Second, the technical and military bureaucracies that often govern nuclear programs have been shown to be susceptible to assumptions and groupthink that may make such innovation difficult, and, indeed, may build and protect bureaucratic structures that ossify and reinforce particular ways of thinking about the utility of nuclear weapons.[49] Third, narratives about the utility of nuclear weapons may be resistant to change given that nuclear weapons are rarely used directly, meaning policymakers are unlikely to be confronted with unambiguous evidence of the utility or lack of utility of nuclear weapons in pursuing their foreign policy goals.[50] Ultimately, however, whether these effects endure is an empirical question. In the case studies, I therefore examine not only whether states change their behaviors in the way the theory anticipates after they acquire nuclear weapons, but also whether these behaviors, and the ideas about nuclear weapons that underpin them, appear to endure over a longer period of time.

Second, it may be argued that nuclear weapons do not cause the behaviors outlined here, but are rather caused by the same factors that lead states to acquire nuclear weapons in the first place. This is likely true, but it does not undermine the validity of the theory—in fact, it is consistent with, and anticipated by, the theory. According to the theory of nuclear opportunism, it may indeed be that states in particular strategic environments face incentives to engage in particular foreign policy behaviors. This in turn leads them both to acquire nuclear weapons to facilitate those behaviors and to engage in those behaviors when they do so. But if states acquire nuclear weapons to facilitate particular behaviors and then use nuclear weapons to facilitate those behaviors, this would be evidence for rather than against the theory: nuclear weapons would be having a direct effect on the state's ability to achieve its political goals as well as having a direct effect on its foreign policies. Indeed, this would be entirely consistent with the vision of nuclear weapons implied by the theory of nuclear opportunism: as useful tools for pursuing a state's preexisting political priorities.[51]

It is also worth emphasizing that the theory of nuclear opportunism is *not* a theory of nuclear acquisition.[52] The theory of nuclear opportunism specifies what a state is likely to use nuclear weapons to try to accomplish conditional on having made the decision to acquire, and acquired, nuclear weapons. In other words, the theory specifies what benefits a state is likely to seek from its nuclear weapons once the state has already concluded that the benefits of nuclear acquisition outweigh the costs. The theory does not have much to say about why some states will conclude that the benefits of nuclear acquisition outweigh the costs, or indeed, what those costs might be, and thus does not make predictions for which states will acquire nuclear weapons. Instead, it seeks to explain why those states that do acquire nuclear weapons behave in particular ways after having done so.

Third, it may be argued that the theory is a significant oversimplification of the complex and probabilistic interactions between a range of international and domestic variables that likely govern a state's response to nuclear acquisition in reality. This is certainly true for at least three reasons. First, by using three simple variables that can be measured prior to a state acquiring nuclear weapons, the theory remains relatively parsimonious. Second, the theory examines only the benefits that nuclear weapons offer states and does not examine the costs that may accompany nuclear acquisition. The process of proliferation can be dangerous for states, and nuclear weapons may also come with disadvantages. For example, Jervis argues that "the possession of nuclear weapons can decrease the state's freedom of action by increasing the suspicion with which it is viewed."[53] Third, the theory is a choice theoretic rather than a game theoretic or strategic one that ignores the actions that other actors can take to try to reduce the benefits that states gain from acquiring nuclear weapons. Naturally, as a result—and as is the case with all theories that aim to simplify a complex world—many potentially important factors are left out. For example, variables relating to civil-military relations, leader psychology, and political ideology and ideas about nuclear weapons, international norms, and regime type are all left out of the theory. This is not to deny that these variables may sometimes matter. For example, as I discuss in chapter 5, the distinctive ideas about nuclear weapons held by Mao Zedong and other Chinese leaders appear to have led to nuclear weapons having a limited effect on Chinese foreign policy.[54] However, any theory must simplify the complexity of the real world. Indeed, and as I discuss further below, if nuclear weapons bring with them serious costs in addition to benefits, or if other states act strategically to take actions that mitigate the benefits a state receives from acquiring nuclear weapons, then this should in fact bias against observing an effect at the point of nuclear acquisition.

Indeed, parsimony has virtues in this context. First, it is clearer whether the behavior of a given state supports or falsifies the theory if the predictions are clear. If a state that does not face serious territorial threats uses nuclear weapons to facilitate aggression, for example, this would clearly count against the theory. If a theory is more complicated, there may be more doubt about whether a given case supports or undermines the theory. Second, a simple theory that uses variables that can be measured prior to nuclear acquisition can be used to predict the effects of nuclear acquisition before it happens. For example, the theory could be used to make predictions about how Iran might behave if it acquired nuclear weapons. Third, given the small number of states to have acquired nuclear weapons, adding additional variables to the theory quickly leads to the problem of "more inferences than observations."[55] More broadly, theorizing inevitably involves a trade-off between explanatory power and parsimony. One could create a theory that was more parsimonious but that could explain fewer cases, and one could equally create a theory that was more complex but that could account for more cases. The theory here aims to offer a middle ground by being flexible enough to explain a range of state responses to nuclear acquisition but nonetheless sufficiently parsimonious to allow the theory to be tested empirically.

Fourth, it may be argued that the theory ignores the diversity of political preferences that exist across states. For example, revisionist state preferences—emphasized in Kapur's account of how nuclear weapons affect foreign policy—are not included in the theory.[56] I choose to omit this variable because the theory suggests that nuclear acquisition may make revisionism of various sorts more attractive to states. Including revisionist preferences in the theory, then, would be close to using the outcome being explained as one of the factors in the explanation (that is, that revisionist states engage in more revisionist behaviors after acquiring nuclear weapons). Instead, the theory of nuclear opportunism tries to *explain* the type of revisionism that different states may engage in after nuclear acquisition using variables that can be observed and measured independently of that behavior.

Fifth, the theory predicts that states will not use nuclear weapons to facilitate one of the six behaviors in the typology: compromise. The behavior is nonetheless retained within the typology for two reasons. First, nuclear weapons do reduce the cost of this behavior, and the typology would therefore not be exhaustive if it were left out. Second, as discussed below, the idea that states will use nuclear weapons to facilitate compromise is a core prediction of the theory of the nuclear revolution: because nuclear weapons make states more secure, compromise should become less costly and more attractive once a state has nuclear weapons. A complete test of the theory of nuclear opportunism against its competitors therefore requires acknowledging the possibility that states may use nuclear weapons to facilitate compromise.

It is also worth making clear *why* the theory of nuclear opportunism does not predict states will use nuclear weapons to facilitate compromise. The theory suggests that states seek to use nuclear weapons to *better* their position in international politics, and use nuclear weapons as a tool with which to do so. This assumption—that states seek to gain benefits from having nuclear weapons—could be justified by reference to a range of theories of international politics, including classical or offensive realism, as well as theories based on bureaucratic politics or leader psychology. However, because of this assumption, it is unsurprising that the theory predicts that states would not acquire nuclear weapons only to then give up territory or other assets that they had previously wanted. While states may be coerced into compromise or make compromises voluntarily for a range of reasons, the theory of nuclear opportunism suggests that states are unlikely to deliberately use nuclear weapons to facilitate this behavior. Ultimately, however, this is an observable implication of the theory that can be tested against the historical record. Consistent with the theoretical expectations, and as discussed above, there are few (if any) clear cases of states using nuclear weapons to facilitate compromise.

Testing the Theory

How should we best examine the validity of this theory? I test the theory using a series of historical case studies. In each case, the goal is to examine the state's foreign policy in the period immediately before and after the acquisition of the relevant nuclear capability, and to assess whether there are changes in the scale and nature of the state's foreign policies that occur at that point. (Exactly what the relevant nuclear capability is in each case is discussed in more detail below.)

If a state uses nuclear weapons to facilitate a particular behavior, this means that the state engages in a particular foreign policy behavior that it would not engage in if it did not have nuclear weapons, that the state engages in a particular foreign policy behavior to a greater degree than if it did not have nuclear weapons, or that a state uses nuclear weapons rather than other military tools to engage in a particular behavior (for example, using nuclear weapons rather than conventional forces to deter an adversary). In each case, using nuclear weapons to facilitate a particular behavior should lead to observable shifts in the way foreign policy is conducted or implemented at the point of nuclear acquisition: in the behaviors a state engages in, the levels or intensity of the behaviors that a state engages in, or the tools that the state deploys to engage in those behaviors. For example, evidence that a state is using nuclear weapons to facilitate aggression may include the state beginning to engage in operations it was previously deterred from undertaking, engaging in operations against an opponent of a type previously undertaken but doing so more frequently or with greater intensity, or explicitly using nuclear weapons to threaten and coerce an opponent it had previously used conventional weapons to threaten and coerce.

Examining changes in behavior at the point of acquisition is a good way to assess the effects of nuclear weapons because to the extent that other factors that might affect foreign policy behavior do not change over the period of acquisition, we can be more confident that any discontinuity we observe is caused by nuclear weapons rather than some other factor. For example, stable (or extremely slow moving) variables such as political institutions, strategic culture, or the polarity of the international system are unlikely to be able to explain any discontinuity that occurs in a state's foreign policy behavior at the point of nuclear acquisition, because such factors are stable over the period being analyzed.[57] Of course, a downside of examining changes in behavior only at the point of nuclear acquisition is that it does not allow us to assess how the effects of nuclear weapons change over time. For this reason, while I focus the case studies on the period immediately before and after nuclear acquisition, I also examine whether the changes in behavior I identify and the ideas about nuclear weapons that underpin them appear to endure over time.

Adopting a historical approach offers additional methodological advantages. First, it allows us to incorporate evidence from the discussions and writings of elites to increase our confidence that it is indeed nuclear weapons that are causing any change in behavior we observe at the point of nuclear acquisition. For example, suppose that a country's elites repeatedly state prior to acquiring nuclear weapons that they wish to gain nuclear weapons in order to allow them greater independence from a patron, and we then observe them behaving more independently of that patron after acquiring nuclear weapons. If we observe this, it is more reasonable to attribute that change in behavior to nuclear acquisition than if we had simply observed the behavior change but did not observe the crucial historical evidence about the beliefs of political elites. Because the way in which leaders think about nuclear weapons represents an important observable implication of the theory of nuclear opportunism, a qualitative approach that allows that evidence to be incorporated provides substantial advantages. Second, the outcomes of interest—the various foreign policy behaviors identified above—are not easily adapted from existing large-n datasets. For example, whether a state pursues additional goals in an existing dispute (aggression) may not be fully captured by a change in the number of militarized interstate disputes (MIDs) or interstate crises (for example, the International Crisis Behavior dataset). While such existing datasets may offer insights into the foreign policy behaviors of states, they are insufficient on their own and do not allow us to test many of the observable implications of the theory of nuclear opportunism.[58]

Indeed, there are several reasons to think that this approach might *underestimate* the true effects of nuclear weapons. First, the fact that the theory largely ignores strategic interaction may lead us to underestimate the effects of nuclear weapons. If states anticipate nuclear acquisition by another state, for example, they may take actions that minimize any benefits that nuclear acquisition has for the acquiring state. For example, adversaries may build up their conventional forces or alter their military doctrines to undercut the benefits of nuclear acquisition for the acquiring state.[59] If so, such efforts by others will likely make it harder to observe the effects of nuclear weapons at the point of acquisition. Second, states may begin to receive some political benefits from their possession of nuclear technologies prior to the point of nuclear acquisition. For example, states may be able to use so-called nuclear latency to extract diplomatic concessions or support from other states.[60] Third, states may rationally and strategically seek to avoid taking full advantage of their nuclear weapons after acquiring them. States may be concerned about provoking reactive proliferation or provoking a balancing coalition forming against them.[61] Again, this would reduce the likelihood of seeing a substantial change in foreign policy behavior at the point of acquisition. All of this would suggest that if we nonetheless see a change in behavior at the point of acquisition, we can be more confident that nuclear weapons are indeed playing a causal role.

I choose cases based on two primary criteria. First, the three cases I use each provide hard cases for the theory. Picking hard cases allows for more confidence in the broader applicability or "external validity" of the findings—if we find support for the theory despite picking cases that we expect the theory will have difficulty explaining, it increases the likelihood that the theory will have some success in cases we do not examine in detail, or in cases that may emerge in the future. In particular, I look for cases with strong "countervailing conditions"—variables whose presence in a particular case makes it less likely that the outcomes posited by the theory of nuclear opportunism will be observed.[62] A second criterion is the availability of primary documents or interview evidence about the foreign policy process at the time of nuclear acquisition. This criterion increases the likelihood of identifying evidence about the precise point at which the state acquired the relevant capabilities, and about the process by which nuclear weapons affected (or did not affect) state foreign policy at the point of acquisition.

Chapter 2 examines the case of Britain. Britain provides a hard case for the theory because many theories of international relations expect a state like Britain—a status quo, democratic, conventionally powerful state with a nuclear-armed patron and large geographic buffers between the state and its primary rival—to have little need to prominently emphasize weapons of mass destruction in its foreign policy or to see a substantial effect of nuclear acquisition on its foreign policy. By contrast, the theory of nuclear opportunism anticipates that Britain would use nuclear weapons to facilitate independence from the United States, steadfastness in responding to challenges, and the bolstering of junior allies.

The second case is that of South Africa, examined in chapter 3. Again, a range of variables suggest that nuclear weapons would have a limited effect in the South African case: apartheid-era South Africa was more militarily powerful than its neighbors and had status quo preferences despite the racism and paranoia of the apartheid regime. South Africa's primary goal was to maintain its domestic political institutions in the face of internal and external pressure. Further, South Africa developed only a small, secret, and unsophisticated arsenal. By contrast, the theory of nuclear opportunism anticipates that South Africa—engaged in an ongoing war in Angola and facing the possibility of direct Soviet intervention in southern Africa that would overturn South Africa's military advantages—would use nuclear weapons to facilitate both aggression and steadfastness against the source of threat.

The third case is that of the United States, examined in chapter 4. The theory of nuclear opportunism anticipates that the United States—engaged in a brutal war when it sought and acquired nuclear weapons—would use nuclear weapons to engage in aggression against Japan (and would have used them for the same purpose against Germany had they been ready before the war in Europe ended). In the aftermath of World War II, the theory anticipates that the United States—not facing any territorial threats and rising in relative power—would use nuclear weapons to facilitate the bolstering of its allies and an expansion of its position and ambitions in world politics. Thus, because the variables that the theory of nuclear opportunism identifies as conditioning the effects of nuclear acquisition change dramatically at the end of World War II, the theory predicts that nuclear weapons would affect US foreign policy differently during World War II and in the aftermath of the war. The case of the United States thus offers an additional set of observable implications of the theory, making it a particularly useful test. The case is also highly historically unusual—the United States was the first nation to acquire nuclear weapons and did so in highly abnormal historical circumstances. If the theory can nonetheless shed light on the way in which nuclear weapons affected US foreign policy, this would provide an important validation of the scope of the theory's explanatory power.[63]

In each case, we need to identify the point in time at which nuclear acquisition occurred. This is important because the point of acquisition provides the point at which to look for changes in the state's behavior. What matters in each case is identifying the point at which the state's nuclear weapons can be deployed and used in the way the state intends. The technological requirements for this will vary from state to state according to its nuclear posture.[64] For example, South Africa—a country that intended to test nuclear weapons on its own territory in order to "catalyze" US intervention on its behalf—did not even require a fully deliverable weapon in order for nuclear weapons to affect its calculations about the risks of different foreign policy options. As soon as South Africa possessed a *testable* device, the country could threaten to conduct a nuclear test and use that threat to raise the probability of US intervention on its behalf, thus reducing the risks associated with a range of foreign policy actions.[65] On the other hand, for a country like Britain, which planned to deliver nuclear weapons to Soviet cities, a far more sophisticated capability was required before nuclear weapons began to affect British foreign policy calculations. Because Britain had to be able to deliver nuclear weapons to the Soviet Union, it was not until 1955 that Britain had the capabilities required—well after its first nuclear test in 1952. Thus, in each case, it is necessary to pay significant attention to the state's intended nuclear posture, the manner in which the state intended to use its nuclear weapons, and the particular technological requirements that such uses require. This enables us to accurately identify the relevant point of acquisition for each state, and therefore the appropriate point in time at which to look for discontinuities in foreign policy behavior.

In each case, I also pay attention to whether alternative explanations perform better than the theory of nuclear opportunism. I examine whether the theory of the nuclear revolution, S. Paul Kapur's theory of "strategic pessimism," or case-specific explanations perform better than the theory of nuclear opportunism. The theory of the nuclear revolution anticipates that states would use nuclear weapons to facilitate steadfastness, compromise, and independence. Nuclear weapons facilitate steadfastness and independence because, according to the theory of the nuclear revolution, these weapons make threats against that state less credible, whether from allies or enemies. States should therefore be able to stand more firmly in defense of what they have (steadfastness), and in defying allies that disagree with them (independence). Similarly, the theory of the nuclear revolution would also anticipate that states with nuclear weapons should be more willing to make compromises than states without nuclear weapons because the security provided by nuclear weapons grants states the freedom to compromise on matters that would previously have been too damaging to the state's security.[66] However, states should not use nuclear weapons to facilitate aggression or expansion, because such theorists of the nuclear revolution view security as the primary goal of states, and view aggression or expansion as behaviors largely driven by insecurity. Because nuclear weapons make states more secure, they should make such behaviors less attractive. Similarly, because alliances are typically viewed as responses to threats and thus defensive in nature, states should not be expected to use nuclear weapons to facilitate the bolstering of allies.[67] S. Paul Kapur's theory of "strategic pessimism" makes predictions about only one behavior in the typology: aggression. He argues that it is only conventionally weak states with revisionist preferences that should be expected to use nuclear weapons to facilitate aggression.[68]

Chapters 2–4 assess whether the theory explains the cases of Britain, South Africa, and the United States. Chapter 5 then assesses the broader applicability of the theory by examining other cases of nuclear proliferation. While these descriptions inevitably contain less detailed analysis and process tracing than the three cases examined in chapters 2–4, they provide an initial assessment of whether the behavior of other states is consistent with the theory.

Independence and Status

The British Nuclear Experience

Britain was the first non-superpower to acquire nuclear weapons after the United States and the Union of Soviet Socialist Republics (USSR), testing its first nuclear weapon in 1952. But despite becoming only the third nuclear-armed state, Britain faced profound uncertainty about its status and prospects as a world power. Britain had been on the winning side in World War II, but its finances and major cities had been ravaged by the war. Britain continued to hold on to much of its empire and remained the preeminent power in the Middle East, but tides of nationalism and decolonization were rising around the world. Britain retained the ambition of a global power but was increasingly dependent on the United States for its own security. What could nuclear weapons offer a state seeking to hold on to what it had as its position became increasingly hard to maintain?

This chapter examines the ways in which nuclear weapons affected British foreign policy after Britain acquired a deliverable nuclear capability in 1955. British elites believed that nuclear weapons helped Britain address two primary political concerns: reducing its dependence on the United States, and maintaining its position in international politics. Britain used nuclear weapons as a substitute for conventional forces it could no longer afford, granting it the ability to bolster its increasingly shaky alliance commitments. And by providing Britain with a source of deterrence under its own control, nuclear weapons allowed Britain to operate more independently of the United States. Ultimately, however, although nuclear weapons were useful to Britain, they were not a "get out of jail free" card. Even with nuclear weapons, Britain could not resist the broader currents of nationalism, decolonization, and political and economic decline indefinitely. Britain's status as a global power would ultimately come to an end despite Britain's nuclear arsenal.

The British case is particularly useful for testing the theory of nuclear opportunism because it represents a "hard case" for the theory. Many theories of, or commonly held intuitions about, international politics expect a state like Britain to have little need to prominently emphasize nuclear weapons in its grand strategy. For example, for scholars who expect that nuclear weapons primarily change the foreign policies of revisionist states, Britain was a status quo state, seeking to hold on to its position in the world. For those who expect that nuclear weapons are most useful to weak and vulnerable states needing to deter severe threats, Britain was relatively secure, with substantial conventional military power, a nuclear-armed ally committed to its protection, and highly defensible sea borders. These factors suggest that Britain would have relatively little need for nuclear weapons, and that acquiring nuclear weapons would have little effect on British foreign policy. If the theory of nuclear opportunism performs well in a case in which we expect that nuclear weapons would have little effect, this would provide an important validation for the theory.

When Did Britain Acquire Nuclear Weapons?

To look for changes in British foreign policy caused by nuclear weapons, we must first identify where to look. When did Britain acquire the relevant nuclear capabilities that might cause it to change its foreign policy?

As discussed in chapter 1, we need to pay attention to the intended British nuclear posture, the manner in which Britain intended to use its nuclear weapons, and the particular technological and military capabilities that such uses required. This enables us to identify the appropriate point in time at which to look for changes in foreign policy behavior.

The British planned to deliver their nuclear weapons to the air bases and cities of the Soviet Union.[1] British doctrine thus required a strategic bomber force with sufficient range to reach targets within the Soviet Union.[2] Britain did not have these capabilities when it first tested nuclear weapons in 1952. As the historian Matthew Jones writes in the official history of the British strategic deterrent: "The success of the first British atomic test . . . although undoubtedly important for reasons of status and prestige, did not yet offer the UK a capability that made any appreciable difference."[3] British leaders understood the importance of delivery capabilities. Indeed, the Air Ministry initiated the procurement process for new and sophisticated bombers capable of carrying nuclear weapons as early as August 1946 (before the final political decision in January 1947 to develop and manufacture a nuclear bomb).[4] In 1954, two years *after* Britain's first nuclear test, Prime Minister Winston Churchill nonetheless acknowledged that "we ourselves have no effective nuclear deterrents [though] we are making progress. . . . British possession of nuclear weapons of the highest quality and on an appreciable scale, *together with their means of delivery* . . . should greatly reinforce the deterrent power of the free world."[5] Anthony Eden, Churchill's successor as prime minister, noted in his memoirs that "alone among the allies of the United States, we were making nuclear bombs *and building air power to deliver them.*"[6] Similarly, the chief of the air staff Sir John Slessor argued in 1954 that Britain's "ability to put those bombs down where we want to" was the crucial capability Britain required to gain benefits from nuclear weapons.[7]

It was in 1955, three years after Britain's first nuclear test, as Britain's new Valiant bombers came into service and trials to match the new weapons to the delivery vehicles were undertaken, that Britain was finally able to deliver nuclear weapons to targets in the Soviet Union.[8] The Canberra bombers that Britain possessed before 1955 were capable of (though had not been designed for) delivering atomic weapons but did not have the range to reach the Soviet Union.[9] On May 31, 1955, a top secret command directive was sent to the air marshal Sir George Mills informing him that he was now responsible for maintaining the Valiant bombers "at the highest standard of operational efficiency" so that they would be ready "to strike immediately [upon] Her Majesty's Government decid[ing] that an atomic offensive is to be launched."[10] Britain's delivery capabilities would improve further after 1955. For example, the Valiants were less capable than the Victor and Vulcan bombers (collectively known as the V-bombers), which came into service in the late 1950s; Britain did not conduct a live drop from an aircraft until October 1956; and it was not until 1960 that British Bomber Command had its full planned complement of V-bomber squadrons. Nonetheless, the Valiants provided Britain with a basic strategic delivery capability from 1955 onward.[11] As a secret Royal Air Force (RAF) history of the development of the strategic nuclear deterrent argues, it was in 1955 that "an A-bomb could have been deployed operationally by the RAF."[12] It is therefore in 1955 that we should expect that nuclear weapons would begin to affect British foreign policy.

Britain's Strategic Environment

What effects should we expect nuclear weapons to have had on British foreign policy? The theory of nuclear opportunism requires us to examine the strategic environment in which Britain found itself in 1955 to make predictions about how nuclear weapons would change British foreign policy, using the sequence of variables laid out in chapter 1.

The first variable in the sequence is the presence of a serious territorial threat or ongoing war requiring the dedication of significant national resources. Britain was not involved in any war at the point at which it acquired nuclear weapons. And as an island nation with considerable conventional power and a particularly powerful navy, Britain did not face serious territorial threats. British strategists were certainly acutely aware of Soviet military power, undoubtedly viewed the Soviet Union as an adversary with aggressive intentions, and feared Soviet nuclear coercion. However, the Soviet Union did not pose a proximate threat to the British mainland, and British strategists recognized that the English Channel and Western Europe (and the large number of US and NATO forces stationed there) provided a substantial buffer between them and the Soviet Union.[13] While Britain certainly faced challenges within its empire, these did not pose threats to the British homeland, and primarily emerged from internal demands for self-determination within the colonies, rather than external foes.[14] And despite Britain's ongoing decline (discussed further below), it remained a conventionally powerful state. It was the third most powerful country in the world and continued to preside over a large empire and network of bases across strategically important regions, including remaining the dominant power in the Middle East.[15] The threats that Britain faced, therefore, do not amount to the level necessary to classify Britain as facing severe territorial threats.

The second variable in the sequence is whether the state acquiring nuclear weapons has a senior alliance partner that helps provide for the state's defense. Britain did possess such an ally: the United States. The Anglo-American relationship, which had grown closer before World War II, transformed during the war. Even before the term "special relationship" was coined in a private communication by Winston Churchill in 1943, the United States had taken a key role in financing British security and supporting the British position in the war through the destroyers-for-bases deal in 1940 and Lend Lease in 1941.[16] Cooperation between the two countries was so significant during the war that US Army chief of staff (and future state and defense secretary) General George Marshall claimed that Anglo-American planning in World War II represented "the most complete unification of military effort ever achieved by two allied states."[17] After the war, as British elites came to recognize the extent of British decline, American ascendancy, and the increasing Soviet threat, a consensus emerged that the partnership with the United States contributed in important ways to British security.[18] Underpinned by a mutual interest in containing Soviet power and reinforced by cultural and linguistic ties, the Anglo-American relationship would play an increasingly important role in providing for British security. The Anglo-American loan of 1946, the Marshall Plan (around 30% of which was invested in Britain), and the formation of NATO all formalized this relationship in the immediate postwar period. By the time Britain acquired nuclear weapons, the United States was a core contributor to British security.

The third variable in the sequence is whether the state is rising or declining in power relative to its key competitors. It is clear that Britain was in long-run relative decline.[19] Britain had emerged from World War II victorious but bloodied and economically weaker than in 1938: the value of British gold reserves had dropped from $864 to $453 million, a quarter of Britain's overseas investments had been sold to help fund the war effort, Britain's external liabilities had risen from £760 to £3,353 million, and exports were down

30 percent.[20] In the immediate aftermath of the war, British officials retained some optimism that Britain could recover its status as a great power.[21] However, Britain could not reverse the downward trends it faced. Britain suffered balance-of-payments crises in 1947 and 1949 and had to turn to the United States for economic support in 1945, 1947, and 1949.[22] Well before the end of the 1940s, British officials had concluded that "weaknesses seemingly provisional in 1945 were . . . permanent. Optimism about the long-term recovery of world power status for Britain was displaced by pessimistic appreciations of ebbing power."[23] This view was shared by American officials, with Secretary of State Dean Acheson declaring bluntly in 1947 that "the British are finished. They are through."[24]

Correspondingly, by the end of the 1940s, Britain was in the midst of retrenchment. India, Pakistan, Sri Lanka, and Burma had achieved independence, and Britain's ability to safeguard its interests around the world was open to serious doubt. The claim that Britain was declining in relative power at the point at which it acquired a deliverable nuclear capability is confirmed by the Correlates of War Project's CINC scores, which provide a measure of a state's share of global power. Britain's CINC score in 1955 was around 20 percent lower than it had been in 1950 and nearly 50 percent lower than it had been in 1939, and this downward trajectory would continue after Britain acquired nuclear weapons.[25] There is therefore no doubt that British power was on a downward trajectory at the point at which Britain acquired nuclear weapons.

Expectations

What predictions does the theory of nuclear opportunism make for a state in Britain's position: not facing severe threats or involved in an ongoing war, dependent on a senior alliance partner, and declining in power? Figure 2.1 shows the application of the theory to the case of Britain.

First, the theory suggests that Britain should not have found it attractive to use nuclear weapons to facilitate aggression. It is only states facing severe territorial threats or engaged in an ongoing war that must make it a political priority to directly improve their position against the source of the threats they face. For states in Britain's position, the security environment is less constricting, and aggression is correspondingly relatively less attractive. The theory therefore does not anticipate Britain using nuclear weapons to facilitate aggression.

Second, the theory of nuclear opportunism suggests that states with a senior ally and not facing serious threats find it attractive to use nuclear weapons to facilitate independence from that ally. States whose security is partly provided for by a senior ally are constrained if they wish to engage in behaviors that the senior ally does not support. This constraint is typically

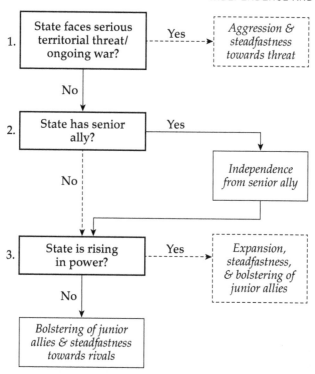

Figure 2.1. The theory of nuclear opportunism applied to Britain, 1955. Dashed lines indicate portions of the theory not applicable in this case.

binding because very few states' interests converge entirely with those of their allies. And, indeed, the United States and Britain did not have the same interests. At the highest level (and most obviously), as a 1955 memo to the British Minister of Defence Harold Macmillan pointed out, "The preservation of the United Kingdom is not of the same importance to the Americans as it is to us."[26] But even well below the level of national survival, Britain and the United States disagreed on a number of policy issues. Most prominently, the United States—itself a former British colony—was generally disinclined to prop up Britain's increasingly shaky hold on its colonies. The constraints imposed by dependence on a senior ally mean that states not facing grave and immediate security threats are likely to be eager to act more independently of their senior ally.[27] As discussed in chapter 1, nuclear weapons facilitate independence because they can serve as a partial substitute for the protection of a senior ally. The theory therefore anticipates that British elites would see nuclear weapons as a useful tool for avoiding dependence on the United States, and that Britain would have fewer qualms about acting independently of the United States after acquiring nuclear weapons.

Third, the theory anticipates that states that are reasonably secure but declining in power are likely to view maintaining their position in international politics as a political priority, and view nuclear weapons as a useful tool in pursuing that goal. The theory therefore predicts that British elites should have found bolstering and steadfastness to be particularly attractive. States in relative decline find maintaining alliances in which they are the senior partner to be increasingly costly and hard to sustain. Nuclear weapons provide a lower-cost way of sustaining an alliance, because by adding a nuclear component to the alliance, the state can make an alliance commitment with fewer conventional forces. States in relative decline therefore tend to see nuclear weapons as a way of making existing commitments of this sort more affordable. Thus, the theory predicts that Britain would use nuclear weapons to bolster existing junior allies. Similarly, steadfastness—standing more firmly in defense of the status quo—is attractive for states trying to hold on to what they have, and the theory therefore predicts that Britain would use nuclear weapons to facilitate steadfastness.

Finally, the theory suggests that Britain would not find expansion attractive. For states declining in power, holding on to what the state already has poses enough of a challenge. Widening a state's goals in international politics is unlikely to be feasible or attractive for such states, even if they acquire nuclear weapons. Similarly, compromise is not attractive to such states. For states seeking to maintain their position in international politics, giving up that position after acquiring an additional source of military power is unattractive.

The theory of nuclear opportunism, therefore, anticipates that Britain would use nuclear weapons to facilitate the bolstering of existing allies, steadfastness in response to challenges, and independence from the United States, but would not use nuclear weapons to facilitate expansion, aggression, or compromise. In addition to these changes in British behavior, the theory also has implications for British elite thinking about nuclear weapons. British elites should have believed nuclear weapons were useful tools for advancing their interests, and, specifically, as tools for facilitating independence from the United States (that is, they should have believed nuclear weapons would help them reduce their dependence on the United States), and for bolstering allies and resisting challenges (that is, they should have believed nuclear weapons would help them maintain their position in international politics).

British Thinking about Nuclear Weapons

Did British elites think about nuclear weapons in the way the theory anticipates? The theory of nuclear opportunism expects that British political and military elites should have viewed nuclear weapons as a solution to specific political problems. In particular, the theory predicts that British elites would view nuclear weapons as a solution to the problem of dependence on the

United States, and as a tool that would help the British maintain their position in international politics despite ongoing British decline. Outside analysts certainly believed that British strategists thought in these terms. As a 1949 memo to the US secretary of state outlined, the British motivations in pursuing a nuclear program were "(a) Freedom of action in terms of national self sufficiency . . . (b) National prestige and position . . . [and] (c) Uncertainty and apprehension as to the attitude (and continuity of attitude) of the U.S. towards the U.K."[28] But did British elites think in this way?

AVOIDING DEPENDENCE ON THE UNITED STATES

It was in the aftermath of World War II that Britain began to pursue nuclear weapons in earnest and in which the most comprehensive thinking took place about what nuclear weapons would offer Britain in the postwar world. But the British program had its origins during the war. It is worth examining British thinking about nuclear weapons during World War II, because at first glance it would seem that the extensive Anglo-American cooperation in the Manhattan Project indicates that concern about British dependence on the United States was not prominent in British thinking at the time.

In fact, even during the war, concern about dependence on the United States was a key theme in British thinking. Indeed, the British had initially been reticent about cooperating with the United States for precisely this reason. The British had been the first government to identify the military potential of nuclear energy (after British officials learned of a memo written by two scholars at Birmingham University[29]), and a committee of scientists concluded in June 1941 that it would "be possible to make an effective uranium bomb" that would be "likely to lead to decisive results in the war."[30] Because the British were ahead of the Americans, President Franklin D. Roosevelt wrote to Churchill in October 1941 proposing a joint venture, stating, "It appears desirable that we should soon correspond . . . concerning the subject which is under study by your MAUD Committee . . . in order that any extended efforts may be coordinated or even jointly conducted."[31] Churchill only responded some two months later expressing a vague willingness to collaborate with the Americans.[32] British officials discussing the possibility of collaboration raised concerns about the possibility of information leaking to the enemy, but this was a largely instrumental excuse. The primary reason to avoid collaborating with the Americans was a desire to retain complete control over the British nuclear program.[33] The British believed (correctly, at that stage) that their bomb project was more advanced than the American one, and were concerned about relying on American goodwill as well as the loss of scientific prestige and intellectual property of potentially significant commercial and strategic value. As Lord Cherwell, Churchill's scientific adviser, had written in advocating for an independent British program, "However much I may trust my neighbour . . . I am very much averse to putting myself completely at his mercy."[34] Churchill agreed, writing to his chief of staff that "action should be taken in the sense proposed [by Cherwell]."[35]

By the summer of 1942, however, the British had reluctantly come around to the necessity of collaboration. British scientists visiting the United States in 1942 realized that the Americans had overtaken the British in understanding the processes for producing fissile material, and concluded that the costs of collaboration were outweighed by the vast resources the Americans could dedicate to the project and the greater protection that they could confer upon a weapons program.[36] In a memo to Churchill recommending pursuing a joint project, the home secretary Sir John Anderson acknowledged that "the Americans have been applying themselves with enthusiasm and a lavish expenditure. . . . In these circumstances I have come to the conclusion [that] work on the bomb project [should] be pursued as a combined Anglo-American effort. I make this recommendation with some reluctance, as I should have liked to have seen the work carried forward in this country. We must, however, face the fact that the pioneer work done in this country is a dwindling asset. We now have a real contribution to make to a 'merger'. Soon we shall have little or none."[37] Ultimately, the British came to conclude that cooperation with the Americans was now the quickest path to possessing nuclear weapons under British control. Dependence on American efforts, however, was never intended to be anything other than temporary.[38] As Anderson explained to Churchill in 1942, cooperating with the Americans would allow British scientists to "take up the work again [after the war], not where we left off, but where the combined effort had by then brought it."[39] In another memo in 1943, he argued that "we cannot afford after the war to face the future without this weapon and rely entirely on America."[40] Britain's unwillingness to make dependence on the United States a permanent feature of its nuclear program was exacerbated by the frustrations it experienced as part of the Manhattan Project, with Churchill complaining to Roosevelt in 1943 about the lack of access to information that British scientists were getting.[41]

British concern about dependence on the United States persisted in the postwar era for three main reasons. First, Britain was concerned that the American commitment to the defense of Western Europe was less than absolute. As Prime Minister Clement Attlee later argued, "There was always the possibility of [the United States] withdrawing and becoming isolationist again. The manufacture of a British atom bomb was therefore at that stage essential."[42] Even though the United States formalized its commitments to Western Europe through the Marshall Plan, the formation of NATO, and the deployment of US conventional forces, debates in the United States made clear that support for an enduring US military commitment to Western Europe was far from unanimous.[43] In the atomic realm, cooperation swiftly stopped after the war. President Harry S. Truman did not feel bound by the Quebec agreement that Roosevelt and Churchill had negotiated during the war, which had guaranteed Britain "full collaboration" on "military and commercial" applications of nuclear technology, and the passage of the McMahon Act in 1946 further prohibited such cooperation.[44] Second, British planners were well aware that British and American interests diverged on important matters. Of course, it was widely known that there were plausible scenarios in which the United States would not be inclined to help Britain prop up its increasingly shaky hold on its colonies. However, even within potential war scenarios in which US and British forces would be on the same side, British elites doubted that the United States fully shared British priorities. As Churchill argued in the House of Commons in 1955, the British could "not be sure that in an emergency the resources of other powers would be planned exactly as we would wish, or that the targets which would threaten us most would be given what we consider the necessary priority in the first few hours. These targets might be of such cardinal importance that it could really be a matter of life and death for us."[45] Third, British elites worried about entrapment and the compromises that dependence forced Britain to swallow. For example, Britain's experience of the Korean War, in which Britain felt forced to back Washington despite substantial Anglo-American disagreements over its conduct, emphasized that reliance on the United States could force Britain into conflicts it would not otherwise need to fight.[46] Similarly, US forces stationed in Britain could be a potentially high-priority target for Soviet forces if a conflict threatened to escalate to the nuclear level, and threatened to suck Britain into a potential US-Soviet conflict. As Churchill stated in 1951, "We must not forget that by creating the American atomic base in East Anglia, we have made ourselves the target and perhaps the bull's eye of a Soviet attack."[47]

British elites viewed an independent nuclear capability as a solution to this problem. In 1946, Foreign Secretary Ernest Bevin declared that "we've got to have this [nuclear weapons]. . . . I don't want any other Foreign Secretary of this country to be talked at by a Secretary of State in the United States as I have just had in my discussions with Mr. Byrnes. We have got to have this thing over here whatever the costs. . . . We've got to have the bloody Union Jack flying on top of it."[48] In 1947, as the final decision to build the bomb was made, Bevin argued that "we could not afford to acquiesce in an American monopoly of this new development."[49] Prime Minister Attlee struck a similar tone, saying "we couldn't allow ourselves to be wholly in their hands. . . . We couldn't agree that only the Americans should have atomic energy."[50] On other occasions, Attlee used more emotive language to communicate the same point, arguing that the Americans "were inclined to think they were the big boys and we were the small boys; we just had to show them they didn't know everything."[51] Such views were shared by

British military leaders. The Chiefs of Staff argued that "it would be most unwise for the United Kingdom to be completely dependent on the United States and to accept the serious political disadvantages of not having a stock of atom bombs under its own control," and that it would not "appear compatible with our status as a first-class power to depend on others for a weapon of this supreme importance."[52] Similarly, Sir John Slessor advised that "we cannot possibly leave to an ally, however staunch and loyal, the monopoly of this instrument of such decisive importance."[53] For the chief scientist of the United Kingdom Ministry of Defence (MOD), failing to keep pace with nuclear technology would leave Britain "rely[ing] on the whim of the United States for the effectiveness of the whole basis of our strategy."[54]

Of course, nuclear weapons were never seen as a full substitute for the relationship with the United States, and Britain continued both to invest in the Anglo-American relationship and to hope that the United States would ultimately protect the British if a major security threat emerged. Indeed, the paradox of Britain's nuclear program was that, in the words of Matthew Jones, "the pursuit of independence also had as a goal the re-establishment of a nuclear relationship with the United States that some—at home and abroad—would see as compromising the exercise of national sovereignty."[55] British officials believed that having an independent nuclear program would allow Britain to gain greater benefits from its relationship with the United States, particularly in the realm of nuclear cooperation and influence over American nuclear choices. As Lord Cherwell wrote in a memo to Churchill, "The possibility of achieving full collaboration concerning plutonium and hydrogen bombs with the U.S. will vanish unless we have something [nuclear weapons] of our own to show."[56] Similarly, Britain hoped that an independent nuclear force would allow it greater influence over US targeting plans.[57] That Britain would seek both independence and influence is not surprising: having more plausible exit options from the alliance (that is, greater independence) should simultaneously have strengthened Britain's voice within the alliance (that is, resulted in greater influence).[58] In this way, British nuclear weapons were both a substitute for the alliance with the United States and a tool of influence within it.

From the earliest days of the British nuclear program, therefore, and despite the pressures of fighting a world war that forced Britain into reluctant nuclear cooperation with the United States, British elites clearly believed—much as the theory of nuclear opportunism expects—that nuclear weapons were a useful tool with which to reduce their dependence on the United States. As I argue below, it is therefore unsurprising that the British became more willing to act independently of the United States after acquiring nuclear weapons. After all, this was an important reason that Britain had acquired nuclear weapons in the first place.

MAINTAINING BRITAIN'S STATUS AND POSITION

Similarly, the desire to maintain Britain's position and status in international politics in the face of its decline regularly appears in British elites' discussions of acquiring nuclear weapons. This argument often took the form of assertions that Britain's status demanded that it remain at the forefront of military technologies: the historian Margaret Gowing, for example, writes that underpinning the British decision to build nuclear weapons were beliefs that "Britain as a great power must acquire all major new weapons, a feeling that atomic weapons were a manifestation of the scientific and technological superiority on which Britain's strength, so deficient if measured in sheer numbers of men, must depend."[59] Lord Cherwell advised Churchill that "it is surely vital, unless we are to become a second-class nation armed with inferior weapons, that we should be in a position to make our own bombs."[60] A draft 1954 air force command directive to Air Marshal George Mills argued that the incoming Valiant squadrons and the nuclear weapons they would carry would provide Britain "the opportunity of again speaking with equal voice with other great powers."[61] Similarly, Sir John Slessor argued that British nuclear weapons were necessary "if we want to remain a first-class power."[62] After acquiring nuclear weapons, British ambassador to the United States Harold Caccia wrote in 1957 that "our acceptance as a great power now rests to a large extent on our having a nuclear program."[63] As discussed above, arguments about the utility of nuclear weapons for maintaining Britain's status combined with concerns about dependence on the United States. It is hard to imagine a more explicit articulation of both of these views than the summary offered by Prime Minister Harold Macmillan, who argued explicitly in a 1958 television interview that Britain's nuclear status gave Britain "a better position in the world and one as a great power . . . [and] made the [United States] pay greater regard to our point of view."[64]

In addition to these somewhat amorphous claims that Britain's status as a global power demanded the possession of nuclear weapons, there were also more concrete strategic arguments made connecting the maintenance of Britain's position with nuclear weapons. In particular, British elites believed they would be able to use nuclear weapons to substitute for conventional forces that were becoming increasingly unaffordable. Nuclear weapons thus provided a way to reduce overall defense expenditures while maintaining Britain's global commitments and allowing Britain to retain its position in the world even in the face of economic decline.

British elites had recognized well before nuclear acquisition that Britain's conventional posture would be profoundly affected by nuclear weapons. For example, a 1945 memo by Prime Minister Attlee recognized that "the emergence of the atomic bomb meant that many of our present ideas on such matters as strategic bases and frontiers . . . must be regarded as obsolete,"[65] and in 1946 the Cabinet Defence Committee "declined to endorse the conclusions reached by the Chiefs of Staff on British strategic requirements in the Middle East" until they were able to assess the importance of "the latest developments in weapons and methods of war."[66] Moreover, British elites were under no illusions about the increasing economic difficulties facing the country, concerns that were exacerbated by the force buildup that occurred after the outbreak of the Korean War. These concerns continued throughout the 1950s, with incoming prime minister Anthony Eden told by his minister of defence in 1955 that "unless existing programs were revised, the cost of defence would rise during the next four years from £1,527 million in 1955 to £1,929 million in 1959."[67] Eden agreed that this was unsustainable as he initiated a reappraisal of British defense policy, stating: "We must now cut our coat according to our cloth. There is not much cloth."[68]

By the time Britain tested its first nuclear weapon, British elites had begun viewing nuclear weapons as a solution to the problem of maintaining the British position despite its increasing economic weakness. By substituting nuclear weapons for conventional forces, Britain could maintain its position at lower costs. In his private notes in 1952, Sir John Slessor was explicit that avoiding retrenchment despite the "economic crisis" facing Britain would require "preserving and increasing the main deterrent—atomic air power."[69] The idea of using nuclear weapons as a substitute for conventional forces was emphasized strongly in the 1952 Global Strategy Paper, one of the first documents to lay out an explicit strategy based on nuclear deterrence.[70] And, indeed, starting in 1955, Britain began to substitute nuclear weapons for conventional forces. Although the 1952 Global Strategy Paper had endorsed nuclear weapons being used as a substitute for conventional forces, the 1952 paper did not result in an immediate shift in Britain's force structure.[71] Reinforcing the argument above that Britain needed the ability to deliver nuclear weapons before British strategy could change, it was in 1955 that the concepts articulated in the 1952 paper began to be reflected in Britain's conventional posture.[72] British conventional manpower stayed between 800,000 and 850,000 between 1951 and 1954, but beginning in 1955, British manpower began to decrease at a significant rate, dropping to 750,000 in 1956, 700,000 in 1957, 615,000 in 1958, 565,000 in 1959, and 520,000 in 1960.[73] After acquiring nuclear weapons, Britain thus reduced its manpower by around a third in five years. Similarly, overall defense expenditure was held constant in 1956 (a decline in real terms and as a percentage of gross national product [GNP]), and subsequently fell as British planners placed greater reliance on nuclear weapons.[74] British elites were clear that this substitution was occurring. As Eden stated explicitly, it is on "the atomic weapons that we now rely, not only to deter aggression but to deal with aggression if it should be launched. . . . We are spending too much on forces of types which are no longer of primary importance."[75] To avoid Britain's defense commitments further damaging the British economy, he believed it essential to continue to move toward greater reliance on nuclear weapons.

The 1957 Defence White Paper ossified these trends. The minister of defence, Duncan Sandys, had his powers strengthened by the prime minister so that he would be able to succeed in securing substantial further reductions in military expenditure and manpower, and reorienting British forces toward nuclear weapons.[76] Sandys was not motivated simply by cost cutting and had a broader strategic vision emphasizing the utility of nuclear weapons and ballistic missiles that emerged leading Britain's efforts against German V-1 and V-2 missiles during World War II.[77] Nonetheless, he aimed to reduce annual expenditure from around £1,600 million to around £1,300 million and proposed further deep cuts in the size of the armed forces from 690,000 to 375,000 and to end conscription, a development Prime Minister Macmillan explicitly stated in the House of Commons "must depend on the acceptance of nuclear weapons."[78]

Crucially, however, nuclear weapons did not simply permit Britain to reduce expenditure on conventional forces. They would allow Britain to do so *without changing* Britain's political commitments or overall strategic position. As an internal RAF history stated: "The nuclear dimension of defence . . . was seen as providing the opportunity for economies in defence . . . without any sacrifices in national security or international influence."[79]

Overall, British elites thought about nuclear weapons in the way the theory of nuclear opportunism suggests. British elites clearly believed nuclear weapons would be useful to them: first, as a solution to the problem of dependence on the United States, and, second, as a tool with which Britain could maintain its position in the world by substituting nuclear weapons for conventional forces.

British Foreign Policy

British elites therefore thought about nuclear weapons in the way the theory suggests. But did British foreign policy actually *change* after acquiring nuclear weapons? Was British elite thinking about how nuclear weapons would be useful to Britain actually translated into British foreign policy? This section asks whether British foreign policy behavior changed in 1955 in the way the theory expects.

Much of this evidence is correlational—it shows that changes in behavior occurred at the time the theory expects that behavior would have changed. In some cases, we can find clear evidence that nuclear weapons *caused* the change; for example, as I show below, Britain was explicit that it was using its nuclear weapons to bolster existing alliances. In other cases, it is less clear that nuclear weapons caused the change. However, even correlational evidence can be powerful if combined with the evidence of British elite thinking discussed above. For example, if British elites repeatedly stated they wanted nuclear weapons to reduce their dependence on the United States, and then began behaving more independently after acquiring nuclear weapons, then the behavior and elite thinking are consistent in a way that suggests nuclear weapons likely caused the change in behavior we observe.

AGGRESSION AND EXPANSION

As discussed above, Britain had status quo preferences when it acquired nuclear weapons: Britain was trying to hold on to what it had. And British elites viewed nuclear weapons in this light—they did not view nuclear weapons as a tool that would be useful for expanding the British position in the world or behaving more aggressively in ongoing disputes. It would therefore be surprising if Britain were to engage in either increased aggression or expansion in the period following nuclear acquisition—merely holding on to what Britain already had was challenging enough.

And, indeed, there is little evidence that Britain began behaving more aggressively after acquiring nuclear weapons. Figure 2.2 shows the MIDs involving Britain over time (for comparison, the disputes of other countries are included). If Britain became more aggressive after acquiring nuclear weapons, we would expect to see Britain involved in more conflict in the period after acquiring a deliverable capability. As can be seen, Britain was involved in between two and three MIDs per year on average, but this did not change substantially after 1955 (restricting the sample to MIDs in which Britain was the revisionist power does not change the results). In the ten years preceding 1955, Britain engaged in an average of 2.6 MIDs per year, and in the ten years following, Britain engaged in an average of 2.3 MIDs per year.[80] While Britain was involved in more militarized disputes than most countries in the world (as would be expected given the British position in the world and its relatively powerful conventional military), there is little evidence of a substantial change when Britain acquired nuclear weapons. If anything, the number of MIDs involving Britain may have decreased slightly after 1955.

Another indication of aggression would be if Britain became substantially more willing in the post-1955 era to aggress against its rivals. Britain's only enduring rivalry over the period was with the Soviet Union, and there is little evidence that Britain became more aggressive toward either the Soviet Union or its proxies.[81] Britain remained committed to resisting encroachment by the Soviet Union—particularly in the Middle East where Britain remained (for the time being) the dominant power. And, as I discuss below, Britain became more willing to stand up to challenges to its position after acquiring a deliverable capability. This behavior certainly led to tensions with the Soviet Union on occasion, most notably during the Suez Crisis, in which the Soviet Union made clear threats to the United Kingdom. But in these cases the Brit-

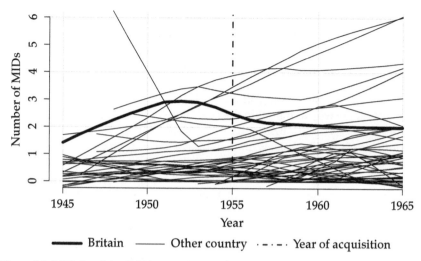

Figure 2.2. MIDs involving Britain over time

ish were responding to what they perceived to be serious challenges to the status quo (in the case of Suez, the nationalization of the Suez Canal), and so these behaviors are more accurately seen as instances of steadfastness than aggression.

Similarly, Britain did not expand its interests over this time period. As I discuss in detail below, Britain sought to use nuclear weapons to bolster its existing allies in Asia, the Middle East, and Europe, but did not seek to widen British commitments. Britain hoped to use nuclear weapons to place increasing emphasis on nuclear weapons at the expense of conventional forces, and thereby reduce the cost of *maintaining* British commitments. Nor did Britain initiate any new rivalries over the period.[82] Little consideration was given to expanding the British position in the world, and such an effort would have been foolish for a declining state such as Britain to engage in.

BOLSTERING

When Britain acquired a deliverable nuclear capability, its military and economic power was far less than that of the Soviet Union and the United States. Despite this, Britain's commitment to play a major role on the world stage remained, and of the eleven and a third British Army divisions, ten and a half were stationed outside the United Kingdom, spread across Europe, Asia, the Middle East, and Africa.[83] This section examines the three major alliance networks of which Britain was a part: the South East Asia Treaty Organization (SEATO) in Asia, the Baghdad Pact in the Middle East (which in 1958 became the Central Treaty Organization [CENTO]), and NATO in Europe. In each of these alliances, beginning in around 1955, Britain sought to use nuclear weapons to bridge the gap between the political commitments that Britain had adopted and Britain's declining conventional military and financial resources. By the late 1950s, all three alliances would see Britain's commitment become increasingly dependent on nuclear weapons. Thus, despite ongoing efforts to reduce defense expenditures, Britain used nuclear weapons to bolster its existing allies. Nuclear weapons offered a cheaper and more affordable way to maintain the credibility of its commitments to allies.

From the early 1950s, Britain had sought to formalize the many alliance relationships it had in Asia, with the hope of better protecting British interests in the region, including maintaining the security of Malaysia and Singapore, and protecting the British position in Hong Kong. Britain had been excluded from joining the 1951 Australia, New Zealand, United States Security Treaty (ANZUS) but succeeded in September 1954 when the United States, United Kingdom, France, Pakistan, Thailand, the Philippines, Australia, and New Zealand created SEATO.[84]

After the establishment of SEATO in 1954, South-East Asian states made a number of attempts to persuade British planners to confirm the details of British conventional deployments to the alliance. However, while British elites believed that SEATO served important strategic and political purposes, Eden and other senior leaders were unable to commit large numbers of conventional forces to the region beyond those in Malaya (now Malaysia), and the alliance lacked the ability to meet a large-scale Chinese offensive with conventional forces. The United States was also unwilling to make any firm commitment of forces to the defense of South East Asia (and certainly not forward-deployed forces as in NATO), or even to participate in an institutional architecture that would facilitate military planning for the region.[85] SEATO member states were well aware of, and uneasy about, the alliance's apparent lack of military capability. The Chiefs of Staff acknowledged that "it has also proved difficult to convince the Australians that the United Kingdom regards the defence of South East Asia . . . of being of equal importance to theatres nearer home."[86] The Philippines complained to the United States about "the utter lack of accomplishment of the organization," feelings shared by other treaty members.[87] Both Britain and the United States were aware of these concerns, with a State Department official telling the British embassy in Washington that "we must breathe life into the blue baby [SEATO]."[88]

Nuclear weapons offered a solution to this problem and were thus used to underpin the credibility of the alliance.[89] Plans to use nuclear weapons, it was concluded, could reassure British allies without producing a greater call on British resources. In February 1956 the Joint Planning Staff concluded that it was "essential that the future strategy for the defence of the treaty area . . . be based on the assumption that nuclear weapons would be used by SEATO" and that "large scale reductions in our conventional forces would not be possible unless . . . it may be assumed that nuclear weapons would be used."[90]

The British Joint Planning Staff emphasized that "the use of nuclear air power must form the basis of our strategy [in the Far East]. Care should be taken, therefore, to avoid undue emphasis being placed on the land campaign in the development of a strategic concept for the region."[91] At the SEATO Council meeting in March 1956, it was agreed that nuclear weapons would be incorporated into SEATO military planning assumptions. In the same year, the British Joint Intelligence Committee stated that "nuclear counter measures will be available" for the defense of British interests in Asia.[92] Britain thus began to draw up plans for nuclear deployments to the region, and in February 1957, it announced publicly that its contribution to the defense of the treaty area would indeed include nuclear-capable delivery platforms, including V-bombers flown from the UK, and carrier-borne aircraft based in Far Eastern waters.[93] British force requirements for SEATO missions included squadrons of nuclear-capable aircraft, and Britain drew up more specific plans to use nuclear weapons in particular scenarios, such as against targets in China or North Vietnam.[94] Such plans appear to have worked as intended by facilitating the withdrawal of conventional forces while simultaneously reassuring allies. For example, when Australian prime minister Robert Menzies visited London in 1957 to be briefed on the implications of the Sandys White Paper (which included plans to reduce British deployments in Malaya from 20,000 to 11,000), he was mollified by plans to deploy three squadrons of V-bombers to the region if a major threat appeared imminent.[95]

The same story played out in the Middle East. Britain remained the most militarily powerful state in the Middle East for much of the 1950s, but British conventional capabilities were increasingly stretched and economically unsustainable as the defense of Western Europe became a relatively higher priority for British planners than the Middle East. The British were well aware of these trends. A 1950 report for the Chiefs of Staff acknowledged "the little the United Kingdom can actually do to protect the Middle East,"[96] and in 1952, the Chiefs of Staff informed the cabinet that "we are faced with the fact that the United Kingdom cannot afford to maintain its present forces [in the Middle East]."[97] In April 1955 Britain sought to reinforce its position in the Middle East by joining the Baghdad Pact. Britain believed the pact served multiple ends: to protect the northern limits of the Middle East against the Soviet Union, to limit Egyptian President Gamal Abdel Nasser's influence throughout the Middle East, to constrain increasing American influence in Iraq, and to protect British oil investments in Iraq and the Persian Gulf.[98] The extent to which Britain hoped to use the pact as a tool for pursuing its economic and political goals in the Middle East irritated the United States, which ultimately declined to join for that reason: as Secretary of State John Foster Dulles noted, "The British have taken it over and run it as an instrument of British policy."[99]

Britain could not, however, afford to contribute large numbers of conventional forces to the alliance, and there was a widespread understanding that a conventional defense of the Middle East in global war was well beyond Britain's capabilities. A Joint Planning Staff paper in 1956 concluded bluntly that Baghdad Pact allies "cannot afford to maintain adequate forces . . . to fight a conventional war with Russia."[100] As in Asia, British reticence to commit conventional forces caused unease among allies, with the Joint Planning Staff noting that "it required a lot of talking to persuade the other planners that the United Kingdom was not trying to avoid helping in the land battle."[101] Ultimately, the Ministry of Defence had to acknowledge that "we have neither the men nor the money . . . to make the Baghdad Pact effective militarily."[102]

Nuclear weapons, as they had in Asia, provided a solution to the problem of maintaining alliance credibility while reducing conventional force commitments. The Chiefs of Staff concluded that "many of the targets selected [in war plans for the defense of the Middle East] are suitable for conventional attack, but nuclear attack would make possible a more economical Allied requirement of forces and munitions."[103] Another report by the Chiefs of Staff on British requirements in the Middle East argued "the implications of nuclear strategy have outmoded a concept embracing large conventional forces."[104] Minister of Defence Harold Macmillan discussed the utility of nuclear weapons for defending the Middle East and Asia explicitly in 1955, when he stated in the House of Commons that "the power of interdiction upon invading columns by nuclear weapons gives a new aspect altogether to strategy, both in the Middle East and the Far East. It affords a breathing space . . . for the assembly . . . of larger defensive forces than can normally be stationed permanently in those areas."[105]

Accordingly, nuclear weapons became increasingly prominent in British plans for the defense of the Middle East. In 1955, a British planning document confirmed that Britain planned to launch nuclear attacks from the Middle East, and in 1956 the Joint Planning Staff wrote that "the main United Kingdom contribution to the military effectiveness of the Baghdad Pact will be nuclear interdiction."[106] A Joint Planning Staff document concluded that "there can be no doubt that it is only by the use of nuclear weapons that the Soviet threat can be reduced sufficiently to bring it within the capability of the Baghdad Pact to withstand. The concept of defence of the Baghdad Pact area . . . is therefore based on the use of such weapons [which] must be provided for them [by the United Kingdom]," while another stated that "the whole concept for the defence of the area in global war relies on nuclear interdiction."[107] Britain sought to use its nuclear weapons as its primary contribution to the Baghdad Pact in 1955, seeking to avoid large force commitments by instead relying on the threat of massive nuclear retaliation to deter aggression.[108] An internal RAF history makes clear that "nuclear strike was seen as the main component of the assistance which could be offered [to the Baghdad Pact]," although there was ambiguity about exactly how and under what circumstances Britain would conduct nuclear operations in support of the Baghdad Pact.[109] However, Britain was not squeamish about deploying nuclear assets close to the Middle East. As early as November 1955, "the plans were for two [British] Canberra B2 squadrons" to be deployed in the Middle East Air Force, and "it was considered that they would then, or shortly afterwards, be capable of carrying nuclear weapons."[110]

As Britain acquired a deliverable nuclear capability, it thus sought to shore up its increasingly shaky alliance commitments in the Middle East, much as it had in Asia. Nuclear weapons allowed Britain to bolster its allies in the Middle East and maintain its position and influence without making conventional military commitments it could no longer afford.

Britain's most important alliance, of course, was NATO—the alliance that played an important role in providing for Britain's own security. Here, too, Britain sought to use nuclear weapons to strengthen the credibility of NATO while reducing British conventional and financial commitments to the alliance. In doing so, Britain also showed greater independence from the United States, by seeking to change NATO strategy in Europe against American wishes.

The MC 48 strategic concept that NATO adopted in 1954 caused unease in London because of its vision of a "two-phase war" in which conventional forces would fight even after a thermonuclear exchange between the Soviet Union and the United States.[111] Britain was unwilling to make the conventional commitments necessary to make such plans for "broken back" warfare credible. Much as it had in Asia and the Middle East, Britain argued that its nuclear weapons allowed it to place less emphasis on its conventional forces, with the cabinet agreeing that while Britain should "express our readiness to maintain, for the next few years, the present fighting capacity of the United Kingdom . . . the introduction of new weapons might call for some variation in the size and shape of our forces." What this meant in concrete terms was that it might be "possible to maintain the present fighting capacity of our forces on the Continent with fewer men."[112] Britain began to increasingly voice disapproval of NATO's strategy and sought to encourage NATO as a whole to change its posture during the Annual Review process. As Eden argued in a letter to President Dwight D. Eisenhower in July 1956, "A 'shield' of conventional forces is still required: but it is no longer our principal military protection. Need it be capable of fighting a major land battle? Its primary military function seems now to be to deal with any local infiltration, to prevent external intimidation and to enable aggression to be identified."[113] The Chiefs of Staff agreed that "as long as we [NATO] have the deterrent and are prepared to use it, it will be effective against lesser forms of war in Europe [in addition to deterring nuclear war]" and that as a result, "it will not be necessary to maintain large conventional forces."[114] Large numbers of conventional forces or other deterrents "do not add materially to the effectiveness of the primary deterrent and their cost weakens the economic strength of NATO states."[115] Similarly, Minister of Defence Walter

Monckton rejected the idea that NATO needed to build up conventional forces sufficient to hold and defeat an all-out attack by the Soviet Union.[116]

The Americans did not appreciate British efforts to change NATO's strategy, expressing concern that British conventional withdrawals would cause other NATO members to make similar withdrawals. Secretary of State Dulles argued that "we find unacceptable any proposal which implies the adoption of a NATO strategy of total reliance on nuclear retaliation" and that "the European nations should increasingly assume a greater share of responsibility for the ready forces required on the Continent to provide the shield which NATO strategy envisages."[117] In a meeting with Macmillan, he was equally blunt: "We do not wish our capability to be so exclusively dependent on atomic weapons that there is no measure of flexibility" and that "the US [could not] accept the idea that there was no need for substantial manpower because any attack would set off massive retaliation and in that provide a sufficient deterrent."[118] Ultimately, neither the United States nor Britain backed down. NATO did not change its strategy in accordance with British preferences, but the British did not give way to American preferences. Britain did reduce its own conventional commitment at the NATO Council meeting in December 1956.[119] Further reductions were made over the next few years, with Britain gaining NATO acceptance for a reduction of 31,500 men (leaving around 63,000) by April 1958.[120] As with its alliances in Asia and the Middle East, Britain's strategic ambition and political commitments to Europe had not changed, but the conventional commitment it was willing to make had been reduced: "The Army's tasks, within and outside Europe, remained; it simply had less with which to meet them."[121] Overall, therefore, British policy toward NATO represents the British using nuclear weapons to facilitate a combination of bolstering and independence from the United States.

The same pattern was therefore observed across Britain's most important alliances in Asia, the Middle East, and Europe. In 1955, as Britain came into possession of a deliverable nuclear capability, it explicitly sought to use its nuclear weapons to bolster its relationships in Asia and the Middle East. Britain used nuclear weapons to increase alliance credibility while reducing British expenditures and conventional commitments to those alliances. In NATO, Britain sought to pursue much the same strategy but ran into American opposition that hindered British efforts to persuade the alliance to move in the direction that Britain sought. In short, British nuclear weapons affected British foreign policy toward its alliances through the efficiency mechanism described in chapter 1: they reduced the costs of Britain's alliance commitments. As an RAF internal history states: "Overall, no overseas commitments had been dropped, but reductions in the level of military support were in prospect and the RAF [the service with the ability to deliver nuclear weapons] was seen as having a major part to play in offsetting their effect."[122] This is consistent with the expectations of the theory of nuclear opportunism.

INDEPENDENCE, STEADFASTNESS, AND COMPROMISE

To assess whether Britain exhibited greater levels of independence, steadfastness, and compromise after acquiring a deliverable nuclear capability in 1955, I examine British behavior in a series of crises in which Britain was challenged by other states between 1950 and 1960. Because the theory of nuclear opportunism anticipates Britain using nuclear weapons to facilitate steadfastness when challenged, we should expect to see Britain respond more forcefully to challenges after 1955. And in crises where British and US preferences diverged, we should expect to see Britain becoming less deferential to US preferences (that is, showing greater independence) after 1955. In order to do this, I examine British responses to crises in the Middle East. I choose the Middle East for three reasons. First, over this period the British position in the Middle East was subjected to numerous challenges. Examining how Britain responded to these challenges offers us a number of crises in a reasonably narrow window before and after nuclearization, thus holding a range of factors constant and making it more likely that nuclear weapons caused any changes in behavior that we observe. Second, the Middle East was a region in which US and British preferences differed substantially. As a result, examining crises in the Middle East allows us to assess whether Britain became less deferential to US policy preferences and willing to respond to challenges more independently of the United States, as the theory of nuclear opportunism would suggest. Third, I use the Middle East because Britain was the dominant power in the Middle East in the early 1950s and determined to retain its position.[123] Any change in behavior associated with nuclear weapons cannot, therefore, be attributed to conventional weakness or revisionism, as Kapur's theory of "strategic pessimism" would suggest.[124]

I examine Britain's response to six challenges to its position: the nationalization of the Anglo-Iranian Oil Company (AIOC) by Muhammad Mossadegh in 1951, efforts by Nasser to eject the British from Suez from 1952 to 1954, the Saudi occupation of Buraimi in 1952, the Suez Crisis in 1956, and subsequent crises in Oman and Jordan. I show that before acquiring a deliverable nuclear capability in 1955, Britain was extremely wary of responding to challenges with force without the support of the United States, and British responses were characterized by compromise and deference to US preferences. After 1955, Britain became more willing to use force unilaterally, paid less attention to US preferences, and was less inclined to compromise. Britain, therefore, exhibited significantly greater levels of independence, steadfastness, and a reduced inclination to compromise after acquiring a deliverable nuclear capability.

Iran, 1951 The nationalization of the AIOC by Mossadegh in 1951 had its roots in the early twentieth century. It was in 1914 that then First Lord of the Admiralty Winston Churchill persuaded the British government to acquire a majority stake in what was then the Anglo-Persian Oil Company (APOC).[125] The shah of Iran had negotiated a sixty-year agreement in 1933 on the terms on which APOC could extract and sell oil, but in the aftermath of World War II, changes in the British government's tax and dividend policy led to an increasing disparity in the revenues that Britain and Iran received from Iranian oil sales.[126] These disparities fueled Iranian anger over Britain's unwillingness to renegotiate the terms of the 1933 agreement. The British were concerned that any change in AIOC's concession could damage the British economy, although the Foreign Office acknowledged internally that the Iranians had "legitimate grievance[s]."[127] In July 1949, the AIOC and Iran signed a new "supplemental" agreement that substantially increased Iranian oil revenues.[128] However, increasing anti-British sentiment within Iran meant that the Iranian parliament never ratified the deal, and on April 28, 1950, the National Front's Muhammad Mossadegh was elected to the country's premiership. With anti-British sentiment at an all-time high and Iranian anger focused on Anglo-Iranian oil, even an offer of a fifty-fifty split by the AIOC was not enough. Mossadegh had declared that "the source of all the misfortunes of this tortured nation is only the oil company," and by early May, Iran had nationalized its oil. The AIOC facilities in Iran, and the oil they extracted, now belonged solely to Iran.[129] The loss of Iranian oil was viewed as a disastrous development for Britain. In the words of the historian H. W. Brands, the nationalization of AIOC "portended the apocalypse, to judge by the reactions of some in London."[130] For three months after the nationalization of AIOC, Britain seriously considered a military response.[131] Ultimately, however, Britain decided against military intervention.

The decision not to undertake military action was not due to a lack of military options. While the British concluded that securing and holding Iran's inland oil fields would be beyond their military capabilities, a more limited plan—known as Plan Y—to occupy Abadan Island and retake control of the refinery was thought to be within British capabilities. A memorandum to the British cabinet stated that "the Chiefs of Staff have concluded . . . that it would be feasible at short notice to occupy and hold Abadan against any opposition which the Persians unaided would be likely to be able to mount."[132] The US embassy in London cabled Washington stating that it was becoming "increasingly concerned . . . [that the] UK [is] preparing [to] use force in Iran."[133] Plans were developed over the summer of 1951, and by September, Britain was in a position to launch an operation to seize Abadan Island within twelve hours of a decision to do so.[134]

Nor was the decision to eschew a military solution made because Abadan was of limited importance to the British. On the contrary, the facility at Abadan was the world's largest oil refinery, Britain's largest single overseas investment, and had played a critical role in supporting the British war effort.[135] Indeed, Abadan was of sufficient importance to the British that the foreign secretary argued that retaining it may be worth risking Soviet intervention in Iran: "The risk of the Russians occupying Northern Persia might be worth accepting provided that we retained full control of the Abadan refinery."[136] As Britain sought to recover economically in the aftermath of the war, "sterling" or "dollar-free" oil extracted from British concessions was viewed as critically important to reducing the British dollar deficit.[137] The British believed that the status of sterling was critical to Britain's international position, to which the dollar deficit on oil posed an important threat.[138] Anglo-Iranian oil was at the center of this strategy to preserve the status of sterling. This was not only because AIOC was an entirely British entity but also because the government itself had a 51 percent stake in the company (unlike other partly British-owned companies such as Royal Dutch-Shell). The money that Britain received from Iranian oil constituted 4 percent of Britain's entire balance of payments.[139] It is no exaggeration to say that British officials both in the Treasury and at the Bank of England believed that the status of the pound as an international currency and Britain's position in the international system depended on British control over Iranian oil.[140] As Chancellor R. A. Butler stated in November 1951, America needed to understand that Britain's "economic viability was at stake."[141] The British ambassador agreed, telling US officials that the British doubted whether the United States "recognized adequately that the British are dealing with a prime strategic necessity."[142] The lack of a British military response to the nationalization of AIOC cannot, therefore, be attributed to the limited importance of the Abadan facility.

Instead, Britain decided against a military response because the United States was strongly opposed to the use of force.[143] For the United States, the dispute over AIOC was subordinate to the broader goal of keeping Iran out of the Soviet sphere, but in 1951 the United States felt too weak to provoke a dispute that might risk war with the Soviet Union. A 1921 Soviet-Iranian friendship pact gave the Soviet Union the authority to intervene if Iran were invaded, and the Americans therefore worried that British military action would "split the free world, would produce a chaotic situation in Iran, and might cause the Iranian Government to turn to the Soviet Union for help."[144] Truman instructed Attlee that "no action should be taken . . . which would result in disagreement between Iran and the free world."[145] Secretary of State Acheson wrote that the only circumstances in which the US government would support the use of force would be to "evacuate British citizens whose lives were in danger. Open Soviet intervention in Iran or seizure of power in Tehran by Communist Govt [sic] would, of course, also create [a] situation where use of force must be considered."[146] And a paper was presented to the British ambassador stating that "we would be opposed to the adoption of 'strong measures' by the British . . . such as the manipulation into office of an Iranian Premier of UK choosing or the introduction of force or the threat of force."[147] Despite understanding that "there is little hope that an acceptable solution can be reached under present circumstances," the Americans insisted that Britain forgo military options.[148]

The Americans were fully aware that the "UK decision whether or not to use force will be in [the] last analysis determined by [the] extent to which [the] US [is] prepared [to] support."[149] As they anticipated, despite British irritation at the United States' reticence to assist them, the British were not prepared to act alone. Harold Macmillan's view in an April cabinet meeting was that the UK could not go against the Americans: "I do not think at this stage we should, merely in deference to the Americans' opinion, go further than that."[150] In July, he made the same argument, that despite "arguments in favour" of using force, "if we were to use force . . . it is most probable that we should . . . alienate American and world opinion."[151] The cabinet was persuaded, concluding that "military action in Persia . . . should not be contemplated unless there were some fundamental change in the situation."[152] In September, by which time Britain had well-developed military options ready to be implemented, the same arguments prevailed again. Attlee advocated against action because of US opposition: "In view of the attitude of the United States Government, [he did not] think it would be expedient to use force to maintain the British staff in Abadan."[153] Attlee's argument carried the day, with cabinet minutes recording that "it was, however, the general view of the Cabinet, in the light of the United States attitude . . . force could not be used. . . . We could not afford to break with the United States on an issue of this kind."[154]

In the absence of US support for military action, Britain was forced to pursue a purely economic approach to dealing with Iran. In particular, Britain threatened to sue anyone who purchased Iranian oil, claiming that they were buying stolen goods.[155] Foreign Secretary Eden, who would later adopt a very different approach in response to the Suez Crisis, was responsible for implementing this approach.[156] The British did, however, continue to try to persuade America to act, but were rebuffed.[157] It was only with an increasingly favorable balance of power resulting from US rearmament, combined with Eisenhower's accession to the White House, that US policy changed. In early 1953, the secretary of state and the director of the Central Intelligence Agency (CIA) informed their British counterparts that the United States was ready to take action against Mossadegh.[158] Thus, although Britain finally participated in covert action to remove Mossadegh, the episode demonstrated Britain's reliance on the United States as it responded to challenges to its position.[159]

Egypt, 1945–1954 Egypt lay at the center of British strategy in the Middle East. In particular, the network of British bases in the Suez Canal Zone constituted a huge military investment with the ability to service and maintain an army of half a million men.[160] Since 1869, the canal had played a critical role in linking Britain to its empire in India and East Asia, facilitating British trade with Africa, Asia, and the Middle East, and in permitting the defense of the empire.[161] Britain had occupied the canal zone since 1860, and its military significance was demonstrated in World War II, when the British defense at El Alamein ended the Axis threat to the canal and, thus, to the Middle Eastern and Persian oil fields.[162] The increasing volumes of Persian Gulf oil and other goods flowing through the canal to Europe meant that the canal remained of high importance in the aftermath of World War II.[163] In the words of a 1953 memo to the prime minister, a British departure from the Suez Canal would have "far-reaching repercussions. . . . An evacuation of the Suez Canal Zone would mean the end of the Commonwealth as an independent force in the world."[164]

However, increasing currents of Egyptian nationalism were challenging the British occupation of Suez. As soon as the war ended, Egypt requested negotiations to end Britain's military presence in the country. For Egyptian nationalists, the Suez Canal was a symbol of imperialism, and a potential source of revenues currently being collected by the British and other European shareholders in the Suez Canal Company.[165] Britain was willing to withdraw forces from Suez, but only if British influence could be preserved and British access to the base during war could be guaranteed, something Nasser was unwilling to grant. Egyptian capabilities remained insufficient to compel British withdrawal, but Britain was increasingly forced to expend manpower and money defending the bases and protecting its soldiers and civilians stationed there.[166]

Despite Britain's continued military strength in the Middle East and the centrality of Egypt within British strategic thinking, the British strategy was to rely on the United States for support. Foreign Minister Eden repeatedly sought American aid, while Churchill bombarded Eisenhower with letters and telegrams pleading for American aid despite his fears that "running to the Americans for help . . . was undignified and did not increase their respect for us."[167] One letter stated that "it seems to me that you might by standing with us . . . bring about a peaceful solution in the truest harmony with the military and moral interests of the anti-Communist front. . . . If an Anglo-American team, military and diplomatic, puts our agreed plan firmly to [Egyptian president Mohamed] Neguib all may come well without bloodshed, and other blessings would flow."[168] A memo from Eden to the British ambassador in Washington stated that it "will be essential that the United States Government shall back us. . . . [The US government] should be left in no doubt that any approach to the Egyptians is unlikely in our view to bear fruit [without their support]."[169] But the British worried that the Americans would not fully support their position. As one cabinet meeting recorded, the prime minister "feared that the position of the British negotiators would be seriously weakened if the American attitude . . . remained uncertain. If there were any risk that the Americans would not support us on some condition regarding the maintenance of the [Suez] base which we thought essential for our security, it would be better that we should enter upon the negotiations alone."[170]

And, indeed, the US position was moving further away from the British one. US officials increasingly viewed supporting the British as inimical to American goals in the region. Many in the Eisenhower administration (particularly in the State Department) favored offering US support to the new Egyptian regime and had little inclination to help prop up Britain's imperial possessions in the face of Egyptian popular opposition. Both sides became increasingly irritated by the other—for example, Dulles complaining that the British were seeking to "put him in a straight jacket [sic]" by forcing the Americans to take part in joint negotiations over Suez, while the British believed the Americans were encouraging Egyptian opposition to joint negotiations.[171] Ultimately, the Americans refused to participate in Anglo-Egyptian negotiations over the canal zone, thus allowing Egypt to conduct bilateral negotiations with the British without the Americans sitting on the other side of the negotiating table, allowing Egypt to play Britain and the United States off against each other.[172] The British were fully aware that they would be pushed toward accepting conditions for their withdrawal that they viewed as unacceptable.[173] Similarly, they understood that Egyptian concessions were unlikely to be forthcoming without US support.[174] According to Churchill, without "whole-hearted support" from the United States, Britain would have to pick from "painful and difficult choices."[175]

Such support was not forthcoming from the United States. Instead, in November 1953, the Americans attempted to use the threat of providing aid to Egypt to coerce the British into making concessions, with Dulles threatening to resume economic aid to the Egyptians and telling Eden that "time is fast running out."[176] Eden tried to convince Dulles that Britain might be prepared to "fight it out or take some other measure unilaterally" if no deal was reached, and Churchill threatened Eisenhower that it would be "difficult for Anthony and me to help you in the Far East if we have to do it in the face . . . of [a] general feeling of indignation."[177] But ultimately, any threats to the Americans were a bluff and Britain could not afford to cross the United States. As Eden acknowledged to Churchill, "The real alternative to an agreement [with Egypt] is a fight which we can ill afford and from which [we] should emerge . . . without a friend left in the Middle East."[178]

Through the spring of 1954, US pressure forced the British to make serious concessions to Egypt on the duration of the agreement, the speed of troop withdrawals, the number of British technicians who might be permitted to stay, and the conditions under which Britain would be able to return to the base. The British were ultimately forced to adopt the humiliating position that the Suez Canal base was no longer even of great importance to them, with Churchill writing to Eisenhower that the canal zone no longer merited "the expense and diversion of our troops."[179] Similarly, Eden instructed the

British negotiating team that maintaining "a concentration of equipment, supplies and facilities in the Canal Zone" was no longer desirable and that Britain could therefore "approach the Egyptian government with, in effect, an entirely new set of proposals."[180] An agreement was swiftly struck: Britain agreed to withdraw its troops without any guarantee that they could return in the event of war.[181] Churchill noted sadly that "the sooner this melancholy business [withdrawal from Egypt] is over the better for all concerned."[182]

British leaders blamed Egyptian intransigence on the lack of US support they were receiving and believed that they could secure a deal that better served their interests if the United States would only stand alongside Britain. Ultimately, however, the British were unwilling to act independently of the United States and were forced to acquiesce to American preferences.[183]

Buraimi, 1952–1954 The Buraimi Oasis, located at the southeastern tip of the Arabian Peninsula, was strategically significant to the British because of the possibility of new oil reserves in the area and its location as a strategically valuable crossroads. As a memo by the foreign secretary to the British cabinet stated: "The retention of this Oasis is essential to our position in south-east Arabia. Whoever controls Buraimi can dominate the British-protected Trucial States and the Sultanate of Muscat Oman, where we believe that big oil deposits lie within easy reach of the Indian Ocean."[184] The territory was disputed, with Saudi Arabia rejecting an agreement that had been negotiated by Britain on behalf of Oman and Abu Dhabi in 1935. Saudi leaders, including the king, Ibn Saud, were well aware of the benefits associated with controlling Buraimi and had asked US officials to assist them in forcing the British to the negotiating table.[185] The United States was eager to avoid antagonizing either the British or the Saudis and viewed both parties' intentions with suspicion: as the US ambassador to Saudi Arabia reported to the State Department, "I do not feel [the] motives of either Brit[s] or Saudis in these matters are beyond question."[186]

US efforts to prevent a British-Saudi dispute from spiraling out of control were dealt a blow when in 1952 Saudi forces occupied the oasis with the support of the Arabian American Oil Company (ARAMCO). British officials viewed this as a significant challenge to their position in the Persian Gulf. Particularly after the nationalization of AIOC and the British "scuttle from Abadan," the Saudi occupation of Buraimi represented a further weakening of Britain's position in the Middle East that would damage British prestige and access to sterling oil.[187] Worse still, given the close ties between the United States and ARAMCO, the British viewed the Saudis as acting with the implicit approval of the United States.[188]

The British had the military capability to remove the Saudi forces and worried that the Saudis were "banking on [the] belief that [the] U.K. will not use force," which might be the "only effective way to counteract [Saudi actions] and restore [the] Brit[ish] position."[189] Indeed, British military options were enhanced by the fact that the sultan of Muscat and Oman had raised a substantial force with which to evict the Saudi forces.[190] However, the Americans requested that the British avoid escalating the conflict and encouraged the British to seek arbitration with the Saudis.[191] One of Churchill's briefing papers emphasized the extent to which the British saw themselves as ineluctably tied to the Americans: "Each power [the United Kingdom and the United States] must support the other fully and be seen by all to do so. Lack of positive support and an affectation of impartiality by either power will be interpreted as disagreement with the other and exploited to the detriment of both."[192]

The British therefore acquiesced to American preferences and persuaded the sultan to pursue a diplomatic solution, agreeing to a temporary "Standstill Agreement" that left the Saudis in control of Hamasa, the primary settlement in Buraimi.[193] Both sides agreed to remain in their current positions and avoid taking actions that might threaten each other or prejudice a future settlement.[194] The Standstill Agreement did not last long, however, with Britain abrogating it in response to perceived Saudi violations. Encouraged by the United States, Britain and Saudi Arabia reopened negotiations on an arbitration agreement that yielded little progress. When Eden took charge of the Foreign Office in 1953, he asked why Saudi forces had not yet been evicted from Buraimi and was told that the British had been reluctant to use force because they required US support.[195] The disagreement continued. Britain insisted that British companies continue their operations in the disputed area, while Saudi Arabia (backed by ARAMCO and the United States) demanded that Britain cease any actions until the case was settled.[196] Again, however, Britain agreed to solve the dispute via arbitration under pressure from the United States, with Churchill making a personal commitment to Eisenhower to this effect.

It is clear that Britain would have liked to pursue a more muscular approach to the Buraimi dispute, but was unwilling to go against the United States. Britain's approach to the Buraimi dispute was heavily constrained by US opposition to a more forceful strategy.

Buraimi, 1955 After obtaining a deliverable nuclear capability in 1955, Britain began to respond more decisively and independently to challenges to its position. Eden bluntly stated the change in British strategy in a cabinet meeting in October 1955: "Our interests in the Middle East were greater than those of the United States because of our dependence on Middle East oil, and our experience in the area was greater than theirs. We should not therefore allow ourselves to be restricted overmuch by reluctance to act without full American concurrence and support. We should frame our own policy in the light of our interests in the area and get the Americans to support it to the extent we could induce them to do so."[197] Britain's newfound independence was demonstrated in responding to challenges in Buraimi, Suez, Jordan, and Oman.

At the point at which Britain acquired deliverable nuclear weapons in 1955, it was in the midst of arbitration with Saudi Arabia over control of the Buraimi Oasis. In the eyes of the British, however, the Saudis were undermining the agreed-upon arbitration process, and several members of the commission resigned in response to Saudi efforts to instruct witnesses appearing before the commission. Eden informed the House of Commons that the British had abandoned arbitration on October 26, 1955.[198]

With the arbitration commission disbanded, Britain shifted its approach. In contrast to the British strategy since 1952 of seeking US political and diplomatic assistance and pursuing a peaceful solution, Britain pursued a unilateral, military approach to change the facts on the ground. Foreign Secretary Macmillan argued that the United States had "a natural instinct to appease the Saudis on account of the American oil company, Aramco" and that Britain "cannot afford to hesitate" to seize back control of Buraimi.[199] Despite the Foreign Office telling Eden two years earlier that Britain could not take military action in Buraimi because of American opposition, Britain was now prepared to ignore the United States entirely. British forces evicted the Saudis from Buraimi and returned the boundaries to the pre-1952 positions. More notable than the fact that British military action occurred was that Britain undertook it without either consulting or informing the Americans. Instead, after Eden had announced in Parliament that action was being taken, the British cabled Washington to let them know that the United States had to accept "that for the United Kingdom the issues are vital. We cannot allow this primitive and expansionist power to seize control of sources from which we draw an essential part of our fuel. Unlike the United States we have no indigenous reserves and in the last resort, we must act firmly to preserve our lifeline."[200]

This "brazen piece of unilateralism" caused outrage in Washington, with under secretary of state Herbert Hoover Jr. rebuking the British ambassador for the absence of consultation.[201] The director of the CIA, Allen Dulles, condemned the "recent British forceable occupation" as "negat[ing] five years [of] U.S. Government effort to get Saudi Arabs and British to arbitrate their boundary controversies."[202] Secretary of State John Foster Dulles vociferously protested the reoccupation of Buraimi to the British foreign office, telling the British that the United States would "state it had no advance knowledge whatsoever of [British] action and if it had would have urged that it not be taken."[203] The British were told that the United States would not support them if Saudi Arabia took the matter to the United Nations (UN) Security Council, and the British officer in charge of the Middle East section of the Foreign Office wrote in his diary: "Today we were thrown into a rage with the Americans upon receiving two notes or messages [from the Americans]— one telling us that we better go back to arbitration on Buraimi ... and the other practically ordering us to call off the Sultan of Muscat's impending clear-up of the rebellious Imam of Oman."[204] Indeed, US displeasure was sufficient that Eisenhower raised the issue personally with Eden during a state visit to Washington in early 1956, acknowledging Britain's legal claims to Buraimi but arguing that world public opinion thought "that the whole Arab peninsula belonged, or ought to belong, to King Saud."[205] Despite this pressure, the British resisted, declaring Dulles's position on Buraimi to be "thoroughly unsatisfactory" and resisting pressure to return to arbitration.[206] Likewise, Eden refused to give ground in his meeting with Eisenhower.[207] Britain and the United States, in the words of under secretary of state Hoover, "agreed to disagree."[208]

The reoccupation of Buraimi indicated an increase both in British independence from the United States and in British steadfastness in responding to challenges, and set a precedent for how Britain would act in response to challenges to its position in the Middle East.

Suez, 1956 It was during the Suez Crisis of 1956 that Britain's newfound independence was most dramatically demonstrated. As with the nationalization of the AIOC, the Suez Crisis involved the nationalization of an asset viewed as critical to Britain's economic and political status. Unlike in the case of the AIOC, however, Britain was prepared to act militarily without the support of (and, indeed, despite the opposition of) the United States.

As discussed above, the Suez Canal had long been viewed as critical to British security. Negotiations over the status of the canal had been a major problem for postwar British foreign policy, and a settlement had been negotiated with Nasser in 1954.[209] This settlement did not last long, however, with Nasser nationalizing the canal in July 1956 in order to raise funds for the Aswan High Dam. As with the case of Anglo-Iranian oil, the nationalization of the Suez Canal was viewed as a crucial challenge to British interests. Concerns about Britain's future ability to trade through the canal further eroded confidence in the pound and made a second devaluation of the currency in less than a decade a frightening possibility. Policymakers also feared that Nasser's rising power and anti-British nationalism would lead him to turn other oil-producing states against Britain and use the Suez Canal as a spigot with which to turn on and off the supply of oil to Western Europe.[210] Indeed, the British interests at stake over the Suez Canal were similar to those at stake over Anglo-Iranian oil. Both were challenges to the British position that would undermine British standing and prestige, both threatened access to British oil holdings, both threatened the British balance of payments and the status of sterling, and both threatened to set a precedent for how Britain would respond to future nationalist challenges.[211]

As in the case of Anglo-Iranian oil, the United States was opposed to military action by Britain to force Nasser to give up the canal.[212] Indeed, US opposition to military action was communicated directly and explicitly to the British. On July 30, Dulles told the British that "Nasser should not now be presented with, in effect, an ultimatum requiring him to reverse his nationalization action under threat of force."[213] Similarly, Eisenhower had communicated to Eden as early as July 31 the "unwisdom even of contemplating the use of military force," and warned that "the American reaction would be severe" if the British took military action without first exhausting peaceful approaches to solving the problem.[214] Britain was under no illusions about US opposition: as a memorandum to Foreign Secretary Selwyn Lloyd made clear, "Britain would have little or no international support . . . [and using] military force would cause a tremendous strain on the British economy." Chancellor of the Exchequer Macmillan also warned of the danger of taking military action and argued that in an extended crisis the pound would come under significant strain due to limited British reserves.[215] The United States was certainly not happy that Nasser had seized the Suez Canal, and Dulles told the British that he believed "a way must be found to make Nasser disgorge."[216] Nonetheless, the Americans believed that military action would play into the hands of both the Soviet Union and Nasser: turning Nasser into an anti-imperialist hero throughout the Arab world and pushing him further into the Soviet sphere of influence.

Despite awareness of these challenges, and in contrast to British behavior in the case of Anglo-Iranian oil, Britain quickly committed to military action in response to the nationalization of the canal. At a meeting at 10 Downing Street shortly after Nasser's announcement of nationalization, Eden made it "clear that military action would have to be taken and that Nasser would have to go. Nasser could not be allowed 'to have his hand on our windpipe,'" and told US under secretary of state Robert Murphy that Suez was a test that "could be met only by the use of force."[217] Similarly, he informed Dulles that "prompt forcible action was necessary" and requested US "moral and economic support," which Dulles refused to offer.[218] Other British officials made similar statements: Chancellor of the Exchequer Macmillan told Dulles that "utmost firmness" was required, and Dulles came away convinced that "the present determination of both the British and French is to move into the Canal area with force."[219]

On October 24, 1956, senior British, French, and Israeli officials (including the British and French foreign ministers and the Israeli prime minister) met secretly outside Paris. Agreement was reached for Israel to launch an attack across the Sinai Peninsula toward the Suez Canal. Britain and France would then make an ultimatum stating that they would protect the canal if fighting continued, and then invade when the fighting failed to stop. The goal was to seize the canal and hopefully supplant Nasser as a side effect.[220]

On October 29, the Israelis launched their invasion, with Dulles telling the president that "British and French intervention must be foreseen" and that "they may in fact have concerted their action with the Israelis."[221] Eisenhower, enraged by Israeli actions and potential collusion among the Israelis, French, and British, wrote to Eden asking for urgent clarification "as to exactly what is happening between us and our European allies" and warning that "we may shortly find ourselves not only at odds concerning what we should do, but confronted with a de facto situation that would make all our present troubles look puny indeed."[222] Dulles and Eisenhower's instincts were correct. Britain and France issued their ultimatum the following day, which Dulles characterized to Eisenhower "as crude and brutal as anything he has ever seen."[223] On October 31, Britain began bombing Egyptian airfields, and on November 5 British and French forces began their assault on the canal zone. The Americans were enraged, with Eisenhower berating one of Eden's aides on the phone thinking it was the prime minister and then hanging up before the mistake could be corrected.[224]

By November 6, however, the British objectives had already been lost: Nasser had obstructed the canal by sinking ships filled with rocks and cement, and the British goal of unrestricted use of the canal was thus gone. The Americans feared the risk of Soviet intervention.[225] Britain and France agreed to a cease-fire, but the United States now demanded a complete withdrawal of their forces. Eisenhower refused to meet with Eden and the French prime minister Guy Mollet in Washington, and stated that he would grant such a meeting only once Anglo-French forces were withdrawn.[226] In addition to diplomatic pressure, the Americans began to turn the economic screws on the British, whose fragile economy was deeply vulnerable to the disruption of oil supplies, the selling of sterling by the Federal Reserve, and restriction of financial support from the International Monetary Fund. Chancellor Harold Macmillan met with the US ambassador on November 18 to tell him that the "British Cabinet is beginning to realize what a terrible mistake has been made" and to plead for US assistance.[227] One day later, Macmillan returned to the US ambassador to report that Eden had had a "physical breakdown and will have to go on vacation immediately" and that the "first action after Eden's departure . . . will be on withdrawal of British troops." He pleaded for an economic "fig leaf to cover our nakedness."[228] Eisenhower refused to do so until the British withdrew.[229] The British, facing no alternatives, buckled under American pressure and on December 2, Foreign Secretary Selwyn Lloyd announced that British forces would be withdrawn from Suez.[230] Eden returned from his vacation and was swiftly forced out as prime minister, informing the cabinet two days before his resignation that "we and the French have been compelled, by a combination of the United States and the Soviet Union . . . to withdraw. . . . This has certainly done us great damage." In the same note he implicitly acknowledged that Britain's greater independence since 1955 had caused a fundamental shift in Britain's relationship with the United States: "The United States attitude to us in the Middle East dates from our refusal to give up Buraimi."[231]

While a detailed examination of the outcome of the Suez Crisis is not necessary here (what is important for testing the theory of nuclear opportunism is how the British responded to the challenge of nationalization, not the overall outcome of the crisis), it is worth noting that the fact that Britain was ultimately humiliated by the United States does not undermine the claim that Britain exhibited greater independence than it did before acquiring deliverable nuclear weapons. In comparison with crises in the pre-nuclear era, such as the nationalization of the AIOC, the British response in Suez exhibited far less concern regarding US policy preferences and a greater willingness to stand firmly in defending challenges to the status quo. The British response is thus indicative of greater independence from the United States, regardless of the fact that the United States was ultimately able to coerce British withdrawal.

Post-Suez: Oman and Jordan In the aftermath of the Suez Crisis, the conventional wisdom is that Britain shrunk, humiliated, away from the world stage and what remained of its empire. *The Times*'s obituary of Eden in 1977 described him as "the last Prime Minister to believe that Britain was a great power and the first to confront a crisis which proved she was not."[232] This position has been echoed in a large body of historical scholarship depicting the Suez Crisis as a decisive turning point in British history.[233]

Other historical scholarship, however, argues that the Suez Crisis was not the turning point in British strategy that it is often portrayed as.[234] Indeed, British independence persisted even in the aftermath of Suez. Britain continued to respond to challenges to its position and was "prepared neither to relinquish its residual interests in the region, nor become subservient to the United States."[235] As Ashton argues, "The British were resolved to pursue the promotion of their interests through the Baghdad Pact with even greater vigour after the Suez debacle, and were certainly not ready to cast off any mantle."[236] And, indeed, Britain continued to act unilaterally in the region when it felt its interests were challenged, often "with little regard for American policy."[237]

First, Britain intervened unilaterally in Oman in 1957 in response to a request from Sultan Said, who was battling the Saudi-backed Ghalib bin Ali. Macmillan wrote to Eisenhower, telling him that "the obligations of friendship seem to us to demand that we should not desert him in times of trouble."[238] The British sought to downplay their intervention, asking the US secretary of state to "take [the] line that Oman affair is 'small stuff' and not considered important by [the] U.S."[239] Nonetheless, the United States had significant concerns about the British intervention, with Dulles informing the president of his "concern that it [British intervention] could not be quickly wound up as a minor incident but that the Arab world would be drawn in in opposition to the UK, Nasser would have a new chance to assert Arab leadership, and we would be caught between our desire to maintain an influence in some of the Arab countries . . . and our desire to maintain good ties with the UK."[240] Ultimately, the United States did not actively oppose the British intervention but was unenthusiastic about the operation, with Dulles irritated by the lack of consultation with the United States given that the deployment of British forces came just days after he received assurances from the British that there "was no question of using British forces there."[241] Despite the humiliation Britain had suffered over Suez a year earlier, Britain nonetheless remained willing to act without US backing.

Second, Britain intervened in Jordan in the aftermath of the July 1958 coup in Iraq by pro-Nasser elements of the Iraqi army that brought down the Hashemite royal family. The coup was viewed as a significant blow to the British position in the Middle East for a number of reasons: because Iraq stood at the heart of the Baghdad Pact; because the revolution appeared to threaten oil interests in Iraq, Kuwait, and the Persian Gulf more broadly; and because of the possibility that the revolution might presage region-wide instability instigated by Nasser.[242] The British sought to encourage US intervention in Lebanon to prop up the faltering president Camille Chamoun, but the Americans worried that popular resistance to any intervention would be exacerbated by British involvement in the aftermath of the Suez Crisis.[243] As a result, the British were excluded from the planning for the operation by Eisenhower, who refused to make the operation a joint Anglo-American one: when Macmillan asked Eisenhower in a telephone conversation if he "wanted us to come with you or do you want to do it alone?" Eisenhower declined his offer.[244] Following the phone conversation with a written message, Macmillan accepted Eisenhower's decision: "I think you are right . . . that our 3,700 men should be held in reserve."[245] Instead, Britain sent its forces unilaterally into Jordan in response to a request from Jordanian King Hussein for assistance.[246] King Hussein had requested that both Britain and the United States assure him that they would come to his aid if he requested: while the British were enthusiastic, the Americans were not, with Dulles telling the British deputy ambassador that "Hussein has a better chance of pulling through without western military assistance than with it" and that the United States had "no clear idea as yet on the desirability of putting troops into Jordan."[247] Dulles expressed more direct opposition to Eisenhower, stating that he had "no enthusiasm for British forces going in," that "pan-Arabism could sweep the country very quickly" in the event of British intervention, and, four days later, that the British were "getting into a dangerous situation in Jordan."[248] Eisenhower agreed that the United States should not "get into the position of supporting Kings against their people."[249] Despite multiple direct requests from the British, the Americans refused to provide forces, though they did provide some logistical support.[250] For the British, however, US military support was not a decisive factor: Britain intervened anyway. British intervention in Jordan thus further demonstrates Britain's continued willingness to intervene militarily in countries without American assistance even in the aftermath of Suez.

What Role Did Nuclear Weapons Play in the Crises? British responses to challenges to its position in the Middle East are thus consistent with the predictions made above. After acquiring a deliverable nuclear capability in 1955, Britain was more willing to respond to challenges to its position more steadfastly, with greater independence from the United States, and showed less inclination to compromise. This evidence is correlational: it shows that British behavior changed in the way the theory anticipates, but does not itself show that nuclear weapons caused the changes we observe. In the discussion of bolstering above, it is clear that British nuclear weapons were causing the changes in behavior: British officials were explicit both in private and in public that nuclear weapons allowed Britain to reduce its conventional military commitments to its alliances and rely to a greater degree on nuclear commitments to strengthen and maintain its alliances. In the crises, however, finding smoking-gun evidence that nuclear weapons caused the change in behavior is harder. Nonetheless, there are reasons to believe that British nuclear weapons caused the change.

First, the change in behavior is consistent with British elite thinking about nuclear weapons discussed above. British elites wanted nuclear weapons in large part because it would reduce their dependence on the United States and help Britain maintain its position in international politics. After acquiring deliverable nuclear weapons Britain behaved in much the way that British elites had anticipated nuclear weapons would allow Britain to behave: with less regard for US preferences and with greater inclination to act militarily to preserve the status quo in the face of challenges. This consistency between British elite thinking and British behavior across a series of crises is suggestive of a causal role being played by nuclear weapons.

Second, we can trace the mechanisms identified in chapter 1 to see the ways in which British calculations may have been changed by nuclear weapons. In this case, it is highly plausible that at least two of the mechanisms identified—the political mechanism and the psychological mechanism—would have been operative in leading British officials to behave differently in the crises after Britain acquired deliverable nuclear weapons.

British nuclear weapons should have meant British officials felt more comfortable taking actions that may have led to escalation because of the effects British nuclear weapons would have on adversaries' calculations. We see examples of this in the crises after Britain acquired deliverable nuclear weapons in 1955: Britain was prepared to take actions after 1955 that it had been careful to avoid before 1955. Indeed, British officials explicitly made reference to a willingness to run the risk of nuclear escalation to pursue the country's political aims. In the leadup to the Suez Crisis, the British foreign secretary Selwyn Lloyd informed US Secretary of State Dulles that the British were fully aware that "they were starting something that might lead to an atomic war" but that they were prepared to take action anyway.[251] Similarly, Chancellor of the Exchequer Macmillan told Dulles that "if we should be destroyed by Russian bombs now that would be better than to be reduced to impotence by the disintegration of [Britain's] entire position abroad."[252]

It is hard to imagine British leaders making such statement in the period before 1955, in which Britain deferred to US preferences in each case.

Similarly, we might expect that British policymakers would have viewed the threat of third-party intervention as less credible given British nuclear weapons. The only crisis in which Britain received such threats was the 1956 Suez Crisis. Soviet Premier Nikolai Bulganin communicated to Eden the "very grave consequence[s]" that would result from Britain's "aggressive war against Egypt" and the Soviet "determination to crush the aggressor," and asked provocatively, "In what position would Britain have found herself had she been attacked by more powerful states possessing all types of modern weapons of destruction?"[253] The French—who lacked nuclear weapons— were "greatly concerned by the threat," communicating to the United States that they "cannot exclude the possibility of an attack by the Soviet Union."[254] By contrast, the nuclear-armed British did not view Soviet nuclear threats as credible. Eden later commented that "we considered that the threats in Marshall Bulganin's note need not be taken literally," and his public relations adviser derided the threat as "twaddle"; the Joint Intelligence Committee concluded that the Russian threat was a bluff; and the immediate effect of the threat was to harden rather than weaken British resolve.[255] The fact that the non-nuclear-armed French took the Soviet nuclear threat more seriously than the British is entirely consistent with the political mechanisms discussed in chapter 1: Britain's nuclear weapons meant that Soviet threats were less credible to the British than they were to the French. As Groom argues, Britain's "store of atomic weapons and a credible delivery system . . . was not something that the Soviet leaders could afford to take lightly."[256]

British leaders during the period in which Britain acquired nuclear weapons also offer highly plausible candidates for the psychological and identity-based mechanisms linking nuclear weapons to changes in foreign policy. Anthony Eden, much like his predecessor Winston Churchill, epitomizes the "oppositional-nationalist" view of Britain that Jacques Hymans identifies as being most likely to view nuclear weapons as a solution to a state's security problems.[257] Eden believed Britain to be an inherently great power with the right to play a pivotal role in global affairs but whose rightful position on the world stage was constantly being challenged and undermined by both allies and adversaries in a dangerous world. Eden's aristocratic family background, the deaths of his elder brother and uncle in World War I, and his vindication after resigning as foreign secretary in opposition to the appeasement of Hitler in the 1930s all contributed to his view of Britain as an important and virtuous state in a dangerous international environment.[258] Such leaders are likely to be particularly inclined to view nuclear weapons as important tools of statecraft, and thus most likely to have their foreign policy calculations influenced by nuclear acquisition.

Overall, therefore, several plausible mechanisms link British nuclear weapons to the observed change in British crisis behavior.

Third, if British nuclear weapons did not cause the change, what did? Britain's responses to challenges in the Middle East seem to have changed dramatically in 1955, but to conclude that nuclear weapons had no effect we need a plausible alternative explanation: an additional factor that also changed in 1955. The most obvious candidate is that Churchill was replaced by Eden as prime minister in 1955: could it be that the changes in behavior we observe are due to the change in leader rather than the acquisition of a deliverable nuclear capability? While it is not possible to rule out this alternative explanation completely, there are reasons to doubt its ability to explain the changes in British behavior. First, Eden was intimately involved in foreign policy making as foreign secretary and deputy prime minister before becoming prime minister, including being the "primary architect" of several of the pre-1955 policies, including the pursuit of US assistance in responding to the 1951 nationalization of Anglo-Iranian oil and the 1954 Anglo-Egyptian Treaty.[259] Second, Eden and Churchill came from the same political party and shared a similar outlook on foreign policy, with Eden recalling Churchill commenting that "you could put each of us in a separate room, put any questions of foreign policy to us, and nine times out of ten we would give the same answer."[260] Both leaders shared the oppositional-nationalist view of Britain's role in the world that Hymans identifies as shaping leaders' views of nuclear weapons.[261] While the relationship between Churchill and Eden was often difficult and fractious, this did not stem from substantive political differences on matters of foreign policy, but rather because Eden was an impatient "heir apparent" as Churchill gradually lost his grip on power.[262] It therefore seems unlikely that Eden and Churchill differed sufficiently on matters of foreign policy to explain the changes in British foreign policy after 1955. Indeed, if anything, Eden was less inclined than Churchill to respond to challenges steadfastly. For example, Eden had argued—against Churchill—that maintaining large numbers of forces in the Middle East and in the Suez base was unnecessary, while Churchill was more inclined to place a high priority on maintaining the British position in Suez.[263]

Overall, there is good reason to think that British nuclear weapons caused the change in foreign policy we see in the crises: a greater degree of independence from the United States, a reduced inclination to compromise, and a greater degree of steadfastness when challenged. These changes are consistent with the predictions of the theory of nuclear opportunism.

Other Explanations

Do other theories explain the British case better than the theory of nuclear opportunism?

The theory of the nuclear revolution predicts that nuclear weapons would make Britain more secure, and thus that Britain would not use nuclear weapons to facilitate aggression, expansion, or bolstering. However, the theory predicts that states may use nuclear weapons to facilitate steadfastness, independence, and compromise. It thus makes several correct predictions in the British case: Britain did indeed use nuclear weapons to facilitate steadfastness and independence, and did not use nuclear weapons to facilitate aggression or expansion. However, in contrast to the predictions of the theory of the nuclear revolution, Britain showed no greater inclination to compromise after acquiring deliverable nuclear weapons, and did use nuclear weapons to facilitate the bolstering of junior allies. Thus, while the theory of the nuclear revolution makes a number of correct predictions, it does not perform as well as the theory of nuclear opportunism.

S. Paul Kapur's theory of emboldenment predicts that weak, revisionist states use nuclear weapons to facilitate aggression. Neither of these conditions is met in the British case. As discussed above, although Britain had suffered substantially in World War II, it had not had its territory occupied and retained a powerful conventional military. Britain had the third largest military in the world and the second largest navy, and it retained a large empire that had contributed considerable military capability to the allied war effort. Britain was not, therefore, a conventionally weak state at the point of nuclear acquisition. Similarly, Britain had firmly status quo preferences: as described above, Britain's political priority was to *maintain* the British position in international politics. Thus, Kapur's theory correctly predicts that Britain would not use nuclear weapons to facilitate aggression. However, Kapur's theory does not offer an explanation for how British foreign policy should have changed: Kapur's theory therefore misses the important ways in which British foreign policy did change after nuclear acquisition.

Finally, the most plausible case-specific alternative explanation would be that the change in behavior observed reflected the change in leadership that Britain experienced in 1955. However, as discussed above, this is not persuasive as an account of the change in behavior we observe: Eden and Churchill came from the same political party, they agreed on most matters of foreign policy, and Eden had been intimately involved in British foreign policy well before he became prime minister.

Nuclear Weapons and Continued British Decline

Nuclear weapons were therefore useful to Britain as it sought to preserve its position in the world and avoid dependence on the United States. But were these merely transitory effects that dissipated over time? Or have these ideas about the utility of nuclear weapons for British foreign policy endured?

It might initially seem that nuclear weapons failed to help Britain maintain its position in the world. It is certainly true that nuclear weapons did not allow Britain to permanently defy geopolitical gravity. In time, Britain was forced to accept a position in the world in line with its capabilities: as a nuclear-armed and active regional power rather than the imperial great power it had once been. Similarly, it is often argued that Britain subjugated its nuclear weapons to the United States, and that after 1958 Britain no longer possessed a fully independent nuclear deterrent.[264] However, the fact that Britain could not ultimately maintain its status as a global power despite acquiring nuclear weapons does not undermine the theory of nuclear opportunism. After all, the claim of the theory of nuclear opportunism is that nuclear weapons are useful and help states pursue goals that they care about, not that they are all-powerful tools of political influence or silver bullets that grant states free rein in international politics.

In fact, the effects that the theory of nuclear opportunism identifies, and the ideas about the utility of nuclear weapons that underpin those effects in the British case, have demonstrated remarkable staying power. Throughout the Cold War and since, British elites have continued to view nuclear weapons as an important component of British power and influence in the world and have sought to avoid dependence on the United States by retaining an independent nuclear capability despite the costs associated with doing so. Despite American efforts to reduce the independence of Britain's nuclear program, Britain has always viewed the right to use nuclear weapons independently as a crucial capability underpinning its position in the world and its independence from the United States, and as a powerful source of influence over the United States and American nuclear choices.

While conceptions of "nuclear independence" have changed somewhat over time, Britain has retained an "abiding adherence to national control and operation."[265] Britain has always retained ultimate control over its nuclear weapons even as it became more dependent on the United States for missile technologies and British strategic targeting became increasingly coordinated with NATO. The United States has certainly sought to reduce the independence of Britain's nuclear arsenal and take advantage of Britain's struggle to afford a fully independent nuclear deterrent: as S. J. Ball argues, US officials "moved to bring planning for [British nuclear] use under an American umbrella and to make the British nuclear force dependent on American nuclear weapons."[266] As McGeorge Bundy told President John F. Kennedy in April 1962, "We would much rather have . . . the British join with the rest of NATO in accepting a single U.S. dominated nuclear force."[267] Nonetheless, the British have always been insistent that they retain the ability to use nuclear weapons independently: as Prime Minister Macmillan told his cabinet, Britain needed to "have within our control sufficient weapons to provide a deterrent influence independent of the United States."[268] And as he argued to Kennedy in negotiating the conditions under which Britain would receive American Polaris submarine-launched ballistic missiles, "The U.K. does not want to be just a clown, or a satellite. The U.K. wants a nuclear force not only for defense, but in the event of menace to its existence, which the U.K. might have to meet; for example: when Khrushchev waved his rockets about the time of Suez" (indeed, Macmillan's invocation of the Suez Crisis as an example of the ways British nuclear weapons can support an independent foreign policy offers further support for the argument made above that nuclear weapons contributed to British independence in the crisis).[269] In the Nassau Agreement and Polaris Sales Agreement that formalized the conditions attached to Britain receiving submarine-launched missiles, Britain secured the right to use nuclear weapons independently if it determined that "supreme national interests are at stake."[270] And, indeed, the Polaris agreement formed the basis of the 1982 deal to provide Britain with the Trident missiles that Britain continues to use, preserving Britain's ability to use nuclear weapons independently of the United States should the British government deem it necessary.[271]

Britain's commitment to nuclear weapons and the ability to use them independently of the United States has therefore continued throughout the Cold War and well into the twenty-first century. Despite British denials, it is now known that British warships carried nuclear weapons during the 1982 war to restore British control over the Falkland Islands.[272] And there was little doubt in the 2000s that the British government would commit to renewing the British deterrent, investing in a new generation of nuclear-armed submarines and extending the life of the Trident missile. The 2006 government white paper announcing its support for such investments declared that "an independent British nuclear deterrent is an essential part of our insurance against the uncertainties and risks of the future,"[273] and large majorities in parliament voted to support the process of renewing the British deterrent in both 2007 and 2016.[274] As Nick Ritchie has argued, a powerful cross-party coalition of British politicians and the permanent civil service continue to view Britain's nuclear weapons as "an essential capability" underpinning Britain's position and status as a "responsible, interventionist, 'pivotal' major power" critical to the "political and military credibility" that Britain has in Washington: precisely the ideas and effects of nuclear weapons that the theory of nuclear opportunism predicts in the British case.[275] The ideas and narratives that motivated British nuclear acquisition and the effects they have on British foreign policy have been "reproduced" by British elites with only minor adjustments in the post–Cold War era.[276]

This level of consensus is particularly notable given that many of the security threats that Britain faces in the post–Cold War era are less obviously amenable to nuclear deterrence than they were in the Cold War era. If anything, it is surprising how little a vigorous debate about the utility of British nuclear weapons among scholars and analysts has permeated the discourse of British policymakers.[277] The theory of nuclear opportunism, by showing how British nuclear weapons are useful even to a relatively secure, declining power, offers an explanation for the cross-party consensus regarding the utility of British nuclear that persists even today.

In short, the basic ideas that underpin the British nuclear deterrent—of both maintaining Britain's position in the world and avoiding dependence on, and gaining influence with, the United States—have persisted over time. They motivated Britain's pursuit and acquisition of nuclear weapons in the 1940s and 1950s, they motivated the changes in Britain's foreign policy after nuclear acquisition, and they continue to shape elite discourse about the utility of Britain's nuclear weapons even in the post–Cold War era. The theory of nuclear opportunism offers a powerful explanation for the persistence of these ideas and for Britain's continued possession of nuclear weapons even as the threats that Britain has faced have changed dramatically over the decades since British leaders first acquired them.

The evidence suggests that nuclear weapons affected British foreign policy in ways that are consistent with the theory of nuclear opportunism. As a reasonably secure state protected by a senior ally and declining in power, Britain saw nuclear weapons as a solution to two fundamental political problems it faced: dependence on the United States and maintaining its position in the world despite its long-run decline. Britain therefore found pursuing independence from the United States, the bolstering of its junior allies, and steadfastness in the face of challenges to be attractive. After acquiring a deliverable nuclear capability in 1955, Britain used nuclear weapons to facilitate these behaviors: bolstering its allies in Asia, the Middle East, and Europe, and responding to challenges to its position more steadfastly and independently of the preferences of the United States, despite simultaneously cutting back on its conventional forces over the same period. These outcomes are consistent with the theory of nuclear opportunism and inconsistent with the theory of the nuclear revolution.

Apartheid and Aggression

South Africa, Angola, and the Bomb

In late 1979, the apartheid South African regime secretly acquired nuclear weapons. A pariah state that excluded the majority of its population from political power, the South African regime faced internal unrest and an increasingly dangerous regional environment. South Africa was surrounded by states eager to see the downfall of the apartheid regime and was fighting an increasingly bloody war in Angola against a potent combination of Angolan and Cuban forces backed by Soviet arms and materiel. Despite these threats, South Africa never publicly tested its nuclear weapons or announced its nuclear capabilities to the world. Some twenty years later, South Africa dismantled its nuclear arsenal—again, in complete secrecy—as a prelude to domestic political reforms and rejoining the international community as a "rainbow nation." It remains the only state to have built nuclear weapons and voluntarily given them up. Based on interviews with members of the political and military elites of the apartheid regime, as well as declassified documents from South African government archives, this chapter examines South Africa's unique nuclear history and the ways in which nuclear weapons affected South African foreign policy.

South African elites from the apartheid regime are often eager to deny that any strategic rationale existed for their nuclear weapons program. According to this narrative, nuclear weapons were of no use to South Africa and had no effect on its foreign policy. For example, David Steward, a former ambassador to the United Nations, head of the Bureau for Information, and chief of staff to President F. W. de Klerk, argues that "the whole idea" that South Africa could have achieved political leverage using its nuclear weapons was "completely cock-eyed" and "the acquisition of nuclear weapons made very little sense at all."[1] Deon Fourie, a consultant to the South African Defence Force (SADF) in the apartheid era and a staff member at the South African Defence College who taught nuclear strategy in the 1970s and 1980s, claims that the entire nuclear program was based on "haywire thinking" by "politicians and soldiers at the top [who] were so unsophisticated politically."[2] This narrative appears plausible. After all, what use would a country fighting guerrillas in a bush war and that had conventional military superiority over all its neighbors have for nuclear weapons?

This narrative, however, is wrong. In fact, for all the paranoia, racism, and nationalism that motivated the apartheid regime, the South African nuclear program was underpinned by a steely strategic logic that South African elites were fully aware of and that affected South Africa's foreign policy in important ways. Perceiving existential threats from both inside and outside South Africa's borders, and fighting a war in Angola with the potential to trigger greater Soviet intervention that could overturn South Africa's military dominance, South African elites viewed nuclear weapons as the ultimate tool for deterring and controlling escalation. If South Africa's security situation were to worsen sufficiently, nuclear weapons provided South Africa with additional leverage to compel assistance from the United States and deter greater Soviet intervention in the region. This, in turn, reduced the risk of acting more aggressively in Angola, something the apartheid regime had long desired. As a result, and much as the theory of nuclear opportunism expects, South Africa became more aggressive in the aftermath of acquiring nuclear weapons.

The South African case provides significant leverage in testing the theory of nuclear opportunism. As with the British case, the South African case is a hard one for the theory because it contains strong "countervailing conditions": factors that would lead us to expect that nuclear acquisition would have a relatively limited effect on foreign policy. South Africa had conventional military superiority over its neighbors, never announced its nuclear capabilities or built a large nuclear arsenal, and had status quo preferences: seeking to hold on to its position in southern Africa and maintain the institutions of apartheid in the face of international and domestic pressure. South Africa also developed nuclear weapons well after the emergence of the norm of nuclear nonuse, which should have made South African nuclear weapons even less relevant to its foreign policy. All of these factors would suggest that nuclear weapons would be relatively unlikely to affect South African foreign policy. The case of South Africa thus represents a hard case for the theory of nuclear opportunism, which predicts that nuclear weapons would have a significant effect on South Africa's foreign policy.

When Did South Africa Acquire Nuclear Weapons?

To look for changes in South African foreign policy caused by nuclear weapons, we first need to know when to look. When did South Africa acquire the relevant capabilities, and when should we expect to see changes occur in South African foreign policy? As discussed in chapter 1, this requires that we pay attention to South Africa's nuclear posture, the ways in which South Africa intended to use nuclear weapons, and the particular technological and military capabilities that such uses require. This enables us to accurately identify the appropriate point in time at which to look for changes in foreign policy.

South Africa adopted a nuclear posture that aimed to threaten a nuclear test as a way to "draw in Western—particularly American—assistance," what Vipin Narang refers to as a "catalytic posture."[3] Most scholars of South Africa's nuclear program agree that this was the way South Africa intended to use its nuclear weapons.[4] This is confirmed by interviews with officials involved in the nuclear program and South African military and political decision making at the time.[5] As former South African ambassador to the UN Jeremy Shearar describes the logic of the strategy, "The thinking was that if the West knew we were going to test, they would want to stop us and they would then pledge support to South Africa."[6] Exactly what conflict threshold would have triggered South Africa to begin implementing the strategy remains unclear, although several members of the South African political and military elite suggested that Cuban or Angolan forces crossing into Namibia (then known as South West Africa, which South Africa controlled and ran as its own territory) would have been sufficient.[7]

The technological capabilities needed to use nuclear weapons in this way are modest. A state does not require the ability to deliver nuclear weapons with reliability, nor does it require a large or sophisticated arsenal.[8] All that is needed for nuclear weapons to affect the policy calculations of a state employing this posture is the ability to conduct a nuclear test: requiring only a crude explosive device and sufficient fissile material to sustain a chain reaction.

South Africa attained this capability in late 1979. André Buys, the future chair of the working group on nuclear strategy within Armscor (the state's arms production agency), recalls that the South Africans had initially thought they would have sufficient highly enriched uranium (HEU) to conduct a nuclear test in 1977. However, progress in producing HEU was slower than expected, and South Africa "only had sufficient material for the first explosion in 1979."[9] By this point, South Africa had already constructed a device with which to conduct an explosion.[10] The factor constraining South Africa's ability to test was therefore HEU, rather than a device with which to explode the fissile material.[11] In Buys's words, "The design was ready, everything was built, we were just waiting for a sufficient quantity of enriched uranium."[12] Although South African plans to conduct a cold test in 1977 had been thwarted by the Soviet discovery of the intended test facility that the South Africans had built in the Kalahari Desert, South African engineers were nonetheless highly confident that the device would work. Buys recalls that "I was convinced [that a cold test was not necessary]. The Little Boy weapon that was used on Hiroshima was never tested, so why would we have to test?"[13] Waldo Stumpf, the head of the South African Atomic Energy Corporation at the time the program was dismantled, confirms that the cancellation of the cold test did "not really" affect South African calculations about whether the device would work, because the device was relatively simple and South African scientists had already "done a lot of other tests— firing one half of the projectile into the other half, criticality tests, etc."[14] From late 1979, South Africa had a device that could be tested within "a few days" of an order being given, and senior political leaders were aware that South Africa had attained this capability.[15] South Africa gained more sophisticated nuclear weapons in the early 1980s, with a ballistic bomb that could be delivered by aircraft in 1982 and glide bombs beginning in 1983.[16] South Africa also began exploring more advanced delivery systems that would have provided South Africa with a more sophisticated nuclear arsenal, including developing plans to deliver nuclear weapons using ballistic missiles and artillery guns.[17] Nonetheless, South Africa acquired the basic capabilities required for its nuclear posture in late 1979. As a result, it is in late 1979 that we should expect nuclear weapons would begin to affect South African foreign policy.

South Africa's Strategic Environment

What effects should we expect that nuclear weapons would have on South African foreign policy? The theory of nuclear opportunism requires us to examine South Africa's strategic environment in order to make predictions about how nuclear weapons would change South African foreign policy.

The first factor to examine is whether South Africa faced severe territorial threats or was involved in an ongoing war. This is straightforward because in 1979 South Africa was involved in a serious ongoing war in Angola. At the point at which South Africa acquired nuclear weapons, it had already conducted a major invasion of Angola in 1975 (Operation Savannah) that had been a tactical success but a strategic disaster that left South Africa diplomatically isolated.[18] In addition, numerous smaller raids inside Angola had been conducted with the aim of destroying South West African People's Organization (SWAPO) camps and supporting South Africa's proxy in Angola, the National Union for the Total Independence of Angola (UNITA). This conflict, known as the Border War, would last until the end of the Cold War.

The war in Angola was only one component of a regional environment (shown in figure 3.1) that had been worsening for South Africa since the 1960s as the African continent experienced widespread decolonization.[19] Reflecting these concerns, South Africa's defense budget increased sixfold between 1961 and 1968.[20] Nonetheless, the immediate threats that South Africa faced remained manageable until the mid-1970s. South Africa (and South

Figure 3.1. Southern Africa

West Africa, which South Africa controlled) was bordered by Portuguese colonies that did not threaten its discriminatory domestic political institutions and were controlled by tens of thousands of Portuguese forces. These "frontline" states provided a buffer against the forces of nationalism, socialism, and black political liberation that worried white South African elites.[21] The colonies of Angola and Mozambique had been an important component of South Africa's forward defense, and the Portuguese government had allowed South Africa to conduct operations against SWAPO forces in southern Angola.[22] The white-minority government in Zimbabwe (then Rhodesia) led by Ian Smith provided an additional sympathetic neighbor.

In the mid-1970s, however, South Africa's security environment dramatically worsened. In particular, the 1974 military coup in Portugal upended South Africa's security environment and removed the *cordon sanitaire* between South Africa and the black majority governments to its north.[23] The new ruling junta in Lisbon granted independence to Mozambique and Angola in 1975, and informed the South Africans that they were no longer allowed to operate inside Angolan territory.[24] Further, in 1979, Ian Smith lost power in Rhodesia to Robert Mugabe.[25] These states now offered safe haven to insurgents seeking the independence of South West Africa (notably, SWAPO) and the dismantlement of apartheid within South Africa. Simultaneously, increasing racial tensions (most dramatically demonstrated in the 1976 Soweto riots), acts of sabotage, and international condemnation of South Africa's internal politics threatened South Africa's stability and the viability of the apartheid regime.

South Africa's new neighbors were hostile to the apartheid government, supportive of the African National Congress (ANC; the banned anti-apartheid party), and enjoyed close relations with the Soviet bloc. By late 1975, Soviet military planes had begun to transfer substantial numbers of Cuban military personnel and Soviet materiel and advisers to Angola.[26] As increasingly large numbers of Cuban forces and Soviet military equipment and advisers began to enter southern Africa, South African elites perceived a far more dangerous security environment. As Waldo Stumpf writes, "During the 1970s, especially the latter half of the decade, the political and military environment around South Africa deteriorated markedly. . . . The large buildup of Cuban military forces in Angola, beginning in 1975, which eventually peaked at 50,000 troops, reinforced a strong perception within the government that it would remain internationally isolated."[27] Victor Zazeraj, a South African ambassador and private assistant to Foreign Minister Pik Botha during the 1980s, recalls that the situation in southern Africa in the aftermath of the Portuguese coup was "perceived and experienced as an existential crisis . . . whereby the country's future existence, as we understood it, was under threat. . . . We had this [hostile] arc across Southern Africa that separated us from the rest of Africa."[28] Deon Fourie remembers that "everybody was shaken rigid [by Cuban and Soviet buildups]."[29]

There was little doubt among South African elites about the hostility of Soviet and Cuban intentions. South African elites perceived that Soviet goals in the region were ambitious and included the overthrow of the apartheid regime. David Steward recalls that "we believed that we were facing an existential crisis and we were extremely worried about the incursion of the Soviet Union into Southern Africa because . . . Southern Africa was a particularly significant target for the Soviet Union. . . . They wanted the SACP [South African Communist Party] to take over."[30] Colonel Jan Breytenbach, who commanded covert operations inside Angola, bluntly states: "When outside powers come to Africa, they don't come here to enjoy a holiday. They come here to expand their influence."[31] Defence Minister Magnus Malan writes in his memoirs that the Soviet goal was "helping the communists to conquer South Africa," and in private he would regularly use a quotation attributed to Leonid Brezhnev: "Our goal is to get control over the two great treasuries on which the West depend—the energy treasury of the Persian Gulf and the mineral treasury of Central and Southern Africa."[32] Similarly, Major General Jannie Geldenhuys, chief of the South African Defence Force from 1985 to 1990, poses a rhetorical question in assessing the motivations of Cuba and the Soviet Union: What "did South Africa have to do with the situation in Angola during the 1970s and 1980s? Obviously, any decent person would ask the much more valid question: What did the island of Cuba and the Soviet Union have to do with Angola?"[33]

The threat that South African elites perceived was not simply the direct military threat then posed by South Africa's neighbors. After all, the SADF had training and equipment superior to that of the opponents it faced in Angola, including the Cuban forces.[34] However, the fear among South African elites was that the Soviet Union had the resources to quickly escalate the conflict with large numbers of forces and advanced equipment that South Africa would have no ability to counter. Thus, while South Africa maintained military superiority over the threats it faced, its superiority was vulnerable to being swiftly overturned. South African elites thus had much to fear. As David Steward recalls, "Even though we were confronted with fairly sophisticated forces in Southern Angola, we never really felt that we were not capable of dealing with them, and we were proved to be right. . . . [But] we were worried that there might be further troops, further Russian troops, further intervention, that would then affect our conventional superiority."[35] Furthermore, South Africa's other neighbors (such as Botswana, Zimbabwe, and Mozambique) posed no offensive military threat but could nonetheless provide a safe haven for the ANC and its military wing Umkhonte we Sizwe (MK), from which it could launch sabotage and terrorist attacks within South Africa. As Major General Gert Opperman, who commanded operations in Angola and served as military secretary to Defence Minister Malan, argues, "We never anticipated that there would be any incursion from Botswana or Zimbabwe or Mozambique of their own forces onto our territories. But they could provide the umbrella under which the ANC could launch incursions. Not armed incursions in the combat sense, but infiltrations—[they would be able to] get through to our infrastructure [and commit acts of sabotage and terrorism]."[36] This combination of the *swart gevaar* (black threat) and the *rooi gevaar* (red threat) thus became the core problem that apartheid South African foreign policy sought to address.

Thus, while apartheid South Africa possessed substantial conventional military power, the threats it faced were significant. South Africa had a large border to defend, could draw on only a small percentage of its population to meet any potential combination of internal and external threats, and faced states whose combined population was far larger than South Africa's and that had a superpower patron with the ability to provide military forces and capabilities that South Africa would be unable to match.[37] This threat was articulated in the apocalyptic concept of "total onslaught" that entered the South African strategic lexicon as early as 1973, and the putative South African solution in the concept of "total strategy" that saw a "reorientation towards a 'landward threat' and away from the traditional role of South Africa as a strategic partner of the West in protecting the sea-lanes around the southern point of Africa."[38]

South Africa was therefore both involved in an ongoing war and faced severe territorial threats when it acquired nuclear weapons. As I discuss in more detail below, the theory of nuclear opportunism predicts that South Africa's political priority should have been to improve its position against the threats it faced and that South African elites should have sought to use their nuclear capability to pursue these goals.

Expectations

The predictions of the theory of nuclear opportunism are straightforward in this case, because South Africa was involved in an ongoing war and faced severe territorial threats when it acquired nuclear weapons. Figure 3.2 shows the application of the theory of nuclear opportunism to the case of South Africa. Both aggression (the more belligerent pursuit of preexisting interests) and steadfastness (standing more firmly in defense of the status quo) against the source of the threats it faced should have been attractive foreign policy behaviors for South Africa. The theory therefore anticipates that South Africa would use nuclear weapons to facilitate both aggression and steadfastness.

Because of the political priority that states facing severe threats or involved in ongoing wars must place on improving their position against the source of the threat, the first variable in the sequence is the only one that matters for the predictions made in the case of South Africa. Aggression and steadfastness are the behaviors that such states should be expected to find most attractive. States facing severe threats, for example, do not have the luxury of pursuing independence (defined as taking actions that allies oppose or do not support), because states in this position require support from anywhere they can get it. As a result, we would not expect that using nuclear weapons to facilitate independence would be an attractive option for South Africa. Similarly, states facing severe threats must improve their own security before they can begin to think about improving the security of others. Using nuclear weapons to facilitate bolstering—strengthening allies or alliances—is therefore an unattractive proposition for states facing severe threats. Considering the scale of the challenges and threats the state already faces, engaging in expansion—the widening of a state's interests in international politics—is also unappealing. Last, while responding to the additional security provided by nuclear weapons by showing an increased inclination to compromise—the acceptance of less in ongoing disputes—might be

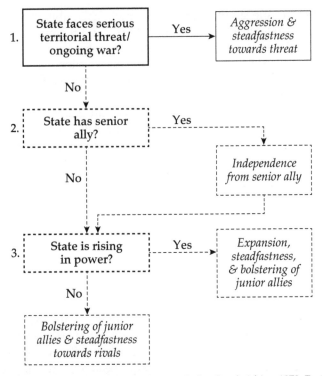

Figure 3.2. The theory of nuclear opportunism applied to South Africa, 1979. Dashed lines indicate portions of the theory not applicable in this case.

predicted by the theory of the nuclear revolution, it is not predicted by the theory of nuclear opportunism. Nuclear opportunism anticipates that states seek to use their nuclear weapons to try to improve their position in international politics, rather than to make concessions that they previously deemed unacceptable. The theory of nuclear opportunism, therefore, does not predict that South Africa would use nuclear weapons to facilitate compromise.

The theory of nuclear opportunism therefore suggests that South Africa should have used nuclear weapons to facilitate aggression and steadfastness but should not have used nuclear weapons to facilitate independence, bolstering, expansion, or compromise in the aftermath of acquiring a testable nuclear device in late 1979. In addition to predictions about South African behavior, we can also make predictions about how South African elites should have thought about nuclear weapons and the benefits that nuclear weapons offered. The theory predicts that South African elites would view nuclear weapons as useful tools for advancing their interests and improving their position relative to the sources of threats that they faced, and more specifically, for facilitating aggression and steadfastness against those threats.

South African Thinking about Nuclear Weapons

This section examines South African elite thinking about the utility of nuclear weapons. Did South Africa view nuclear weapons as a useful tool for improving its position against the threats it faced? Did it think about nuclear weapons as a way of facilitating aggression and steadfastness, and if so, how?

In examining this question, there are limits to the certainty of conclusions we should expect to draw. First, only a small group of South African elites actually knew about the nuclear program. Second, the renunciation of South Africa's nuclear program and the strategic rationale behind it, and South Africa's subsequent commitment to nonproliferation, were a core part of South Africa's efforts to rejoin the international community in the early 1990s. As a result, and as discussed earlier, South African officials are often reluctant to acknowledge that South Africa's nuclear weapons had any strategic value at all. Third, many documents from the apartheid regime relating to the nuclear program were either destroyed or remain classified.[39]

Nonetheless, from the statements of military and political elites one can piece together a coherent strategic rationale for South African nuclear weapons that is consistent with the expectations of the theory of nuclear opportunism. First, South African foreign policy and conduct in the Border War were heavily constrained by the need to avoid triggering potential escalation, and, in particular, to reduce the risk of further Soviet intervention that might overturn South Africa's conventional military advantage. In short, South African elites wanted to act more aggressively in Angola but were deterred from doing so by the risk of escalation. Second, nuclear weapons would be helpful in solving this problem by reducing the risk of such escalation. The logical implication of these two beliefs is that by reducing the risk of escalation, nuclear weapons reduced the risk associated with South African aggression.

First, there is little question that South African elites wanted to act more aggressively in Angola, but were restrained from doing so by fears of Cuban and, especially, Soviet escalation. Furthermore, those actions that South Africa did take were constrained in various ways by the need to reduce the risks of escalation and to avoid triggering further Soviet intervention.

Apartheid-era South African elites are consistent that fears about conflict escalation were a major constraint on South African behavior throughout the 1970s and 1980s, and those fears of escalation frequently prevented South African aggression. The fear was primarily due to the Soviet Union, which had the ability to flood the conflicts on South Africa's borders with advanced equipment and further forces. As Major General Johann Dippenaar remembers, "Right from the beginning we were aware that there were Russian advisors and Cuban advisors, we realized that advisors could escalate to forces."[40] As a result, South Africa consistently sought to avoid giving the

Soviet Union any excuse to escalate the conflict. As Major General Opperman recalls: "Right throughout the war there was an element of restraint . . . the types of weaponry used; the sort of targets engaged . . . would it result in unnecessary escalation?"[41] Major General Roland de Vries, who commanded operations in Angola, argues similarly that "it had to be played very carefully because the conflict could have developed into a regional war."[42] Dippenaar recalls that "politics put a lot of restrictions on all operations . . . so there was a constant caution."[43] These constraints affected South African conduct of the Border War in a number of ways. Concerns about escalation did not always prevent South Africa from taking military actions, but the fear of escalation by the Soviet Union was a constant constraint. As one 1981 Department of Foreign Affairs memo stated with respect to covert South African operations in Mozambique, "It must be borne in mind that every attack upon the ANC will be interpreted as an attack on Mocambique sovereignty and thus provide a pretext for Russia to sink her bear-claws deeper into that state. This should not stop us from raiding ANC bases in the future, but such action should be carefully considered in the light of its potential for escalating the Russian presence in Mocambique."[44]

These fears not only constrained South African choices about which operations to conduct, but also constrained South African goals within individual operations. For example, South Africa sought to restrict the geographical zones in which it operated to reduce the fears of escalation. Major General Opperman recalls commanding "an operation 250 kilometers deep inside Zambia [in which] I was forced to withdraw overnight, although at that stage we had not yet achieved all the things that we wanted to achieve militarily. In fact, I would have liked to stay there for another week or two, but we were told to withdraw overnight. . . . Instead of continuing and doing what you believed had to be done from a military point of view, you had to withdraw. . . . One of the constant factors to be considered was: would it result in unnecessary escalation of the war?"[45] Colonel Breytenbach confirms that although South Africa had the capacity to hold significant territory, it did not, for fear of escalation, arguing that "we could have taken over the Cunene Province, for instance—we used to go in there quite often to go sort out SWAPO. So we could have gone in there with three battalions and keep them there, but then of course the Russians would come back *en masse*," escalating the conflict.[46] Major General de Vries recalls similar constraints: "There were constraints . . . in terms of how far you could go. Can you attack Menongue? No. Can we attack Cuito Cuanavale from the west? No. Rather, stay on the eastern side of the river so that the war does not escalate."[47] These constraints hampered South Africa's ability to achieve tactical military goals. Major General Opperman recalls that visiting US commanders "could not understand how we could accept a situation where the ground of tactical importance on the other side of the river was in the hands of the Zambian forces. They suggested we take over and control that ground, because in the process we would have greater security. But I said, 'No, I have to live with that risk.' If I take over that ground, it might make sense from a military point of view, a tactical point of view, but from a strategic point of view that would be exactly the type of escalation that we would like to prevent."[48]

South Africa also conducted its operations in ways that aimed to minimize the threat of escalation. In many cases, this meant secrecy. In Operation Savannah, Major General Opperman recalls that "our government had hoped that by going in covertly, we would prevent the situation from escalating much more rapidly."[49] South African forces "had the capability" to take the Angolan capital Luanda in that operation, but restrained themselves in large part out of fears of the escalation that overtly capturing the capital city would trigger.[50] Ambassador Shearar confirms that going to Luanda "would have opened the door for anyone else to come in," and recalls that this concern was expressed explicitly by the foreign minister at the prime minister's residence.[51] In other cases, the desire to control escalation meant ensuring that exit routes existed for South African advisers to other participants in the Angolan war. As an adviser to both the National Front for the Liberation of Angola and UNITA, Colonel Breytenbach recalls that "the first thing you get sorted out is your escape route to get out. . . . You must be able to get away quickly. . . . When things start getting wrong, then you must get out. . . . You always have a standby plane or vehicle or something that you can get into and be gone."[52] The South African government also sought to control information in the public domain about South African activities in Angola, restricting reports published in South African media outlets, and seeking to discredit those appearing in foreign sources as "Communist propaganda."[53]

Targeting was also carefully calibrated in order to minimize the threat of escalation. In particular, the South Africans sought to avoid direct conflict with Russian forces in order to avoid triggering deeper Soviet involvement in the region. As Ambassador Victor Zazeraj recalls, "Very often there were Russian pilots flying . . . at the same time as our pilots, who could hear them on the radio communications and knew the markings on the planes. There was an unspoken rule that if it was a Russian pilot or even a Cuban pilot, the South African Air Force wouldn't interfere with them too much. . . . You don't want to scratch the bear and create a problem that you can't solve. We would not have wanted to draw them in, or create a pretext that would allow them to do us more harm than we could cope with."[54] Indeed, Soviet forces may have intentionally facilitated this mutual restraint by separating themselves from the Angolan and Cuban forces. Ambassador Zazeraj noted that "the Russians were no worse at apartheid than we were. . . . Their officers were not living in the same camp as the rest of them [and] made sure you could see from the air which was their camp—they had big hammers and sickles on their tents." This enabled South African restraint: "Our Air

Force would be told not to hit the Russian camp. . . . You don't want to have a missile go in and upset them, because then you would have a crisis."[55]

The South African government also sought to centralize control over military operations. Some South African elites involved in decision making at the time claim that Pretoria exercised only weak control over what the SADF was doing in the field, and that many SADF operations were not officially sanctioned by Pretoria. David Steward, for example, argues that "very often [the SADF] didn't tell the Department of Foreign Affairs about their adventures."[56] Such claims must be evaluated with skepticism because of the incentive that members of the apartheid regime have to claim they lacked knowledge about, and did not authorize, specific operations. The weight of evidence, however, suggests exactly the opposite: that Pretoria exercised very tight control over individual operations and did so precisely because of concerns about escalation. As Major General Opperman recalls, "We never had carte blanche. We were always very aware . . . that the politicians were in charge."[57] Major General Dippenaar recalls that "every time before operations could take place, we had to have approval—and there was no chance you could have done anything without political approval from our side. And then all those approvals came out with very strict conditions: you can't be longer than this, you can't take more than that kind of vehicle [etc.]."[58] Colonel Breytenbach confirms that "every time we went across the border it was planned at the highest level, and there were Generals sitting there on this planning committee with the Minister of Defence," while Major General Geldenhuys writes that "a decision to cross the border was a political one for which the government and the Minister of Defence carried the responsibility."[59] Colonel Breytenbach recalls that new orders were given on a daily basis to keep commanders on the tightest possible leash, and individual commanders were often unaware of the ultimate goals of the missions they were undertaking.[60] While former military commanders may have an incentive to claim they were under strict orders so as to minimize their personal responsibility for the less savory activities that occurred during the Border War, some political elites also agreed that tight political control was exercised over military operations. Ambassador Zazeraj confirms that "control [by Pretoria] was very much the case—they really did not want the situation to get out of control. . . . The political elite was dead scared that something would create an international incident."[61] This micromanagement of operations by Pretoria caused tensions in civil-military relations. Major General de Vries recalls that "the high command started micromanaging the battlefront, which was highly infuriating for the commanders on the ground."[62] And officers who exceeded the bounds of their authority were punished. Major General Opperman recalls that "Colonel Jan Breytenbach—who was one of our best tactical commanders on the ground—he decided on his own to undertake patrols in Zimbabwe, and he was severely reprimanded because he was told that, 'your undisciplined actions, your initiative, might make military sense, but it would escalate the war and we don't want that.'"[63]

Overall, the fear of escalation constrained South African aggression in the Border War in a number of ways: South Africa was cautious about the nature, scale, and scope of its operations in order to avoid provoking potential Soviet intervention. South African elites wanted to act more aggressively in Angola but were deterred from doing so by the fear of escalation.

Crucially, South African elites understood that nuclear weapons offered South Africa a solution to this problem. In particular, they allowed South Africa greater ability to control the risks associated with escalation. In examining South African thinking surrounding the utility of the nuclear program, it is important to note, as mentioned above, the limited number of people involved in discussions of South Africa's nuclear strategy. Very few officials even knew of the existence of the nuclear program, and there was little discussion of the nuclear program within the South African government. Thus, while many in the South African Department of Foreign Affairs were skeptical of the utility of nuclear weapons for a state like South Africa that never lost its conventional military advantage,[64] their views were marginalized within the South African decision-making process. After 1978, the State Security Council "replaced the cabinet as the dominant institution in the formulation of foreign policy."[65] The State Security Council was dominated by the more hawkish views of President P. W. Botha and Defence Minister Magnus Malan and was staffed primarily by military officers.[66] Major General Opperman, who served in the State Security Council as the military secretary to Defence Minister Malan, confirms that the views of President Botha and Defence Minister Malan "dominated the discussion" and that both believed that nuclear weapons served a "clear political purpose."[67] That political purpose was, in large part, to grant South Africa greater capacity to control the dangers of Soviet escalation. As early as 1977, a CIA assessment argued that "the [South African] rationale for going ahead in the development of nuclear weapons stems from a fear that ultimately South Africa faces the threat of being invaded by Communist-backed black regimes and perhaps even by Soviet and Cuban forces."[68] Similarly, in 1984, the CIA concluded that it was the "threat of a [Soviet] invasion of South Africa [that required] the added protection of a credible nuclear deterrent."[69] These external assessments are mirrored by the recollections of South African officials. As Major General Opperman recalls, "I think . . . the fear of [Soviet] escalation, from a nuclear point of view, was also very prominent [in the reasons for nuclear acquisition]."[70] In the words of Major General de Vries, the purpose of South African nuclear weapons was to create "a silent fear on the side of the Cubans and the Russians" to constrain their temptation to escalate the conflict.[71]

Indeed, the nuclear strategy that South Africa adopted—the so-called three stage strategy—was explicitly designed to provide multiple points within a conflict at which nuclear weapons could influence the escalation calculations of opponents and allies.[72] According to André Buys, the strategy was "absolutely" aimed at improving South Africa's ability to deter and control escalation.[73] As described in an internal memo, the first stage of the strategy aimed to seek some deterrent effect from uncertainty: South Africa should pursue "a 'strategy of uncertainty' whereby a conflicting set of perceptions regarding SA's nuclear weapons capability is created. The greater the uncertainty created, the greater the deterrent effect of South Africa's presumed capability. Only once a situation is reached where the military threat against SA increases to a point where the conventional balance of power tilts against us, should consideration be given to moving into a posture of covert disclosure and eventual overt displays of strength."[74]

As described, the strategy was designed so that it would "go live" only if the conflict in Angola escalated to a point at which South African elites felt it threatened the survival of the state. Thus, South African nuclear weapons aimed to provide South Africa with more options should the conflict on South Africa's borders begin to escalate beyond Pretoria's control. As Major General Dippenaar described the purpose of South Africa's nuclear weapons, "Even if things go terribly wrong, there is some way of responding and reacting."[75] André Buys confirms that "the concern was that this [the Angolan conflict] would escalate to a point where we would not be able to curtail it. And so the question was then, what do we do then?"[76] Buys continues: "The first stage was that we would keep it secret, and for that, you don't need any physical hardware—the strategy of uncertainty, just keep them guessing. The second stage was that if the military threat escalates to the point where we want to start activating the deterrent strategy, we would tell the United States—you had Ronald Reagan as president, we had Margaret Thatcher in Britain, these were people our politicians could talk to and they could be informed: 'we've got this problem, but we've got nuclear weapons, so please try and intervene and get the pressure off.'"[77]

This is the catalytic nuclear posture that Narang and others identify.[78] At a particular conflict threshold—perhaps the invasion of South West Africa (Namibia) by large numbers of conventional forces—South Africa would have communicated to Washington its intention to conduct a nuclear test.[79] Indeed, Foreign Minister Pik Botha explicitly promised President Reagan that South Africa would not test a nuclear weapon without first informing Washington.[80] The purpose of such a threat would have been to use the American desire to avoid overt proliferation to persuade the United States to intervene—whether diplomatically to persuade the Soviet Union to restrain its own clients, or militarily by providing South Africa with conventional reinforcements: "It was a way of getting a reluctant party to become involved and stop this thing from getting out of hand."[81] South African officials were well aware that Washington was opposed to South Africa acquiring nuclear weapons,[82] and paid careful attention to US responses to other proliferators, including India.[83] This led South African officials to believe that the United States may well be prepared to offer South Africa support—whether military or political—in order to prevent South Africa from becoming an overt nuclear power. At the very least, the ability to threaten to test a nuclear device would, in the words of a 1984 CIA assessment, "put the United States in an awkward position."[84]

However, South Africa's nuclear strategy included plans beyond mere threats of testing, because, in Buys's words, such threats "might not work. . . . If that [threatening to test] didn't work, the third strategy was then the open strategy—we would detonate one underground. If that brings sense to the military threat, if the threat is relieved, then OK. If it is not, the idea was that we would demonstrate a nuclear weapon. And what we had in mind was to actually go and do a mock attack with a nuclear weapon over the ocean—fly out and actually detonate a nuclear weapon a thousand kilometres south of South Africa in the ocean."[85] This basic strategy—which had been approved as early as April 1978—thus provided opportunities for South African elites to control escalation and deter further Soviet intervention at several points in a potential conventional conflict.[86] Indeed, South African officials considered adding a fourth stage to the strategy, which would have provided another point at which South Africa's nuclear capabilities could have been used to control escalation. As Buys describes, "There was a lot of discussion about whether we should add a fourth step or not—it was never officially added, but the debate was, if that [a test over the ocean] doesn't work and they still attack South Africa—do we actually use it tactically? It was never approved by the politicians and thank God we never got near that—but it was certainly discussed. . . . We said that there might be a need for a fourth stage to the strategy, but it was never approved, which would have entailed tactical use on troops when they crossed our borders."[87] Consistent with these ideas of tactical nuclear use, South Africa also toyed with designs for tactical nuclear weapons and alternative delivery systems including ballistic missiles and artillery guns, but such devices were never approved for construction.[88]

At the time, South African elites also made public but ambiguous threats that aimed to dissuade South African opponents from escalating the conflict. P. W. Botha, for example, gave a speech in 1979 in which he stated that "South Africa's enemies may possibly find out that we have military weapons they don't know about." A UN report noted that the South African interior minister stated that if South Africa were attacked, "we will use all means at our disposal, whatever they may be. It is true that we have just completed our own pilot plant that uses very advanced technology, and that we have major uranium reserves."[89] Other ministers also made public reference on other occasions to a "secret weapon."[90]

US analysts also believed South Africa's ambiguous nuclear status would affect its adversaries' calculations. A 1984 CIA assessment argued that South

Africa's nuclear posture granted it "a number of benefits, particularly for a pariah state such as South Africa. It forces Pretoria's adversaries to assume that South Africa has a weapons capability and to factor that assumption into their policy formation."[91] And, indeed, the ambiguous threat of nuclear escalation did in fact reduce the willingness of Cuban forces to take particular escalatory steps in Angola, thus easing the dangers associated with South African aggression. Ambassador Zazeraj recalls that "we only had confirmation [that the Cubans had changed their behavior out of fear of South African nuclear weapons] in 2010—we had a meeting with Jorge Risquet [Fidel Castro's point man on Africa] who confirmed that the Cubans in Angola were convinced that South Africa had nuclear warheads attached to its G5 and G6 artillery. And for that reason, Cuban troops never came anywhere near the Namibian border, and never came near the South Africans. They were also split up in different areas, so that if we did attack them with nuclear weapons, we wouldn't wipe all of them out."[92] Indeed, Fidel Castro himself acknowledged the role of nuclear weapons in constraining Cuban behavior, writing: "Our troops advanced at night . . . in groups of no more than 1,000 men, strongly armed, at a prescribed distance from one another, always keeping in mind the possibility that the enemy might use nuclear weapons."[93]

Overall, therefore, nuclear weapons were seen as providing South Africa with a tool that enabled it to deter escalation by its adversaries. Consistent with this aim, South African elites set up their nuclear strategy in a way that allowed them to attempt to control escalation at several different conflict thresholds within an escalating conflict. If nuclear weapons allow a state to better control escalation, they also reduce the risks associated with engaging in aggression. First, nuclear weapons can deter an opponent from escalating a conflict in response to aggression. Second, even if an act of aggression does lead to substantial escalation, or leads to a response from the adversary that the state is unprepared for, possessing nuclear weapons provides a state with additional options in responding to, and controlling, such a situation. As a result, nuclear weapons can reduce the expected costs of engaging in activities that risk such escalation, such as aggression.

Apartheid-era officials are, unsurprisingly, reluctant to state explicitly that they believed that nuclear weapons facilitated South African aggression. Nonetheless, a clear causal chain—with each stage verified by South African elites—links South African nuclear acquisition to an increase in South Africa's tolerance for escalation and ability to engage in aggression. Given that South African aggression was constrained by fears of escalation and that South African officials believed nuclear weapons helped them control escalation, the logical conclusion would be that nuclear weapons would facilitate South African aggression. And, indeed, at least some officials are prepared to make ambiguous statements that suggest nuclear weapons were not a purely defensive capability. Ambassador Victor Zazeraj states that "the military felt that nuclear weapons had a purpose. The military thought that as long as their enemy believed that South Africa had nuclear weapons and acted accordingly, *it made their lives a whole lot easier*. In some ways I think they were right. . . . It did work."[94] A memo written in 1975 by the chief of the defense staff Lieutenant General Raymond Fullarton Armstrong argues nuclear weapons could serve as a "positive weapon in our defense."[95] That nuclear weapons might facilitate aggression was also understood by outside observers: a 1980 UN report concluded that South African nuclear weapons "could also help to support extended involvement and intervention elsewhere in the region," even if South Africa never revealed its capabilities and chose to "covertly stockpile weapons and rely . . . on unconfirmed but widely credited rumours that it had those weapons in order to further its purposes."[96]

Even if former South African officials are generally (and unsurprisingly) unwilling to confirm explicitly that they viewed nuclear weapons as a tool to facilitate aggression and steadfastness, one can piece together a causal chain that reinforces that conclusion. South African elites felt constrained by concerns about escalation *and* viewed nuclear weapons as a tool that could be used to deter and control escalation. Nuclear weapons may therefore have been seen as reducing the risks associated with both aggression and steadfastness. But if so, did South African behavior change as the theory expects? Did South African tolerance for escalation, and willingness to engage in behaviors that it had previously eschewed for fears of escalation, rise after acquiring nuclear weapons?

South African Foreign Policy

We are therefore able to trace a logic in how South African officials thought about nuclear weapons that seems consistent with the theory of nuclear opportunism. However, did South Africa's foreign policy behavior change in the way that the theory suggests? The theory of nuclear opportunism anticipates that South Africa should have used nuclear weapons to facilitate aggression and steadfastness after late 1979. I first examine South Africa's behavior in its primary ongoing conflict during the 1970s and 1980s to assess whether South African behavior changed at the point of nuclear acquisition. I then examine the other foreign policy behaviors in the typology. I look at South Africa's foreign policy with respect to its (few) allies to assess whether South Africa behaved more independently or sought to bolster allies to a greater degree in the aftermath of nuclear acquisition. Finally, I examine whether South Africa's ambitions in the region widened in a way that indicates South African expansion in the aftermath of nuclear acquisition.

Did South Africa become more aggressive in its conduct of the ongoing Border War in 1979, as the theory of nuclear opportunism would suggest?

Did South Africa defend its position more steadfastly? Or did South Africa become more willing to compromise after nuclear acquisition? This section examines South Africa's conduct in its most important ongoing conflict, the civil war in Angola, and the broader Border War. I assess whether in the aftermath of nuclear acquisition, South Africa became more willing to make compromises, whether South Africa pushed more aggressively in pursuit of its goals, and whether South Africa became more willing to fight to defend the status quo.

We can first examine how the macro-level patterns of conflict that South Africa was involved in changed over time. In the ten years preceding South African nuclear acquisition, South Africa was involved in an average of 1.25 MIDs per year. Consistent with the idea that South Africa behaved more aggressively in existing disputes, in the ten years following nuclear acquisition, the number of conflicts rose by 25 percent to 1.55 MIDs per year. Similarly, we can examine the military operations that South Africa undertook in Angola in the few years before and after acquiring nuclear weapons. As table 3.1 shows, in the three years before South Africa acquired nuclear weapons (1977, 1978, and 1979), it engaged in just three major military operations in Angola—Seiljag, Reindeer, and Rekstok—and (with the exception of a paratrooper raid at Cassinga as part of Operation Reindeer) kept its operations close to the Angolan border. In the three years after acquiring nuclear weapons (1980, 1981, and 1982), South Africa engaged in many more major military operations in Angola and became more comfortable conducting military operations deeper inside Angolan territory.

We can also examine South African conduct in individual operations in more detail. In the years preceding nuclear acquisition, South Africa was relatively cautious in the operations it undertook in Angola (with Operation Savannah providing a notable exception, which is discussed further below). South Africa generally conducted its operations covertly, staying close to the border between Angola and Namibia, and generally limited the manpower and heavy weaponry dedicated to them.

South African efforts to undermine the ongoing insurgency in South West Africa had been under way since the 1960s, but it was in 1974 that the SADF took over responsibility for counterinsurgency operations from the South African Police, just weeks before the coup d'état overthrowing Portugal's fascist dictatorship.[97] In the aftermath of the coup, South Africa could no longer rely on Portuguese forces to prevent SWAPO fighters from setting up bases within Angola from which to conduct raids inside South West Africa, and could no longer count on support in conducting anti-SWAPO patrols north of the border. For SWAPO, this provided an enormous benefit: SWAPO leader Sam Nujoma wrote that "it was as if a locked door had suddenly swung open," and SWAPO moved its headquarters to the Angolan capital of Luanda.[98] Within weeks, southern Angola and north South West Africa were "swarming with SWAPO armed bands."[99]

Table 3.1 South African military operations in Angola before and after nuclear acquisition

Three years before nuclear acquisition (1977, 1978, 1979)

Operation	Date	Location(s)	Distance to border (km)
Seiljag	Feb. 1978	Yati Strip	14.0
Reindeer	May 1978	Chetequera	29.2
		Dombondola	6.5
		Cassinga	253.2
Rekstok	Mar. 1979	Oncocua	36.4
		Mongua	73.6

Three years after nuclear acquisition (1980, 1981, 1982)

Operation	Date	Location(s)	Distance to border (km)
Sceptic	May 1980	Ionde	118.8
		Chifufua	180.0
		Chitumba	90.0
Vastrap	July 1980	Cuamato	35.0
Klipklop	July 1980	Chitado	5.0
Wishbone	Dec. 1980	Ongiva	33.8
		Xangongo	68.6
Konyn	Aug. 1981	Cahama	121.9
		Chibemba	154.5
Carnation	June 1981	Ongiva	33.8
Protea	Aug. 1981	Ongiva	33.8
		Xangongo	68.6
		Cahama	121.9
Daisy	Nov. 1981	Ionde	118.8
		Indungo	300.0
		Mupa	134.7
Mispel	Nov. 1981	Ongiva	33.8
Kerslig	Nov. 1981	Luanda	890.6
Makro	Dec. 1981	Ongiva	33.8
Super	Mar. 1982	Cambêno Valley	24.2
		Iona	33.3
Meebos I	Mar. 1982	Ongiva	33.8
		Evale	93.3
Meebos II	July 1982	Ongiva	33.8
		Xangongo	68.6
		Cassinga	253.2

Hawks in the SADF wanted to cross the Angolan border at this stage to "clobber SWAPO on the other side."[100] But South Africa held back, with Prime Minister John Vorster remaining particularly cautious. It was only when the United States and the Organisation of African Unity (OAU) encouraged South Africa to take action to prevent the Marxist Popular Movement for the Liberation of Angola (MPLA) from taking power in Luanda that South Africa undertook a significant military operation deep inside Angola, in Operation Savannah. The precise role that the United States played in encouraging South African action is disputed, and US records downplay the

US role.[101] Nonetheless, South African elites had no doubt that the United States had encouraged action. David Steward recalls that South Africa went into Angola "with the support of the United States," a claim confirmed by Major General Opperman, who argued that "one of the conditions of the American promises to become involved [was that] their role should not be [revealed]."[102] Ambassador Victor Zazeraj is adamant that South Africa went into Angola "at the request of the US" and that South Africa would not have considered doing so without American encouragement and the promise of American reinforcements, a suggestion that is backed up by the serious misgivings that many South African cabinet members (including the prime minister) held regarding the operation.[103]

Although US officials have sought to play down the American role, Chester Crocker, the Reagan administration's senior official working on southern Africa, acknowledges that "our winks and nods formed part of the calculus of Angola's neighbors."[104] Piero Gleijeses, a historian generally unsympathetic to the apartheid regime, confirms that Pretoria "might otherwise have hesitated" had it not been for American encouragement.[105] And, indeed, US officials made public statements that implied support for South African intervention. In a speech that the South African embassy forwarded to the secretary for foreign affairs, US secretary of state Henry Kissinger stated that "the forces in control of the capital city of Luanda achieved this position through a very substantial inflow of communist arms. . . . The United States does not feel that it will recognize the faction [the MPLA] that has . . . seized that capital city [of Luanda] by foreign assistance. . . . We would support any move that keeps outside powers out of Angola, and we would participate in such a move."[106]

South Africa's initial objectives in Operation Savannah were rather modest: to help UNITA reclaim territory it had previously controlled. Furthermore, South Africa hoped to accomplish these goals while maintaining the secrecy of its role, due to fears that an overt invasion would create significant escalation dynamics.[107] However, South Africa achieved tactical successes well beyond what was expected. Despite using mostly World War II–era equipment and materiel, South African forces achieved quick and dramatic advances, with a CIA operative describing it as "the most effective military strike force ever seen in black Africa, exploding through the MPLA/Cuban ranks in a blitzkrieg," and with one commander moving "more than 3,100km up a hostile coast in a mere 33 days of movement" for the loss of just one South African life.[108]

South African forces even ended up within striking distance of Luanda, although the cabinet was informed that several hundred casualties would likely result if South Africa attempted to take the Angolan capital.[109] But South Africa's efforts to maintain secrecy failed, and its intervention in Angola was widely reported around the world. More importantly, the escalation that South Africa feared transpired: within weeks, thirty-six thousand

Cuban troops and three hundred tanks had arrived on Angolan territory, making further advances increasingly challenging for South African forces.[110] In addition, the United States abandoned its tacit support for South Africa, with Congress passing the Clark amendment, forbidding aid to groups fighting in Angola.[111] An OAU vote recognizing the MPLA as the legitimate government of Angola removed any trace of international legitimacy from the South African intervention, and South Africa was forced to withdraw.[112]

In the aftermath of Operation Savannah, SWAPO was "in a stronger military position than ever before. . . . It could set up an open training, administrative and logistics structure inside Angola and launch its insurgents southwards as it chose," and South African elites were aware that the "security commitment on our borders is likely to get bigger, not smaller."[113] Despite these threats, for the rest of 1976 South Africa restricted itself to minor operations, fearful of triggering further escalation.[114] South African forces stayed mostly on the South West African side of the border, particularly in Northern Ovamboland, where they achieved some success against SWAPO insurgents.[115] The same pattern continued throughout most of 1977, despite SWAPO achieving increasing lethality and operational skills due to the training it was receiving from Cuban advisers.[116] However, attacks against South African forces in northern South West Africa by insurgents, who would often fall back across the border into Angola when South Africa responded, became increasingly common and difficult for South African forces to deal with.[117] One incident in October 1977 led to South Africa crossing the Angolan border in a more substantial way. South Africa responded to an unusually large group of around ninety insurgents crossing into Ovamboland that attacked a South African patrol. At the end of the skirmish, the South Africans had penetrated twenty-one kilometers into Angola and killed sixty-one insurgents, for a loss of five South African forces.

Thus, overall, South Africa continued to behave in a relatively restrained manner inside Angolan territory. Nonetheless, it continued to respond when attacked, harried insurgents in South West Africa, and gave short shrift to a peace proposal made by Britain, the United States, France, West Germany, and Canada (the "Western Five") that it viewed as unacceptable because it would have required a substantial South African drawdown from South West Africa without corresponding concessions on the Angolan side of the border.[118]

At the end of 1977, however, Prime Minister Vorster and advisers met in the resort of Oubosstrand with the belief that it was necessary to take stronger actions against SWAPO. In spite of this, Vorster was hesitant to take the war into Angola and concerned about the possible escalation that might result. Ultimately, a compromise was reached: tanks could be used but not aircraft, operations must be kept clandestine, and any military operations had to be approved at the highest level to reduce the risk of escalation.[119] No immediate actions were taken, however, and a planned operation (Operation Bruilof) that would have taken place twenty-five kilometers inside

Angola was abandoned for reasons that remain unclear.[120] Some of the planning for Bruilof was expanded and folded into a more ambitious plan, labeled "Reindeer," that was implemented in early May 1978 and hit three geographically separate targets simultaneously. Two of these targets, Chetequera and Dombondola, were close to the Angolan border, but the third, a camp near the town of Cassinga, was deeper inside Angolan territory. The attack on Cassinga was conducted by air, with South African special forces parachuted in and flown out to avoid the need for a substantial invasion of Angolan territory that would have risked escalation.[121] The South Africans viewed the attack as a success, although it ignited controversy over whether the camp attacked was a SWAPO military installation or a refugee camp protected by SWAPO forces, with critics accusing the South Africans of massacring hundreds of civilians, including many women and children.[122] In the aftermath of Operation Reindeer, up until the point at which South Africa acquired nuclear weapons, South African actions were again more restrained, although two "modest" operations took place in March 1979 (Operation Rekstok and Operation Saffraan) inside Angola and Zambia.[123]

Overall, therefore, South African behavior in the period leading up to nuclear acquisition was relatively restrained in terms of avoiding escalatory interventions inside Angola. While South Africa responded forcefully to attacks inside South West Africa, it did not generally conduct operations inside Angola with two exceptions, Operation Savannah and Operation Reindeer. In the former, South Africa had an increased tolerance for escalation because it anticipated support from the United States that failed to appear. The latter was a swift raid followed by a quick withdrawal of South African forces designed to minimize the risk of escalation. Although Operation Savannah demonstrated that South Africa had the military capabilities to conduct operations deep inside Angola, and South Africa was acquiring new conventional military capabilities over this period that *increased* its ability to project military power into Angola, South Africa generally sought to avoid conducting operations inside Angolan territory, and certainly avoided leaving forces in Angola for substantial periods of time.[124]

After acquiring nuclear weapons, however, South Africa became considerably more comfortable going deeper inside Angolan territory, doing so with greater regularity, and using heavier weaponry and larger numbers of forces to do so. Starting in 1979, South African officials began to take actions that would escalate the conflict in Angola, and began to adopt more ambitious goals in the conflict. A 1979 State Security Council document by Defence Minister Malan proposed a new strategy for Angola. He argued that "the political situation in Angola must be kept as unstable and fluid as possible," with the objective being the creation of "an anti-Marxist government in Angola."[125] P. W. Botha also approved "a more pro-active stance for the SA Defence Force."[126] As Robert Scott Jaster argues, "The war against SWAPO began in earnest in 1979."[127] This change in strategy was noticed by the outside world: a UN report from 1980 noted that a "significant reassessment and shift of South Africa's military and political posture" had occurred and that South Africa was dedicating significant resources to "extensive military operations on or across its borders."[128]

In May 1980, a few months after South Africa had acquired nuclear weapons, a decision was made that "SWAPO had to be taken on and beaten in its lair [Angola]."[129] This operation, code-named "Sceptic," was to take place in June 1980, and unlike in any operation since Savannah, the plan was that South African forces would stay inside Angolan territory for a significant period of time to deal with any SWAPO forces that escaped the initial assaults on bases at Chifufua, Ionde, and Chitumba. This marked a change from the pre-1979 South African modus operandi of quick strikes inside Angolan territory followed by a swift exit. Major General Geldenhuys described the new strategy as "comparable to what happens when an ant-hill is kicked open. The ants scatter, you search for them around their nest and they lead you to new nests. . . . A combination of area operations, follow-ups, and search-and-destroy operations [is] launched to locate and destroy them."[130] Such an approach required a considerably higher South African tolerance for keeping forces inside Angolan territory than it had typically had before 1979 (with the exception of Operation Savannah, in which South Africa believed it had US support). Scholtz summarizes the change: "Operation Sceptic . . . was an important development in the Border War. Its predecessors, operations Reindeer, Rekstok and Saffraan, had been limited in scope and time. Sceptic evolved into a much longer operation, during which People's Liberation Army of Namibia (PLAN) was hunted deep within its own rear areas in Angola for about three weeks. Apart from Savannah, this was the biggest and longest operation the SADF had been involved in since 1945."[131] Steenkamp concurs: Sceptic was "a far more ambitious venture than any of the previous external operations."[132]

South Africa's greater comfort with escalation continued after Operation Sceptic and is confirmed by participants in the conflict. Both Major General Opperman and Ambassador Zazeraj, for example, confirm that South African tolerance for escalation increased in the 1980s, while the historian Piero Gleijeses argues that South African elites "ratcheted up the pressure on South Africa's neighbors."[133] Throughout the rest of 1980 and early 1981, South Africa launched operations inside Angola, including Operation Klipklop in July 1980 and Operation Carnation, which ran from June to August 1981.[134] In May 1981, senior SADF officials concluded that they had to operate in Angola on a more sustained basis and "dominate a territory, instead of going in after specific bases and leaving again afterwards."[135] The resulting discussions led to Operation Protea. Protea used over four thousand troops and would be the largest SADF operation in the entire Border War and the largest mechanized operation by the South African Army since World War II.[136] Protea marked a further increase in South African aggression. For the first time, South African forces took a semi-permanent occupying role within the province of Cunene, and the invasion was "so brazen that it provoked widespread condemnation from Western governments."[137] Such operations could not be undertaken without escalating the conflict. And, indeed, the Angolan army, the People's Armed Forces for the Liberation of Angola (FAPLA), joined in the conflict between PLAN and the SADF on PLAN's side. The Cubans also began to play an increasing role, with Cuban pilots flying MiG-21s close to the combat zone (with one Cuban-piloted MiG-21 shot down by a South African Mirage), and the Soviet Union delivered T-54 and T-55 tanks and antiaircraft missiles to FAPLA.[138] While South Africa had previously sought to avoid such escalation, such concerns appeared less binding after 1979. South Africa followed Operation Protea with further operations "like waves in the wake of Protea."[139] Operation Daisy, a major operation targeting territory three hundred kilometers inside Angola (the deepest into Angola that the SADF would ever seek to strike during the Border War), was followed by other significant operations—Operation Makro in December 1981–January 1982, Operation Meebos I in March 1982, and Operation Meebos II in July and August 1982—all aimed at destroying SWAPO capabilities but with far less sensitivity to escalation than South Africa had previously exhibited.[140]

While 1982 saw some largely unsuccessful efforts to negotiate a cease-fire, the war continued at a low level with regular contacts between the SADF and SWAPO on and around the Angola-Namibia border, occasional South African operations over the Angolan border, and continued South African violations of Angolan airspace, something that South African officials no longer sought to hide. While such sorties were primarily for reconnaissance purposes, they occasionally engaged Angolan forces, and shot down an Angolan MiG-21 in October 1982. South Africa also continued to assist UNITA, facilitating a large expansion of the territory under its control and supporting a full-scale UNITA assault on an Angolan garrison at Cangamba, killing 120 Cuban forces.[141] Further, the escalation that South Africa most feared and had previously sought to avoid—a larger-scale Soviet involvement in Angola—was becoming increasingly likely. Increasing quantities of Soviet materiel were flowing into Angola, and a South African official in the United States was handed a note in November 1983 from a Soviet diplomat stating that "South Africa's continued occupation of Angolan soil and support for UNITA was unacceptable. . . . The USSR would give Luanda all the support it needed to protect its sovereignty and territorial integrity."[142] Whereas before 1979 South Africa sought to avoid such escalation and controlled its operations accordingly, South Africa responded to this Soviet threat by launching Operation Askari, a large-scale operation aimed at destroying SWAPO's ability to launch an assault into South West Africa in early 1984. In particular, South Africa sought to force FAPLA forces in the Angolan provinces of Cahama, Mulondo, Caiundo, and Cuvelai to retreat, and sought to dominate the approach routes that SWAPO would use in the event of an assault on South West Africa.[143] Askari was a significant operation, requiring large numbers of forces deep inside Angola. South African military leaders anticipated that the operation would last for two months, and an SADF planning document acknowledged that achieving South Africa's goals in the conflict would be "time-consuming."[144] Again, the result of South African aggression was escalation: "With the growing role of the Soviet Union . . . outside factors grew in importance, while South African control over the course of the war diminished."[145] As in the aftermath of Operation Protea, Askari led to a short-lived and unsuccessful effort to achieve a peace settlement.[146] This did not stop further SADF actions deep inside Angolan territory: in July 1984, South African Special Forces Commandos destroyed an oil pipeline in Angola's northernmost province, which led to the loss of forty-two thousand barrels of oil, and an Angolan and East German ship were damaged by mines that had been laid by the South Africans in the Luanda harbor.[147] Major conventional operations also continued, in addition to acts of sabotage and covert operations, with Operation Boswilger and Operation Egret being undertaken inside Angolan territory in 1985, and the war continuing to escalate until the late 1980s.

Overall, therefore, South Africa became more aggressive in the period after acquiring nuclear weapons. This change in behavior does not itself prove that nuclear acquisition *caused* the change. However, in combination with the evidence that South African elite thinking viewed nuclear weapons as a tool for reducing the risk of escalation associated with aggression, it suggests that South Africa both thought and behaved in a manner consistent with the expectations of the theory of nuclear opportunism.

Did South Africa also become more willing to compromise in the aftermath of nuclear acquisition? Overall, there is little evidence to suggest this. While periodic peace initiatives were launched throughout the period, South Africa's demands remained constant. The basic South African negotiating position throughout the period, as articulated by Foreign Minister Pik Botha, was that "we were not ready to exchange [a war] on the Cunene [River, marking the border between Namibia and Angola] for a war on the Orange [River, marking the border between Namibia and South Africa]. . . . If Southwest Africa was governed by SWAPO there would be a serious risk that the Russians would threaten South Africa from that territory."[148] While South Africa accepted an independent Namibia in principle, it did not want to withdraw from South West Africa as long as doing so might increase the threat to South African territory. This position later became known as the principle of "linkage": that the withdrawal of Cuban forces from Angola and an end to SWAPO attacks within South West Africa were a prerequisite for a process that would lead to Namibian independence.[149] In reality, this meant that negotiations over the future of South West Africa were something of a sham. South African elites recognized that a free election in Namibia would lead to SWAPO coming to power, an outcome that was unacceptable for South Africa and that precluded a full-scale South African withdrawal from South West Africa.[150] Overall, therefore, South Africa did not become more willing to compromise in the aftermath of acquiring nuclear weapons.

It seems reasonably clear that South Africa engaged in increased aggression in the aftermath of nuclear acquisition, and did not engage in greater efforts to compromise. However, whether South Africa also engaged in greater steadfastness in the aftermath of nuclear acquisition, as the theory of nuclear opportunism anticipates, is less clear. Even in the period before nuclear acquisition, South Africa responded forcefully to SWAPO attacks inside South West Africa but merely restrained itself in terms of operations inside Angolan territory that aimed at degrading SWAPO's capability to launch attacks. In the aftermath of nuclear acquisition, South Africa continued to respond forcefully to SWAPO attacks but also engaged in more aggressive preemptive actions aimed at destroying SWAPO's military capabilities and reducing its capacity to plan and execute attacks. Thus, it is hard to identify any substantial changes in South Africa's steadfastness over the period of nuclear acquisition. Instead, the change in South Africa's foreign policy seems to have largely been an increase in aggression. Thus, this expectation of the theory of nuclear opportunism is not confirmed—nuclear opportunism anticipates an increase in South African steadfastness that we do not see in the historical evidence.

What about the remaining three behaviors? Did South Africa engage in greater levels of independence, defined as becoming more willing to take actions that its allies opposed? Did South Africa seek to strengthen its allies and thus engage in greater levels of bolstering? And did South Africa engage in expansion—widening its interests in international politics? South Africa's increasing international isolation over the time period makes assessing these claims reasonably straightforward, because South Africa lacked allies that it would have sought independence from, and allies that it could have plausibly sought to bolster. South Africa was "the skunk of the world," and South African foreign policy calculations were made on the assumption that "we were on our own."[151]

The only actor that could have plausibly restrained South Africa in the prenuclear period, and from which South Africa might have sought independence from in the aftermath of nuclear acquisition, was the United States. And indeed, as discussed above, South Africa's nuclear posture was in large part aimed at encouraging US intervention in southern Africa if the conventional situation escalated beyond South Africa's ability to control it. In truth, however, South African elites did not view the United States as in any way committed to providing for South Africa's security. Indeed, this assessment of US ambivalence about South African security was part of the reason for the catalytic nuclear strategy, since it was believed that absent South African nuclear weapons, the United States would be highly unlikely to assist South Africa.[152]

As discussed above, the South Africans felt that the United States had left them in the lurch during Operation Savannah, and from that point on they regarded the United States as (at best) a fickle and unreliable ally. In Major General de Vries's words, "I don't think the United States was seen as an ally for our counterinsurgency war in South-West Africa and southern Angola. They dropped us with Operation Savannah. . . . They weren't our allies; there was no support from Americans on the ground. So we didn't like them that much."[153] As Major General Opperman recalls, "I think the United States lost all their credibility as an ally during Operation Savannah. We realized that the United States had only one interest, and that was their personal interest in the situation. . . . I don't think we ever considered the Americans to be reliable."[154] Major General Dippenaar describes the lack of reliability of US patronage, saying "One day they [the United States] will support you, the next day there will be a vote and they will say, 'Stop the support.'"[155] These sentiments were also expressed by South African leaders at the time, with Vorster telling the Rhodesians soon after Operation Savannah that "anyone who relied on the USA has his deepest sympathy," and P. W. Botha telling parliament that "we [went into Angola] with the approval and knowledge of the Americans. But they left us in the lurch."[156]

South Africans recognized that although there were factions in the US Congress and executive branch who were inclined to support them, there were also powerful forces pushing in the opposite direction, both inside and outside the government.[157] South African diplomat Pieter Snyman, who served in Washington, recalls that "we had good friends in Congress and in the administration, but [we knew that] they [might] succumb to the pressure of their own [antiapartheid] constituencies."[158] While the United States might sometimes offer support to South Africa, South African diplomats were well aware that such support could never be relied on. A memo from the South African ambassador to the minister for foreign affairs in 1977 summarized South Africa's view of the United States: "South Africa will always be available as a target [because of apartheid]. . . . In the circumstances South Africa can expect little overt understanding and no assistance."[159]

As a result, South Africa did not feel constrained by the need to maintain support from Washington, because it did not feel it was getting much US support, and certainly did not believe that the United States could be relied on to contribute to South African security. Major General de Vries confirms that South Africa did not, therefore, fear the loss of US support. South Africa was able in large part to "ignore the bad reputation and the snide remarks that came from countries such as the Western powers," because it did not cost South Africa anything to do so.[160] A 1981 CIA assessment concurred that South African elites believe they "can no longer rely upon the West for its security" and that "South Africa's policies on nuclear weapons will be made fairly independently of any U.S. security interests. Whether to develop and display a nuclear weapons capability will depend almost entirely on the Afrikaners' sense of domestic and regional security."[161]

South Africa certainly imposed constraints on its actions in the Border War, as discussed above, but these were imposed by fears of escalation rather than by fears of a withdrawal of Western support. As a result, after acquiring nuclear weapons, South Africa did not become more independent of the United States. In fact, the South African relationship with Washington became closer in the 1980s. The Reagan administration placed a lower priority on domestic reform within South Africa; sought to "nurture evolutionary change" by working with, rather than isolating, the South African regime;[162] fought against (and vetoed) congressional legislation to impose sanctions on South Africa; and had greater tolerance for South African efforts to circumvent international sanctions. This shift in the US–South African relationship was not due to South Africa's nuclear weapons but due to the Reagan administration's greater ideological sympathy for the apartheid regime, its greater concerns about Soviet influence in the region, and the reduced priority it placed on human rights promotion within its foreign policy. An internal 1985 memo to Patrick Buchanan, Reagan's communications director, described the administration's position as "We don't like apartheid but we're just afraid to be too hard on S. Africa if the likely outcome will be communism," while also acknowledging that the Reagan administration had sometimes "sounded like lazy apologists for apartheid."[163] As the South African foreign minister put it in a memo to colleagues: the Reagan administration's assessment of its interests in Southern Africa was "more clinical and less a function of moral outrage [at apartheid]. . . . This will bring an end . . . to the acceptance as an article of faith of the need to promote, irrespective of the cost, political liberalisation in South Africa."[164] Nonetheless, both parties remained wary of each other. In the words of a US State Department briefing paper preparing the secretary of state for a meeting with the South African foreign minister early in the Reagan administration, "The South Africans are deeply suspicious of us. . . . South African truculence (which can be coated with great charm) is compounded by the fact that, as an international pariah, the country has had no meaningful, balanced bilateral relations in recent memory."[165]

South Africa also lacked allies that it would have felt any inclination to bolster. As Theresa Papenfus concludes in her biography of Pik Botha, "After Operation Savannah it was clearer than ever that South Africa had no friends."[166] While South Africa had proxies that it supported in pursuit of its regional goals (notably UNITA in Angola and the Liberation Front of Mozambique in Mozambique), these were not states that South Africa could use nuclear weapons to bolster.

Aside from the United States, South Africa's most meaningful relationship over the period was with Israel, with which South Africa enjoyed an important, though highly secretive, relationship.[167] The South Africa–Israel relationship bought South Africa access to Israel's advanced conventional weaponry and nuclear technologies, and South African military officials frequently found themselves in Israel to shepherd through such deals. Major General Dippenaar, for example, recalls being posted to Israel as an "agricultural adviser," although in reality he was there to learn from the way the Israelis conducted mobile warfare and to facilitate "transferring technologies which would then help with the development of other weapon systems."[168]

Despite its importance, the South African–Israeli relationship was largely transactional and based on mutually beneficial material exchanges: technology and arms transfers from Israel to South Africa, and natural resources (including uranium) and currency transfers in the opposite direction. As Sasha Polakow-Suransky summarizes the relationship, "Israel profited handsomely from arms exports and South Africa gained access to cutting-edge weaponry at a time when the rest of the world was turning against the apartheid state. . . . Israel denied its ties with South Africa, claiming that it opposed apartheid . . . even as it secretly strengthened the arsenal of a white supremacist government."[169] The transactional nature of the relationship, the vast distances between the two countries, and the more immediate defense priorities that both countries felt meant that South Africa felt no inclination to directly provide for Israel's security. As a result, South Africa did not consider it politically attractive to seek to bolster Israel's position in the Middle East in the aftermath of nuclear acquisition, and there is little evidence that the relationship changed in its aims or scope as South Africa acquired nuclear weapons: substantial conventional arms transfers continued much as before. Indeed, the secrecy of the South African–Israeli relationship in both countries meant that any public bolstering of either state by the other would have been deeply politically challenging.

As a result, and in line with the expectations of the theory of nuclear opportunism, South Africa did not use nuclear weapons to facilitate either bolstering or independence in the aftermath of nuclear acquisition.

Nor did South Africa give any thought to engaging in expansion. South Africa was a state seeking to hold on to its position in southern Africa. Over the period of nuclear acquisition, South Africa was being buffeted from both within and without as it faced Soviet and Cuban forces in neighboring countries, diplomatic isolation, stringent antiapartheid sanctions, and increasing domestic instability and economic turmoil. For South Africa, merely maintaining its international position and domestic political institutions was becoming more and more challenging. As a result, it would have been highly surprising if South Africa had significantly expanded its interests in world politics in response to nuclear acquisition. And, indeed, while South Africa frequently went on the offense in Southern Africa, its strategic goals were ultimately defensive and status quo oriented: to hold on to what it had. In Scholtz's words, "The South African posture was offensive on the tactical, operational, and military strategic levels, but defensive on the security-strategic level. . . . The government wanted primarily to preserve the status quo, but realised that a defensive military strategy and operational and tactical approach would not be sufficient."[170] No new alliances were entered into in the aftermath of nuclear acquisition, nor did South Africa initiate disputes with countries within which it did not already have long-standing conflict. In the aftermath of nuclear acquisition, South African foreign policy thus remained firmly focused on the Frontline States, on its long-standing relationship with Israel, and on its fractious relationship with the United States, and held the ultimate goal of maintaining, not expanding, South Africa's position. This expectation of the theory of nuclear opportunism, therefore, is confirmed: South Africa did not use nuclear weapons to pursue expansion.

Other Explanations

The theory of nuclear opportunism thus performs well but not perfectly. It correctly anticipates that South Africa would use nuclear weapons to facilitate aggression and would not use nuclear weapons to facilitate compromise, independence, bolstering, or expansion. However, it incorrectly anticipates that South Africa would use nuclear weapons to facilitate steadfastness, which we do not see in the historical record. How do other theories perform in explaining the South African response to nuclear acquisition?

The theory of the nuclear revolution predicts that nuclear weapons would make South Africa more secure, and thus that South Africa would have less need to engage in aggression, expansion, or bolstering—all of which are behaviors driven by insecurity in the view of the theory of the nuclear revolution. However, the theory predicts that states may use nuclear weapons to facilitate steadfastness, independence, and compromise after acquiring nuclear weapons. The theory of the nuclear revolution thus makes several correct predictions in the South African case: South Africa did not use nuclear weapons to facilitate expansion or bolstering. But, in contrast to the predictions of the nuclear revolution, South Africa used nuclear weapons to facilitate aggression, it did not use nuclear weapons to facilitate steadfastness or independence, and it did not exhibit a greater inclination to compromise after acquiring nuclear weapons. The theory of the nuclear revolution does not, therefore, perform as well as the theory of nuclear opportunism.

S. Paul Kapur's theory anticipates that South Africa would not have used nuclear weapons to facilitate aggression.[171] Kapur anticipates that only conventionally weak, revisionist states use nuclear weapons to facilitate aggression. South Africa was conventionally strong relative to its neighbors at the point at which it acquired nuclear weapons. As discussed above, although South Africa faced serious threats during the period in which it acquired nuclear weapons, it never lost its conventional military superiority over its opponents.[172] Because Kapur's theory requires both conventional weakness *and* revisionist preferences to predict increased aggression, Kapur would therefore predict that South Africa would not have used nuclear weapons to facilitate aggression.[173] Kapur's theory thus misses the important way in which nuclear acquisition affected South African foreign policy: by facilitating conventional aggression.

A case-specific alternative explanation would be that the increase in South African elites' tolerance for escalation occurred not because of nuclear weapons but because of South Africa's increasing conventional military capabilities, which gave them greater power projection capabilities. As Colonel Breytenbach points out: "It depends on capability—how deep you can go."[174] Similarly, David Steward argues that South Africa stopped its advance in Operation Savannah in 1975 because "our defence force was completely unprepared for an operation of this scale—it didn't have artillery at that time, it had rudimentary 25 pounder cannons from the Second World War and it had overextended itself. . . . By the 80s we had significantly improved our operational capability . . . and this increased the capability of the SADF to operate."[175] It is certainly true that South African defense expenditure and military manpower rose dramatically throughout the 1970s and 1980s. South African military expenditure rose from $359 million in 1970 to $2.24 billion in 1979 and $3.6 billion by 1989.[176] This increase included expenditure on major new weapons systems (including the G5 and G6 artillery pieces, and the Cheetah fighter jet) that were commissioned and integrated into South Africa's force structure over this period.[177]

The weight of evidence, however, would argue against this explanation. First, South African capabilities were growing constantly over the entire period, and there was not a discontinuous change in capabilities in 1979 that might explain the change in South African behavior observed. Second, the evidence suggests that capabilities were not the relevant constraint on South African behavior. After all, Operation Savannah proved that South Africa could conduct operations deep inside Angolan territory, but Savannah was undertaken only because South African elites anticipated US support that failed to materialize. Such large-scale operations were not tolerated again until after South Africa had acquired nuclear weapons, despite South Africa's demonstrated ability to undertake them. Third, the military capabilities that a state chooses to deploy are in large part the result of the state's tolerance for escalation: South Africa's investments in conventional weaponry were the result of a desire to engage in increased aggression rather than a cause of it. And in the South African case, it is clear that at the point at which the South Africans wished to escalate, they provided their forces with the required military capabilities to do so. Colonel Breytenbach confirms that the government was willing to provide "equipment that would allow you to go further in" when it wanted to do so.[178] And, indeed, it was not simply the case that the war escalated in 1979 for reasons that were unrelated to

South African actions. The conflict escalated in 1979 because South Africa chose to escalate it. In short, South Africa took actions after 1979 that it knew would escalate the conflict and that it had not been willing to undertake before it acquired nuclear weapons.

Thus, although the theory of nuclear opportunism does not perform perfectly in the South African case, none of the alternative explanations do better in explaining the ways in which South African foreign policy changed after South Africa acquired nuclear weapons.

The Abandonment of South Africa's Nuclear Weapons

Although South Africa's aggression continued well after it acquired nuclear weapons, the war in Angola ultimately came to an end with the withdrawal of Cuban and Soviet forces from the region. At this point, in the late 1980s, South Africa made the decision to abandon its nuclear weapons, first freezing and then dismantling its nuclear program. In doing so, South Africa became the first and, thus far, only state to give up indigenously produced nuclear weapons. Does this not count against the theory of nuclear opportunism, demonstrating the lack of utility that nuclear weapons offered to South Africa?

In fact, the reasons underpinning South Africa's nuclear abandonment reinforce rather than undermine the theory of nuclear opportunism. In the late 1980s, South Africa's security environment improved markedly. Cuban forces had left Angola, and the Soviet Union was in the process of abandoning its global ambitions. Thus, the primary factor that had motivated South African nuclear acquisition and engendered the particular political benefits that South Africa acquired from possessing nuclear weapons—the threats it faced—had dissipated. In this more permissive international environment, South African elites concluded that the benefits of nuclear weapons no longer outweighed the costs. Reform-minded South African elites recognized that persuading the international community to remove the crippling economic and political sanctions that South Africa faced would require progress both on domestic political reform and on nonproliferation: joining the Treaty on the Nonproliferation of Nuclear Weapons (NPT) as a nonnuclear weapons state. As F. W. de Klerk was coming into office as president, Waldo Stumpf recalls a meeting in which de Klerk stated that "in my term of office, I'm going to take South Africa back to being a respected international member of the community. And that means two things, it means we're going to unban Mr. Mandela [and] dismantle the apartheid policy, and we're going to accede to the NPT."[179] South Africa acceded to the NPT in 1991 and disclosed the existence of its nuclear program in 1993.

As discussed in chapter 1, the theory of nuclear opportunism emphasizes the benefits of nuclear weapons but does not make any claims about the circumstances in which those benefits will outweigh the costs of possessing them. In the case of South Africa, it is clear that in a less restrictive security environment, the benefits of nuclear weapons no longer outweighed the costs of the program: in the words of Peter Liberman, "Pretoria's sensitivity to the economic and diplomatic liabilities of the program" grew over the 1980s.[180] Second, from the perspective of the theory of nuclear opportunism it is unsurprising that states would reevaluate the value of their nuclear programs at the point at which the key variable determining the foreign policy benefits they acquire from nuclear weapons changes. In South Africa's case, the severe threats the regime faced had motivated nuclear acquisition and determined the ways in which South Africa used nuclear weapons to facilitate aggression in Angola, but those threats had disappeared, opening up the political space for a fundamental reevaluation of South Africa's nuclear policy. In the words of André Buys, when F. W. de Klerk terminated the nuclear weapons program, "I was very happy. Some of my friends said, 'Shouldn't we have kept them?' but I said, 'We've had the strategy all along—it was threat based, and the threat has disappeared.'"[181]

The evidence, therefore, suggests that nuclear acquisition did affect South African foreign policy, even if apartheid-era political and military elites are often reluctant to acknowledge it. South African aggression in the Border War increased in the aftermath of acquiring nuclear weapons, with South Africa becoming more willing to undertake military operations deep inside Angolan territory than it had previously been willing to do. The fears of provoking escalation that had previously constrained South Africa became less binding after the acquisition of nuclear weapons.

This effect is consistent with South African elite thinking: South African elites wanted to engage in greater aggression in Angola but were deeply worried about triggering escalation, and viewed nuclear weapons as a way of reducing the risk of such escalation occurring. Even if South African elites are disinclined to state explicitly that nuclear weapons facilitated South African aggression, the evidence supports that conclusion. That South Africa would respond to nuclear acquisition in this way is consistent with the theory of nuclear opportunism but inconsistent with other explanations.

South Africa did not use nuclear weapons to facilitate the other possible behaviors: steadfastness, expansion, bolstering, compromise, or independence. This is largely, though not fully, consistent with the expectations of the theory of nuclear opportunism, which would have anticipated South Africa using nuclear weapons to facilitate steadfastness in addition to aggression. Nonetheless, the theory of nuclear opportunism performs better than other explanations, such as the theory of the nuclear revolution or S. Paul Kapur's theory of emboldenment, neither of which expects to see South Africa using nuclear weapons to facilitate aggression. As with the British case, the theory of nuclear opportunism outperforms the alternative explanations as an explanation for how states use nuclear weapons to achieve their goals in international politics.

The Foundations of a New World Order

The United States and the Start of the Nuclear Era

During World War II, in the deserts of New Mexico, US and allied scientists sought to create a new kind of weapon that could single-handedly win the war. They succeeded in creating the most powerful explosives known to humankind. Having used nuclear weapons to compel Japanese surrender, the United States sat atop a new international order. Nuclear weapons would powerfully shape the way in which US elites envisaged, built, and sustained the postwar order, and they continue to profoundly affect US foreign policy and grand strategy.

The theory of nuclear opportunism anticipates that during World War II, the United States' political priority would have been to improve the US position against its enemies, and that the United States would use nuclear weapons to escalate and seek to end the war against Japan. In the aftermath of World War II, the theory anticipates that the United States would use nuclear weapons to engage in expansion—the widening of the United States' interests—and bolstering of allies as a result of the favorable geopolitical environment in which the United States found itself. Although the theory of nuclear opportunism does not perform perfectly, I argue that the theory nonetheless sheds significant light on the US case.

The case of the United States is useful for testing the theory of nuclear opportunism. First, the variables that the theory identifies as conditioning the effects of nuclear acquisition themselves changed dramatically at the end of World War II. As a result, the US case offers extra leverage in testing the theory of nuclear opportunism because the theory suggests that nuclear weapons should affect US foreign policy *in different ways* before and after the end of World War II. The US case offers an extra set of expectations with which to assess the performance of the theory: it is, in essence, two cases. Second, this means that it offers a hard case for the theory, because it is one in which a state may have acquired nuclear weapons for a particular purpose during the war but then faced incentives (if the theory is correct) to use them for a very different set of purposes after the end of the war. If US policymakers changed the way they thought about the utility of nuclear weapons at the end of the war in the way the theory of nuclear opportunism suggests, that would provide particularly good evidence for the theory. Third, the US case is in many ways an outlier and unusual relative to subsequent cases of proliferation. The United States was the first state to acquire nuclear weapons, meaning that US policymakers lacked well-established understandings of the ways in which nuclear weapons could be used or experiences of the ways in which other countries had thought about the utility of nuclear weapons. More broadly, the United States acquired nuclear weapons under historically unusual circumstances—at the conclusion of a brutal world war that transformed international politics. Similarly, the United States acquired nuclear weapons at a point at which it occupied a highly unusual position in the international system as the most powerful state in the world by some distance. Thus, if the theory sheds light on the US case, in addition to cases in which states acquired nuclear weapons under more historically normal circumstances, that would offer significant validation of the theory.

Nonetheless, the US case also presents two important challenges because the international system saw dramatic changes with the end of World War II.

First, because the geopolitical circumstances of the United States changed dramatically, there are reasons to think that US foreign policy would have changed in important ways during this time even if the United States had not acquired nuclear weapons. This means that identifying the effects of nuclear acquisition is somewhat harder, and a simple before-and-after comparison of US behavior is likely to be less convincingly attributable to the effect of nuclear acquisition than in other cases where few other factors change simultaneously with nuclear acquisition. This concern does not invalidate the research design, but it demands that we pay particular attention to the mechanisms through which nuclear weapons affected US foreign policy, the way in which leaders thought about US nuclear weapons, and the relevant counterfactuals (that is, how the United States would have behaved in the absence of nuclear weapons) in the period after US nuclear acquisition. The availability of a rich array of documentary evidence and a vast historical literature on US foreign policy during this period means that this is feasible.

Second, in a contested and fast-changing international system, distinguishing between several of the behaviors in the typology is difficult. For example, establishing the nature of the status quo—necessary to distinguish between aggression and steadfastness—is extremely difficult in a situation of flux in which a range of political actors were seeking to define exactly what the status quo was (or should be). Similarly, defining the nature of the United States' preexisting interests—key to distinguishing between expansion and aggression—is extremely challenging, because of the vast changes in the international system that were occurring.[1] As a result, I focus less on categorizing behaviors that could plausibly be interpreted in different ways and instead show the ways in which nuclear weapons affected these behaviors, regardless of how one labels them. In this way, the US case offers a less clean test of the theory than other cases, but nonetheless allows for a rich description of the ways in which nuclear weapons influenced the foreign policies of the United States.

When Did the United States Acquire Nuclear Weapons?

To look for changes in US foreign policy caused by nuclear weapons, we first need to know when to look. When did the United States acquire the relevant capabilities? As discussed in chapter 1, this requires that we pay attention to the ways that the United States intended to use nuclear weapons, and the particular technological and military capabilities that such uses require. This enables us to accurately identify the appropriate point in time at which to look for changes in foreign policy.

In the case of the United States, this is simple. The purpose of the Manhattan Project was to produce a usable weapon that could have an important impact on the outcome of the war and to deliver it by air to the cities of Germany or Japan. It is not surprising that US military elites found the idea of nuclear weapons attractive. The use of conventional strategic bombing—and of area bombing of cities and civilians, rather than targeting exclusively military assets—had grown in importance as the war progressed. By the time strategic bombing began in Japan, it was seen by US policymakers as a vital part of the overall US effort to force Japanese surrender.[2] The promise of nuclear weapons played into this broader enthusiasm for strategic bombing.[3] For President Franklin Roosevelt and his head of military research and development, Vannevar Bush, nuclear weapons offered primarily offensive advantages, and there was little question that the bomb would be used against America's enemies.[4] In 1944, Churchill and Roosevelt had agreed that the bomb could "be used against the Japanese, who should be warned that this bombardment will be repeated until they surrender."[5] The Interim Committee, set up to advise Secretary of War Henry Stimson and the president on the use of the atomic bomb, recommended that "the bomb be used against Japan as soon as possible" and "without prior warning."[6]

Given that the United States already had aircraft capable of reaching Japan and Germany, all that was needed was a nuclear explosive that could be dropped out of them. Rehearsals for the use of the gun-type "Little Boy" bomb that would be used on Hiroshima were completed by the end of July 1945.[7] The twenty kiloton Trinity test of July 16, 1945, demonstrated to US military and political leaders that the "Fat Man" implosion device that would be used on Nagasaki would also work successfully.[8] It is therefore in late July 1945 that we should expect that nuclear weapons would have begun to affect US strategic calculations.

The United States' Strategic Environment

What does the theory of nuclear opportunism expect to see in the US case?

As described in chapter 1, the first factor to examine is whether the United States faced serious territorial threats or was involved in a war that required the dedication of significant national resources. When the United States acquired a deliverable nuclear capability in 1945 it was in the midst of World War II. The United States did not face ongoing fighting on its own territory (although it had, of course, suffered the 1941 attack on its territory at Pearl Harbor), and by this point US victory in the Pacific was virtually inevitable (though the timing and manner of that victory were not) and victory in Europe had been achieved. Nonetheless, World War II represented a brutal war that had demanded the expenditure of significant American blood and treasure, and the United States was prepared to pay considerable further costs to achieve a complete victory should an invasion of Japan prove necessary. Because the United States was involved in an ongoing war, the other variables in the decision tree do not come into play. Under such conditions, the theory anticipates that the United States' political priority would be to improve its position against its enemies, and predicts that the United States would use nuclear weapons to facilitate aggression and steadfastness. Figure 4.1 shows the application of the theory to the US case in the summer of 1945.

The theory also expects that the same logic would be reflected in elite thinking about nuclear weapons. American elites should have viewed nuclear weapons as a tool with which to improve their position against their opponents in World War II, and should have planned to use them for this purpose within the conflict. Last, the theory anticipates that because of the war the United States was engaging in, and the political priority that the United States would accord to improving its position in the war and against its enemies, the other behaviors would be less politically appealing. As a result, the theory predicts that the United States would not seek to use its nuclear weapons to facilitate the remaining behaviors in the typology: expansion, independence, bolstering, or compromise.

With the end of World War II, however, the circumstances facing the United States changed dramatically. The geopolitical situation transformed from one in which the United States was involved in a brutal and all-out war to one in which the United States was by far the most powerful state in the world and faced no serious threats. Because several of the factors identified as important by the theory of nuclear opportunism changed with the end of World War II, the theory predicts that the United States would use nuclear weapons differently in the aftermath of World War II than during the war.

Measuring the first factor—the presence of serious territorial threats or an ongoing war—is straightforward. With the passing of World War II, the United States was no longer involved in a war and faced no serious threats

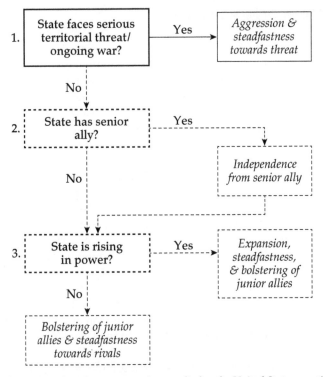

Figure 4.1. The theory of nuclear opportunism applied to the United States, wartime. Dashed lines indicate portions of the theory not applicable in this case.

to its territory. US elites were certainly suspicious of the intentions of the Soviet Union, but the Soviet Union had been decimated by war, was thousands of miles away, and had no capacity to project power against the US homeland. The United States thus emerged from World War II in an extraordinarily secure position: a hegemon in the Western Hemisphere and a state whose potential peer competitors either were under occupation or had been ravaged by the most destructive war in human history. The United States thus faced no serious threats of the kind described by the first variable.

Because the United States did not face threats of this sort, the second and third factors come into play in determining the expectations of the theory of nuclear opportunism. Measuring the second factor—whether the United States had a senior ally committed to its protection—is also straightforward. Because the United States was now by some distance the most powerful state in the world, it could not have a senior ally by definition. The third factor is whether the United States was increasing in relative power. Here, too, the coding is clear. The United States was unique among the great powers in becoming richer, stronger, and more powerful during World War II. By the end of the war, the United States had a higher standard of living and per capita productivity than any other country in the world, its gross domestic product (GDP) had risen by two-thirds, it controlled nearly two-thirds of the world's gold reserves, and it possessed the world's most potent military and power projection capabilities.[9] US gross national product (GNP) at the end of the war was three times that of the Soviet Union and five times that of the United Kingdom.[10] Finally, the United States ended World War II holding a historically unusual concentration of military power. In the historian Melvyn Leffler's words, the United States' "strategic air force was unrivaled. Its navy dominated the seas. Its aircraft carriers and marine divisions enabled it to project its power across the oceans.... The United States had preponderent power."[11] The claim that the United States was rising in relative power at the end of World War II is confirmed by the Correlates of War's CINC scores, which provide a measure of a state's share of global power. The United States' CINC score rose every year from 1937 until 1946. Thus, as World War II came to an end, US relative power was on an upward trajectory. Figure 4.2 shows the application of the theory to the United States in the aftermath of World War II.

As a result of this uniquely favorable geopolitical environment, the theory predicts that the United States' political priority should have been

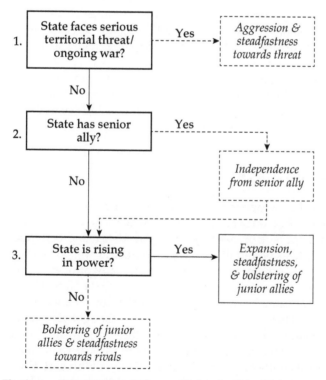

Figure 4.2. The theory of nuclear opportunism applied to the United States, postwar. Dashed lines indicate portions of the theory not applicable in this case.

to expand its influence in international politics—forming new alliances, initiating new adversarial relationships, and developing a greater ability to project power and influence—and that the United States should have used its nuclear weapons to facilitate these behaviors. States that are rising in power and in a secure environment do not face tight resource constraints, and the favorable geopolitical environment in which they find themselves affords them the latitude to expand their influence in international politics. The theory therefore predicts that in the aftermath of World War II, the United States would use its nuclear weapons to facilitate expansion, to bolster existing allies, and to stand more firmly in the face of any challenges. Additionally, the theory predicts that US elites would view nuclear weapons as useful in facilitating these behaviors.

Because of the favorable geopolitical circumstances that the United States faced, the theory anticipates that the United States would not seek to use nuclear weapons to facilitate aggression, independence, or compromise. The theory anticipates that using nuclear weapons to engage in independence would be unnecessary because the United States possessed no allies with the ability to constrain its behavior. The uniquely favorable position in which it found itself meant that the United States was already able to set an independent course in foreign policy, regardless of nuclear weapons. Similarly, states that are both rising in power and facing few threats have less need to engage in aggression. As discussed in chapter 1, rising states can afford to be patient in dealing with any threats that they face, because their permissive security environment affords them the latitude to do so. Using nuclear weapons to facilitate compromise is also unattractive because states in this position have the wind at their back: they have little reason and feel little pressure to engage in compromise.

The United States during World War II

How did nuclear weapons affect US foreign policy during World War II? The United States used nuclear weapons to escalate the war vis-à-vis Japan but used them to pursue preexisting goals—the defeat and surrender of Japan. The United States would likely have used nuclear weapons for similar purposes against Germany had the bomb been ready prior to German surrender. Although the extreme circumstances in which the United States acquired nuclear weapons make categorizing this behavior somewhat tricky, within the typology of behaviors I argue that it is best thought of as aggression. Aggression includes the escalation of a conflict through the introduction of new weapons or technologies, and the use of nuclear weapons for the first time in armed conflict represented an escalation of this sort. US policymakers understood the use of nuclear weapons in these terms. However, there are also ways in which the acquisition of nuclear weapons facilitated compromise. Nuclear weapons allowed the United States to avoid a long and bloody invasion of Japan that would likely have ended with little US inclination to compromise on any aspects of the terms of Japanese surrender, including the retention of the emperor. Nuclear weapons also facilitated US independence from the Soviet Union by obviating the need for Soviet assistance in a potential invasion of Japan.

AGGRESSION

On one level, it seems obvious that the United States used nuclear weapons to facilitate aggression during World War II: after all, the attacks on Hiroshima and Nagasaki continue to represent the only instances of direct use of nuclear weapons against an enemy. However, at the point of nuclear acquisition, the United States was already making maximal demands for an unconditional Japanese surrender, was engaged in a total and brutal war against Japanese forces in the Pacific, was tightening the blockade of the Japanese home islands, and was engaging in a systematic effort to destroy Japan's cities from the air. The extreme circumstances in which the United States acquired nuclear weapons make categorizing US nuclear use against Japan within the typology somewhat tricky. After all, given the way in which the United States was waging the war in the Pacific during the summer of 1945, did nuclear weapons really make the United States *more* belligerent in pursuing the defeat and surrender of Japan?

Ultimately, however, the use of nuclear weapons is best seen as an example of aggression. This is not because the United States was unable to defeat Japan without nuclear weapons. As Schelling argues, "With a combination of bombing and blockade, eventually invasion, and if necessary the deliberate spread of disease, the United States could probably have exterminated the population of the Japanese islands without nuclear weapons. . . . It would not have strained our Gross National Product to do it with ice picks."[12] However, as discussed in chapter 1, aggression can include the escalation of a conflict through the use of new tactics, forces, military doctrines, or technologies. The use of nuclear weapons against Hiroshima and Nagasaki meets this definition because it crossed an important technological focal point from the perspective of the United States, meeting Richard Smoke's definition of escalation as "a step of any size that crosses a saliency."[13] While the political goals that the United States was pursuing—the complete defeat of Japan— did not change with nuclear acquisition, nuclear weapons allowed the United States to introduce a significant new military technology that radically increased the efficiency with which the United States could destroy Japanese targets. The United States' Strategic Bombing Survey, conducted in the aftermath of the attacks, estimated that the single most effective night of conventional bombing—against Tokyo on March 9, 1945—killed 83,600 people using 279 planes and 1,667 bombs, while the attack on Hiroshima killed a comparable number using a single plane and a single bomb.[14] Crucially, nuclear weapons offered a plausible path to Japanese surrender without first having to engage in a brutal effort to conquer Japanese territory: what Truman feared would be "an Okinawa from one end of Japan to the other."[15] While the incendiary bombing of Japanese cities was nothing new, the explosive power of the nuclear attacks on Hiroshima and Nagasaki was still three to four times greater than that which could be delivered in a conventional strategic bombing raid, and, of course, such a conventional attack required hundreds of bombers instead of the single bomber required for each of the nuclear attacks.

The Strategic Bombing Survey concluded that "the survivors were not aware at the time that a radically new bomb had been used. . . . Even the Government had no conception, until President Truman's announcement was broadcast, of the new principle of operation."[16] While it is reasonable to question whether the Japanese recognized the nuclear attacks to be dramatically different in scope from the attacks they had already experienced during the spring and summer of 1945, it is clear that from the perspective of the United States, nuclear weapons offered a sea change in destructive efficiency.[17] "From the U.S. perspective," Ward Wilson argues, "the atomic bomb was clearly different."[18] The United States had dedicated some $2 billion and enormous human capital to developing nuclear weapons, and US policymakers spoke about the weapon in terms that suggest they did not simply view nuclear weapons as a marginal improvement on existing capabilities.[19] In briefing the newly inaugurated Harry Truman, for example, future secretary of state James Byrnes spoke "in quiet tones which did not disguise his feeling of awe, that the explosive emerging from American laboratories and plants might be powerful enough to destroy the world."[20] Secretary of War Stimson believed that the Manhattan Project "should not be considered simply in terms of military weapons, but as a new relationship of man to the universe. . . . While the advances in the field [of military technology] to date had been fostered in the needs of war, it was important to realize that the implications of the project went far beyond the needs of the present war."[21] Truman, announcing the use of nuclear weapons, spoke in terms that indicated he considered nuclear weapons to be fundamentally different from preexisting forms of warfare, stating, "It is a harnessing of the basic power of the universe. The force from which the sun draws its power has been loosed against those who brought war to the Far East."[22] Although there were always voices that sought to "normalize" nuclear weapons, in general, US officials recognized that nuclear weapons were special and that using them would represent an important escalation of the conflict. As the director of the Bureau of the Budget and future under secretary of state James Webb would write in a memo to President Truman, "The atomic bomb is no ordinary piece of ordnance."[23]

It is true that unlike in the South African case, the United States used nuclear weapons directly rather than using them to facilitate greater *conven-*

tional military aggression. But both behaviors represented—in different ways—escalation of the conflicts each state was undertaking, and both fall under the category of aggression.

Using nuclear weapons in this way was consistent with the thinking of US officials since the beginning of the Manhattan Project. Given the brutality of the war and the political importance of achieving a rapid US victory, there was little doubt that the United States would choose to use nuclear weapons once it had them in its possession.[24] Secretary of War Stimson stated after the war that "at no time, from 1941 to 1945, did I ever hear it suggested by the President or any other responsible member of the government that atomic energy should not be used in the war. . . . We were at war, and the work [of the Manhattan Project] must be done. . . . It was the common objective throughout the war to be the first to develop an atomic weapon and to use it."[25] Senior US policymakers, in Martin Sherwin's account, "asked whether it would be ready in time, not whether it should be used if it was."[26] Similarly, General Leslie Groves, who oversaw the Manhattan Project, and had initially been skeptical of the war-winning potential of nuclear weapons, wrote after the war that the Manhattan Project and potential use of nuclear weapons were subject to "basic military considerations. . . . If we were successful in time, we would shorten the war and thus save tens of thousands of American casualties."[27] Neither did the British government present any obstacles or question the wisdom of using nuclear weapons against the Japanese.[28] Three days after the bombing of Hiroshima, Truman declared that the logic of nuclear use was straightforward: "Having found the bomb we used it."[29]

Indeed, it was the assumption that nuclear weapons would be used, and the belief that using them might be decisive in the war effort, that led to the dedication of such immense resources to the Manhattan Project. In Stimson's words, "The entire purpose was the production of a military weapon; on no other ground could the wartime expenditure of so much time and money have been justified."[30] The Manhattan Project was accorded the highest priority as a result, and the rush to produce a working device was considerable. As President Roosevelt stated, "I think the whole thing should be pushed not only in regard to development, but also with due regard to time. This is very much of the essence."[31] And James Conant, the chairman of the National Defense Research Committee, argued that "if the possession of the new weapon in sufficient quantities would be a determining factor in the war," then "three months' delay might be fatal."[32] General Groves's instruction from Stimson was to produce a bomb "at the earliest possible date so as to bring the war to a conclusion."[33] The United States, therefore, built nuclear weapons with the full intention of using them and aware of the fact that to do so would cross an important threshold in destructive efficiency.

The intended target of America's nuclear weapons was both the Japanese and the Germans. There were several reasons that the United States planned to target Japan with its first atomic attack, including the fact that German scientists would be better able to accurately analyze a "dud" explosion if it occurred and the initial absence of B-29 bombers in Europe.[34] Nonetheless, Groves reported that "President Roosevelt asked if we were prepared to drop bombs on Germany if it was necessary to do so and we replied that we would be prepared to do so."[35] Coming into the presidency after Roosevelt's death in April 1945, Truman did not challenge the assumption that the bomb would be used. Within four months of coming into office, and a week after the successful Trinity test in New Mexico on July 16, 1945, Truman authorized the dropping of nuclear weapons on Japanese cities as soon as the weapons were ready. The purpose of doing so was clear: to escalate—and end—the war. As Truman wrote, the Japanese "will fold up before Russia comes in. I am sure they will when Manhattan appears over their homeland."[36] Although Truman would later claim to have had no doubts about his decision to use nuclear weapons, there was at least some ambivalence about the course of action he had authorized. As he wrote in his diary, "It seems to be the most terrible thing ever discovered, but it can be made the most useful."[37] In short, not only did the United States use nuclear weapons in the way the theory anticipates, but it had thought about using nuclear weapons in that way since the start of the Manhattan Project.

Overall, the United States' use of nuclear weapons against Hiroshima and Nagasaki comes under the category of aggression. While the United States was already making maximal demands of Japan and engaged in a brutal war against its forces in the Pacific and its cities from the air, the use of nuclear weapons nonetheless represented (and was seen at the time to represent) an important escalatory step that could potentially prove decisive in ending the war.

COMPROMISE

Nuclear weapons may have allowed the United States to engage in compromise, defined as accepting less in ongoing disputes. Ultimately, the United States backed down somewhat from the demands articulated at the Potsdam conference for a completely unconditional Japanese surrender, and made modest concessions to the Japanese regarding the status of the emperor.[38] In some ways, nuclear weapons hardened the resolve of US policymakers and made them less inclined to compromise. For example, at the meeting discussing the initial Japanese offer of surrender (on terms much more favorable to Japan than those the Japanese ultimately accepted), the secretary of state asked why the United States should "go further [in offering concessions] than we were willing to go at Potsdam when we had no atomic bomb, and Russia was not in the war."[39] And as US negotiations over the terms of Japanese surrender were ongoing, the US military was preparing for a third atomic strike against Tokyo in late August on the assumption that further nuclear attacks would allow the United States to drive a harder bargain rather than facilitate US compromises.

On the other hand, nuclear weapons offered the United States a tool with which it could potentially achieve Japanese surrender without fighting a bloody invasion of Japan, and do so without the assistance of the Soviet Union. This may have made the United States more willing to accept limited compromises on the status of the emperor in order to avoid US casualties and wrap up the conflict sufficiently quickly to keep the Soviet Union out of the postwar occupation. Before nuclear acquisition, the United States had anticipated requiring Soviet assistance to invade and defeat Japan. It is hard to imagine that having fought a bloody and costly invasion of the Japanese mainland, the United States would have accepted anything other than a completely unconditional surrender. Once they had acquired nuclear weapons, however, US policymakers sought to end the war before the Soviet Union could invade Japan, and thus reduce Soviet influence over the postwar settlement (as I discuss further below). US policymakers were therefore prepared to accept the modest compromises on the status of the emperor necessary to quickly secure Japanese agreement to the terms of surrender.[40] In this limited but nonetheless important way, US nuclear weapons facilitated US compromise.

INDEPENDENCE

Similarly, there are also ways in which nuclear weapons facilitated US independence—defined as taking actions that allies oppose or do not support. As discussed, before nuclear acquisition, the United States had anticipated requiring (or at least desiring) the assistance of the Soviet Union to invade and defeat Japan, and at Yalta, Roosevelt had obtained a Soviet pledge to enter the war against Japan once the war in Europe was terminated. The price of Soviet assistance, of course, was that the Soviet Union would receive a more favorable postwar settlement in the Pacific across a range of issues and territories. Roosevelt had agreed that if the Soviets would enter the war against Japan, the United States would allow them to annex southern Sakhalin and the Kuriles, establish a naval base at Port Arthur, and recover Russia's pre-1904 rights in Manchuria, including its "preeminent interests" in the region's railroads and the port of Dairen. While many US policymakers had misgivings about the Yalta agreement, they were disinclined to abandon the agreement while Soviet support might still be needed in Asia. Until US nuclear weapons had demonstrated their utility, US officials believed it would be foolish to eschew assistance from the Soviet Union that might still be required to ensure Japanese defeat.[41]

US nuclear weapons obviated this dependence on the Soviet Union by offering a path to Japanese surrender that would not require Soviet assistance. Truman believed that the Soviets "needed us more than we needed them," that "our new weapons" meant that Soviet participation in the Pacific war was no longer needed to conquer Japan, and that the United States should no longer feel bound by the Yalta agreement. As Secretary of War Stimson argued, "They can't get along without our help and industries and we have coming into action a weapon which will be unique."[42] Instead, the United States used its nuclear weapons to end the war before the Soviet Union could invade Japan, enabling the United States to govern Japan alone in the aftermath of the war. Indeed, the Soviet Union had recognized in the aftermath of the Hiroshima bombing that it would have to accelerate its intervention into the war in case the atomic bomb prompted an immediate surrender, launching an attack on Japanese forces in Manchuria.[43] It is true that the Soviet Union had supported the US use of nuclear weapons: Stalin had told Truman at Potsdam that he hoped the United States would make "good use" of nuclear weapons against Japan.[44] Nonetheless, the Soviet Union was dissatisfied with the way in which the war in the Pacific ended and the nature of the postwar settlement. Even after the United States had announced Japan's surrender, the Soviet Union continued fighting Japanese forces in Sakhalin with the intention of occupying Hokkaido, before ultimately backing off after a "firm" response from President Truman on August 18.[45] Overall, therefore, it seems fair to conclude that US nuclear weapons reduced US dependence on the Soviet Union in the Pacific, and thus that the United States used nuclear weapons to facilitate independence.

EXPANSION

The United States did not use its nuclear weapons to engage in expansion during the war, defined in chapter 1 as the widening of a state's interests. The United States' goals in using nuclear weapons against Japan were the same as they had previously been during the war: to destroy Japanese cities, demoralize the Japanese population, and achieve victory and Japanese surrender on favorable terms and with the loss of as few American lives as possible. Nuclear weapons were perceived to offer a higher likelihood of achieving these ends than continued conventional bombing, but the goals remained constant. It might be argued that the United States used its nuclear weapons against Japan to intimidate the Soviet Union and thus lay the groundwork for more expansive postwar ambitions. While most scholars agree that Truman did not choose to use US nuclear weapons against Japan in order to intimidate the Soviet Union, "he was fully conscious of its diplomatic ramifications and eager to reap its anticipated benefits."[46] However, such effects were secondary to the primary intended outcome of forcing Japanese surrender. More importantly, such aims were prospective—they sought to influence how the *postwar* world would operate. As a result, such a claim would support the argument I make below that the United States used its nuclear weapons to engage in expansion *in the aftermath* of World War II.

BOLSTERING

The United States did not use its nuclear weapons to bolster allies during the war—defined as taking actions to strengthen an existing alliance or alliance partner. While President Roosevelt had agreed with Churchill that the United States would consult with the British before using its nuclear weapons, this was not an effort to strengthen the British position but merely an acknowledgment of their shared investment in the Manhattan Project and the fact that both leaders agreed that nuclear weapons should be used (meaning that such an agreement would not in fact constrain the United States). The United States had no intention of providing Britain (and certainly not other allies) with nuclear weapons or otherwise using nuclear weapons to strengthen the British position during the war.

STEADFASTNESS

Finally, there is little evidence that the United States used nuclear weapons to facilitate steadfastness—defined as standing more firmly in defense of the status quo. Instead, US officials viewed nuclear weapons as a weapon that offered offensive opportunities, and intended to use them in this way during the war.[47] The theory of nuclear opportunism thus incorrectly predicts the United States would use nuclear weapons to facilitate steadfastness in addition to aggression. This counts as a strike against the theory. However, given the circumstances in which the United States acquired nuclear weapons, it is not necessarily surprising that the US response to nuclear acquisition would be overwhelmingly characterized by aggression rather than steadfastness. Because the United States was on the offensive in the war when it acquired nuclear weapons, it was simply not required to defend the status quo. Instead, when it acquired nuclear weapons, the United States was engaged in a more or less constant effort to *revise* the status quo and achieve victory in the war. The lack of challenges to the US position makes assessing any change in the level of steadfastness difficult, but it is clear that US officials saw nuclear weapons as offering primarily offensive rather than defensive advantages. This goes against the expectations of the theory of nuclear opportunism.

The United States after World War II

Assessing the role that nuclear weapons played in US foreign policy in the aftermath of World War II is a complicated task. The sheer breadth of US foreign policy activity, the unstable and changing nature of international politics in the postwar period, and the contradictory and complex ways in which the United States acted in the aftermath of World War II make isolating the effect of any single factor on US foreign policy challenging. This is particularly true with respect to nuclear weapons, a technology that had only just been invented and the implications of which were not well understood by US policymakers. In addition, the vast historiographical debate surrounding the origins of the Cold War and the many plausible historical interpretations of particular events in the early Cold War mean that any conclusions drawn from this case are necessarily tentative. Nonetheless, the theory of nuclear opportunism makes clear predictions about the behaviors that should be expected, and it is reasonable to assess whether they seem to be realized in the historical record.

The theory of nuclear opportunism predicts that the United States—a hegemon in the Western Hemisphere and a state whose potential peer competitors were all either defeated and under occupation or ravaged by the effects of the most destructive war in human history—should have used nuclear weapons to bolster its junior allies and to expand its interests in international politics. Consistent with the theory of nuclear opportunism, I argue that there is good evidence that the United States did use nuclear weapons to bolster its allies, expand its interests, and respond steadfastly to challenges. However, the United States also used nuclear weapons to engage in foreign policy behaviors that can be reasonably characterized as aggression, against the expectations of the theory.

The extent to which the United States expanded its interests, engaged in aggression, or merely defended the status quo in the aftermath of World War II has been the subject of a vast historiographical debate. During the 1960s and 1970s, disputes between "orthodox" and "revisionist" historians generated considerable heat on the question of whether the United States or the Soviet Union was the more belligerent and expansionist power and thus primarily responsible for the onset of the Cold War.[48] Over thirty years after John Lewis Gaddis claimed to identify a "post-revisionist synthesis" that recognized that the United States was neither the ideal form of the "Leninist model of imperialism" nor "naive and innocent" in its conduct of the Cold War, historical debates over US motivations and behavior in the immediate postwar period continue.[49]

This historiographical debate combines with (and perhaps results from) the extraordinarily complex and contested postwar international environment to make analyzing the effect of nuclear weapons on postwar US foreign policy challenging. In particular, distinguishing between several of the behaviors identified in the typology is harder than in previous cases. For example, identifying the status quo is critical to distinguishing between aggression and steadfastness. However, in the immediate postwar period, what constituted the status quo in the Soviet-US relationship was open to significant disagreement. Similarly, distinguishing between "preexisting" and "new" interests—crucial to distinguishing between expansion and aggression—in the context of an international environment characterized by extraordinary upheaval is extremely tricky.

Instead of trying to categorize US foreign policy into the behaviors in the typology, I examine four interconnected and crucially important aspects of US foreign policy in the immediate postwar period: the institutionalizing of an unprecedented global network of alliances, the United States' installation of a worldwide peacetime network of overseas bases, US interactions with the Soviet Union, and the use of economic power for political ends. In each case, I show the ambiguity of these behaviors and the different ways these behaviors could be categorized. I do not seek to conclusively assign a label to each behavior. However, regardless of the label one assigns to each behavior, I argue that each behavior was facilitated in important ways by nuclear weapons. The United States thus offers a less clean test of the theory than the other cases in which the international environment was more stable and distinguishing between the behaviors in the typology is easier. Nonetheless, the case reinforces the view of nuclear weapons implied by the theory of nuclear opportunism: as useful tools of political statecraft that can facilitate a range of foreign policy behaviors.

STRENGTHENING ALLIANCES AND INITIATING NEW ONES

In the aftermath of World War II, the United States eschewed its traditional skepticism of entangling alliances in favor of establishing a globe-spanning network of alliances. In this section, I show the important role that nuclear weapons played in supporting and sustaining these alliances. This shift in US foreign policy is best seen as a combination of both bolstering and expansion. Many of the security treaties that the United States signed and alliances that the United States entered into in the aftermath of World War II were entirely new (such as that with Japan) and are perhaps better considered as examples of expansion, which includes the initiation of new alliance relationships. However, many of the alliances that the United States entered into represented the formalization of existing and long-standing relationships (such as with the United Kingdom) and thus fall under the category of bolstering—the strengthening or formalizing of existing allies or alliances.

The motivation behind this shift in US foreign policy is much debated among historians and political scientists. In one view, the United States aimed to build up its allies in Europe (and elsewhere) so that they could ultimately take the lead in providing for their own defense. In this view, the United States' commitment to Europe would be temporary, and the United States would ultimately seek to reduce its defense commitments over time and withdraw from Europe and Asia.[50] For example, Mark Sheetz argues that "post-war [American] leaders engaged in strenuous efforts to avoid a permanent military involvement in Europe."[51] Similarly, Brendan Rittenhouse

Green writes that "the United States aimed to establish an independent European pole of power that could contain the Soviet Union with minimal U.S. aid."[52] In another view, however, US alliances had a more hegemonic, suppressive character and aimed to maintain the United States' position in Europe indefinitely.[53] For example, Christopher Layne argues that soon after World War II, the United States "intended to remain in Europe permanently, even if the threat of Soviet aggression disappeared."[54] Similarly, Francis Gavin notes that Washington's alliances in the nuclear era "appear to be permanent [and] to persist regardless of threat."[55]

Regardless of the ultimate motivations underlying US actions, however, in the aftermath of World War II, the United States entered into, and then formalized, a series of alliance commitments to prop up the economies and military capabilities of countries sympathetic to the United States. In 1949, the United States signed the North Atlantic Treaty with eleven countries (Belgium, Canada, Denmark, France, Iceland, Italy, Luxembourg, the Netherlands, Norway, Portugal, and the United Kingdom). This was followed in 1951 by the ANZUS agreement with Australia and New Zealand and a bilateral security treaty between the United States and Japan, the expansion of NATO to Greece and Turkey in 1952, the Mutual Defense Treaty between the United States and South Korea in 1953, and the Sino-American Mutual Defense Treaty with Taiwan and the expansion of NATO to West Germany in 1955. Within ten years of the end of World War II, therefore, the United States had built a globe-spanning alliance network underpinned by US military power and a willingness to play an active role in the defense of each of its alliance partners. Secretary of State Acheson remarked that this amounted to "a complete revolution" in the foreign policy of a country that had traditionally eschewed potentially entangling alliances.[56]

This alliance network was being built up, however, in the context of the demobilization of the US armed forces that occurred in the aftermath of World War II. Despite concerns expressed by military leaders about the dangers associated with too quickly degrading US military capabilities, President Truman and other elected officials demanded a swift demobilization in response to powerful domestic political demands to bring US military forces home. US carriers were converted into giant passenger ships to transport US service personnel overseas back to the United States, and in January 1946 thousands of US soldiers rioted in an effort to hasten their return to civilian life.[57] US military personnel fell from over 12 million in 1945 to around 1.5 million in 1947, and military expenditure fell by around a factor of six (after adjusting for inflation) over the same period.[58] Even after this fall in capabilities, US military personnel and expenditure were around five and thirteen times higher, respectively, than they had been in 1937, but sustaining US alliances with a vastly reduced military force nonetheless presented a critical challenge for US policymakers in the immediate aftermath of World War II. Even in West Germany, for example, the United States had only two divisions present, and those forces were dispersed throughout the country in order to administer the occupation. The conventional balance was so precarious that Secretary of State George Marshall requested that the secretary of defense not make the details of the military balance public, to avoid demoralizing the Europeans because "the picture which this presents is one of such hopelessness."[59]

Nuclear weapons offered a solution to this quandary. Nuclear weapons allowed the United States to maintain, strengthen, and extend US alliance commitments while US conventional military capabilities declined. The role of nuclear weapons was most explicit in Western Europe, although the same logic was implicit elsewhere as well. The crucial role that nuclear weapons played in facilitating America's alliances in Europe had been recognized by US policymakers even in the immediate aftermath of World War II. In 1946, George Kennan wrote that "it is important that this country be prepared to use them . . . for the mere fact of such preparedness may prove to be the only powerful deterrent to Russian aggressive action."[60] A 1947 CIA report argued that a key reason why the Soviet Union would not "resort to overt military aggression" despite its "overwhelming preponderance of power" was that "the USSR would be exposed to early long range air bombardment with conventional and atomic bombs."[61] A 1948 National Security Council (NSC) report stated that "if Western Europe is to enjoy any feeling of security at the present time . . . it is in large degree because the atomic bomb, under American trusteeship, offers the present major counterbalance to the ever-present threat of the Soviet military power."[62] According to Secretary of Defense James Forrestal, nuclear weapons were "the only balance we have against the overwhelming manpower of the Russians."[63]

Such was the impact of nuclear weapons on US strategy in Europe that George Kennan ultimately worried that the United States was placing too much reliance on them. As he wrote in 1949, "We are so behind the Russians in conventional armaments, and the attraction of the atomic bomb to strategic planners has been such that we are in danger of finding our whole policy tied to the atom bomb."[64] Nonetheless, the trend of increasing reliance on nuclear weapons continued. In 1950, NSC-68 made the reliance on nuclear weapons to compensate for conventional military shortcomings explicit, and embraced a policy of using nuclear weapons first in a conflict to make America's alliance commitments credible: "In our present situation of relative unpreparedness in conventional weapons, such a declaration [of no first use] would be interpreted by the USSR as an admission of great weakness and by our allies as a clear indication that we intend to abandon them."[65] If US nuclear use was not credible, and a war in Europe had to be fought with conventional forces only, the consequences were simple: "an early Soviet conquest of Western Europe."[66]

Similarly, once the Soviet Union had developed its own nuclear weapons, the same logic dictated the development of tactical nuclear weapons.[67] In the words of a memo to the chairman of the Joint Chiefs of Staff, "Atomic weapons used tactically are the natural armaments of the numerically inferior but technologically superior nations. They are the natural answer to the armed hordes of the Soviet Union and its satellites."[68] Marc Trachtenberg summarizes the role nuclear weapons played in facilitating US alliance commitments to Europe in the absence of large conventional forces: nuclear weapons meant that "the United States did not have to maintain a massive military establishment, or deploy forces in western Europe capable of defending that area on the ground. The West could settle for a tripwire strategy. Very powerful, and very expensive, forces in being—in particular, ground forces in Europe—were not absolutely essential."[69] In Wilson Miscamble's words, by 1949 "American conventional forces were deemed capable of defending only the Western Hemisphere and the main Japanese Islands and perhaps of retaining communication lines to some bridgeheads in Great Britain, the Iberian Peninsula, and North Africa. The Americans depended on the deterrent quality of their atomic monopoly."[70] In short, nuclear weapons were the only way that the United States could make credible commitments to Europe—and beyond—without the kind of conventional deployments that had quickly become politically unacceptable after World War II.

US plans were certainly not ideal from the European perspective: as a *Newsweek* article from 1948 claimed, "The temporary overrunning of Europe by the Red Army is taken for granted."[71] In the words of one 1948 assessment sent to the president, "If war should come within the next few years, this could result in the loss of the bulk of our ground forces in Europe, heavy casualties to the naval and air units employed in evacuation, capture of most, if not all, of our heavy equipment and all ground installations there, and the detention of American civilian personnel."[72] In short, US war plans were essentially that Europe would be lost in the event of a Soviet invasion, but that this would be followed by an inevitable and sustained US campaign of nuclear attacks.[73] Even US war plans that dryly acknowledged that "atomic bombing will produce certain psychological and retaliatory reactions detrimental to the achievement of Allied war objectives" nonetheless concluded that "the advantages of its early use would be transcending" and recommended the "prompt and effective delivery of the maximum numbers of atomic bombs."[74] Despite the grim nature of a potential European conflict that US plans implied, a reliance on nuclear weapons was the only politically feasible option for US policymakers. As Secretary of State Marshall argued, "The country could not, and would not, support a budget based on preparation for war," and the United States was therefore unable "to build up U.S. ground forces for the express purpose of employing them in Western Europe."[75] Relying on nuclear weapons to sustain US alliance commitments was, in short, the only game in town in the immediate aftermath of World War II.

Given the importance of nuclear weapons in sustaining US alliance commitments, it is unsurprising that even while the United States was undergoing a substantial conventional military demobilization, it was dedicating considerable resources to expanding its nuclear arsenal. The Joint Chiefs of Staff in 1947 called for an enlargement of the US nuclear arsenal, and substantial effort was dedicated to overcoming production problems and building up both the nuclear weapons stockpile and the B-50, B-36, and B-29 bombers necessary for their delivery.[76] Similarly, it is unsurprising that the Berlin crisis of 1948 triggered internal discussions about who controlled US nuclear weapons during crises, as well as limited US nuclear signaling in an effort to deter further Soviet actions.[77] Three days after the Soviet Union shut off ground access into Berlin, the Strategic Air Command was placed on alert, and by the middle of July the US government announced the deployment of two B-29 squadrons (explicitly described as "atomic capable") to the United Kingdom at the request of the British government. These bombers were not in fact equipped to deliver nuclear weapons, but those B-29s in the United States that had been modified to deliver nuclear weapons were placed on a twenty-four-hour alert.[78] The fact that the United States agreed to Britain's request for nuclear signaling of this sort despite Truman's concern that "this is no time to be juggling an atomic bomb around" is further evidence of the role that nuclear weapons played in bolstering US allies in the immediate aftermath of World War II.[79]

From shortly after the end of World War II, therefore, the United States used its nuclear weapons to underwrite a host of new and existing alliances. By using nuclear weapons as a substitute for conventional forces, the United States avoided having to choose between a return to its traditional foreign policy of isolationism, on the one hand, and retaining a large standing army and an economy dedicated to large-scale war fighting, on the other. Without nuclear weapons, the United States would have been forced to confront this dilemma directly, sacrificing either the postwar demobilization of the US military or the United States' new forward position in the world.

OVERSEAS BASES

US policymakers had concluded during the war that US dominance of the Western Hemisphere was no longer sufficient to guarantee US security, and that the United States required a permanent and extensive network of overseas bases for both offensive and defensive operations. The attack on Pearl Harbor, the rise of strategic bombing as a tactic of great power war, and the possibility of other states using nuclear weapons against the United States all pointed in the direction of a more forward defense and an extensive system of overseas bases. Such bases would allow the United States both a greater chance of interdicting attacks on the homeland and a greater ability to project power against potential adversaries. As the Joint Chiefs of

Staff argued, in the aftermath of World War II, "neither geography nor allies will render a nation immune from sudden and paralyzing attack should an aggressor arise to plague the peace of the world."[80] As Army chief of staff George Marshall stated, "It no longer appears practical to continue what we once conceived as hemispheric defense as a satisfactory basis for our security. We are now concerned with the peace of the entire world."[81] As the US envoy to Moscow had informed Stalin in 1945, "The interests of the United States were worldwide and not confined to North and South America and the Pacific Ocean."[82] In 1943, defense officials therefore started to examine the number of overseas bases that the United States would need in the aftermath of victory. In November 1945, months after the Japanese surrender, the Chiefs of Staff provided the secretary of state with a list of thirty-five bases deemed "essential" or "required."[83] As Leffler summarizes the outcome of the process: "After extensive discussion, the Joint Chiefs of Staff (JCS) defined a set of primary, secondary, and minor base sites. The primary areas stretched to the western shores of the Pacific, encompassed the polar air routes, and projected U.S. power into the Eastern Atlantic as well as the Caribbean and the Panama Canal zone. Dozens of additional sites were denoted as secondary and minor base areas." In short, US "military planners [had] redefined the U.S. strategic perimeter."[84]

Putting in place a globe-spanning network of overseas bases could be plausibly interpreted either as aggression, expansion, or steadfastness. Certainly, these bases were part of a broader US strategy to play a larger role in world affairs and increase the US ability to project power. Compared with any previous period of peace, they represented a significant expansion of US interests. In Layne's words, in planning for a peacetime network of overseas bases, "American policymakers were laying the grand strategic foundations of a post-war international system in which U.S. power would be predominant."[85] General Groves encouraged the United States to take advantage of its predominant power to expand its position: "We are now in a favorable position. . . . We should get our bases now and plan not for 10 years but for 50–100 years ahead."[86] However, an argument could be made that such behaviors represented aggression: the United States was generating greater offensive capabilities to guarantee a long-standing interest—the ability to protect the US homeland—from developing threats and the increasing power projection capabilities of adversaries. Certainly many US documents framed the importance of overseas bases in such terms. For example, a 1946 report stated that "unless warfare itself is abolished or atomic warfare is effectively prohibited, it will be necessary for the United States to maintain . . . forward bases from which attacks against the United States could be intercepted and counter-attacks could be delivered against possible enemies." The report concluded that "our armed forces must seize upon these new developments and utilize them fully."[87] A 1949 report for the NSC on Japan argued that "United States control of Japan . . . will not only deny to the USSR an extremely important strategic base . . . it will provide us with staging areas from which to project our military power to the Asiatic mainland and to USSR islands adjacent thereto."[88] Similarly, if one views these bases as simply allowing the United States to respond more quickly to acts of aggression by others, the creation of the US base network could also be viewed as an instance of steadfastness.

Regardless of whether establishing a permanent peacetime network of overseas bases constituted an instance of aggression, steadfastness, or expansion, nuclear weapons played an important role in facilitating this behavior. Of course, plans for overseas bases had been initiated before the United States acquired nuclear weapons. Nonetheless, the relationship between nuclear weapons and a more extensive basing system went in both directions and was mutually reinforcing. In other words, an expanded basing system increased the potency and deliverability of US nuclear capabilities, and US nuclear capabilities increased the utility of an expanded basing system. As a 1945 report argued: "[The] advent of the atomic bomb . . . greatly increase[s] the importance of [advance] bases. This is true both offensively and defensively. Offensively, it is essential to transport the bomb to the internal vital areas of the enemy nation. The closer our bases are to those areas, the more effectively can this be done. . . . All of this points to the great importance of expanding our strategic frontiers in the Atlantic and Pacific Oceans and to the shores of the Arctic."[89]

Similarly, a 1947 report on the broader military implications of nuclear weapons recommended the "establishment of a system of strategically located overseas bases from which all our offensive weapons may be employed, thus enhancing our security by extending the range of those weapons."[90] Nuclear weapons may not, therefore, have reduced the costs of an expanded system of overseas bases. But nuclear weapons increased the military value of such a system, making it more attractive to US military planners. Overseas bases and nuclear weapons also combined to serve the broader political imperative of postwar conventional demobilization. The way in which nuclear weapons facilitated this goal was discussed above. But overseas bases were similarly critical to minimizing the military risks associated with a rapid demobilization, and the combination of the two was particularly valuable. As a Chiefs of Staff report had described, the challenge for the United States was to balance the priority of "maintenance of the United States in the best possible relative position . . . ready when necessary to take military action abroad" with the recognition that "the United States, relative to other great powers, will maintain in peace time as armed forces only a minimum percentage of its war time potential." To do this required that US forces be "disposed strategically [so] that they can be brought to bear at the source of enemy military power, or in other critical areas in time."[91] This meant stationing US forces closer to potential theaters of military operation. Overseas bases— and the increased potency that they offered when combined with nuclear weapons—thus allowed the United States to engage in postwar demobilization while maintaining significant power projection capabilities.

FOREIGN POLICY TOWARD THE SOVIET UNION

Nuclear weapons also facilitated the way in which the United States conducted its foreign policy toward the Soviet Union. Again, the circumstances of the immediate postwar period make it hard to unambiguously conclude whether these behaviors should be characterized as aggression, expansion, or steadfastness. The status quo was ill defined and open to conflicting interpretations, and the extent of the United States' preexisting interests was far from clear. As a result, different scholars have very different interpretations of certain US actions.

For example, was the provision of aid to the governments of Turkey and Greece—subsequently articulated as the Truman Doctrine and a core part of the early postwar effort to contain Soviet influence—an example of expansion, aggression, or steadfastness? In one view, the policy was an example of steadfastness. Gaddis argues that the provision of aid to the Turkish and Greek governments simply sought to defend the status quo. The Truman Doctrine was "the ultimate expression of the 'patience and firmness' strategy . . . that the United States could allow no further gains in territory or influence for the Soviet Union."[92] This was certainly how some US officials saw the policy. In the words of a State Department memo, the purpose of US aid was to maintain the status quo by preventing an otherwise certain "breakdown in the Greek economy . . . which would have resulted in domination of Greece by the Communists."[93] But in another light, US policy appears expansive: the Americans were shedding the last vestiges of isolationism and expanding their interests to gain increased influence in the Mediterranean and Middle East as British power waned. Stephen Xydis argues that the Truman Doctrine initiated "an authentically revolutionary phase in the nation's experience [that] ended the epoch of isolation."[94] Leffler argues that "the real problem was that there loomed gaping vacuums of power. . . . While British power foundered, the American desire for access to the airfields and petroleum resources of the Middle East mounted."[95] In another view, the policy was aggressive because it aimed to push more forcefully in pursuit of the preexisting interest of resisting and rolling back communist expansion: Howard Jones argues that the Truman Doctrine indicated "the administration's willingness to engage in the struggle against communism on all fronts—social, political, and economic as well as military."[96]

As discussed above, I do not seek to resolve these debates by affixing particular labels to these behaviors. Instead, I describe the basic features of US interactions with the Soviet Union in the immediate postwar period, and the ways in which nuclear weapons influenced them. What were the key features of US foreign policy toward the Soviet Union? I discuss three aspects of US foreign policy: the willingness to engage in vigorous and sometimes escalatory diplomacy in response to perceived Soviet aggression, offensive covert actions aimed at undermining the Soviet Union in Eastern Europe and within the Soviet Union itself, and the prominence of thinking about preventive war in US foreign policy discourse. I argue that nuclear weapons contributed to each of these components of US foreign policy toward the Soviet Union.

First, the United States engaged in active and sometimes belligerent diplomacy in response to, and to deter, perceived Soviet aggression and misbehavior. In 1946, the United States had become increasingly angered by Soviet maintenance of troops in Iran. In Truman's words, this represented an "outrage if I ever saw one," and ultimately coerced the Soviet Union into withdrawing forces from the country.[97] Also in 1946, Truman had declared himself willing to follow "to the end" advice that recommended using "the force of American arms" in the event of any Soviet aggression in Turkey.[98] Scholars disagree over whether such Soviet intervention was in fact likely— Leffler argues that such fears were "contrived" to justify the American desire for access to the airfields and oil of the Middle East, while Mark argues that they were "sincere and justified within the context of the strategic premises that informed American foreign policy."[99] In March 1947, Truman laid out the Truman Doctrine, providing support for the Greek and Turkish governments in response to Britain withdrawing its aid to the two states.[100] And in 1948, in response to the Soviet blockade of West Berlin (which in turn was in response to the announcement of the deutsche mark) the Western allies undertook the Berlin airlift to transport food and fuel to the city's population, flying over two hundred thousand flights over the eleven months of the blockade. The Joint Chiefs of Staff concluded in October 1948 that to go to war over Berlin "would be neither militarily prudent nor strategically sound," and urged the civilian leadership to consider withdrawing from West Berlin.[101] But despite the United States' relative military weakness and the vulnerability of Berlin to Soviet military action, the United States was nonetheless prepared to engage in escalations that risked Soviet escalation.

This is not to suggest that the United States always chose to escalate conflicts in its dealings with the Soviet Union. For example, while the president had proclaimed that it was "the policy of the United States to support free peoples who are resisting attempted subjugation,"[102] this policy was certainly not pursued universally: the United States did not seek to oppose the Communists in Czechoslovakia in 1947, decided to withdraw from Korea in the same year, and took a "middle road" in seeking to prevent communist takeovers of Italy and Greece.[103] Nonetheless, the escalation of disputes with the Soviet Union was a key feature of US foreign policy in the aftermath of the war.

Second, the United States undertook actions aimed at undermining the Soviet Union within the eastern bloc and Soviet territory: what one report to

Truman recommended as "dynamic steps to reduce the power and influence of the Kremlin inside the Soviet Union and other areas under its control."[104] Historians are increasingly documenting the extent to which the United States used covert efforts to weaken the Soviet position within its own territory and sphere of influence.[105] Covert operations began with an effort to suppress the Communist vote and ensure a Christian Democrat victory in the Italian elections in 1947.[106] The perceived success of this effort led to the approval by Truman in 1948 of NSC 20/4, which stated explicitly that America's goals "in times of peace as well as in time of war" were to "reduce the power and influence of the USSR to limits which no longer constitute a threat," ambitions that would require the United States to "place the maximum strain on the Soviet structure of power."[107] This was accompanied by NSC 10/2, which concluded that "the overt foreign activities of the U.S. government must be supplemented by covert operations" and demanded that operations be "planned and executed [so] that any U.S. Government can plausibly disclaim any responsibility."[108] This directive provided the basis for a range of policies: broadcasting propaganda into the Soviet Union and Eastern Europe, the deployment of paramilitary forces to develop underground resistance movements, the attempt to disrupt Kremlin decision making, the funneling of support to East European liberation groups, sabotage and demolition, encouraging defections to the West, and attempting to provoke power struggles and personal animosity within the Communist leadership. The Office of Policy Coordination (OPC), created by NSC 10/2 and attached to the CIA, was authorized to engage in covert operations, and by 1952 its budget had grown to $82 million, with over 2,800 employees and an additional 3,142 operatives under contract.[109] The goals of these efforts were explicitly offensive: "to increase confusion, suspicion and fear among the Communist leaders" and to "encourage mass defections from Soviet allegiance and to frustrate the Kremlin design in other ways."[110] Undermining the Soviet Union's influence in Eastern Europe proved harder than US policymakers hoped: the OPC's James McCargar had anticipated that "we had only to shake the trees and the ripe plums would fall."[111] But offensive actions inside the Soviet sphere of influence were nonetheless a part of US foreign policy toward the Soviet Union.

Third, arguments for preventive war against the Soviet Union were surprisingly prevalent in the United States—both inside government and outside.[112] As the philosopher Bertrand Russell wrote at the time, "If America were less imperialistic, there would be another possibility. . . . It would be possible for Americans to use their position of temporary superiority to insist upon disarmament . . . everywhere except the United States. . . . During the next few years this policy could be enforced."[113] These ideas were not confined to philosophers and public intellectuals. As Trachtenberg documents, leading journalists, US senators, and high-ranking military officers all made preventive war arguments.[114] While such ideas were not implemented for a range of practical, strategic, and normative reasons, their existence is notable.

Regardless of whether one views these features of US foreign policy toward the Soviet Union as instances of expansion, aggression, or steadfastness (or some combination of all three), what role did nuclear weapons play in facilitating them? In short, it is hard to overemphasize the importance of nuclear weapons. As a 1946 State Department report had stated, "It would be strange indeed if the perfection of such a revolutionary weapon did not have great political effects."[115] In a situation of conventional weakness relative to the Soviet Union, US nuclear weapons were the only capability that gave the United States some degree of escalation dominance, and thus facilitated the United States taking actions that ran some risk of leading to conflict. The importance of nuclear weapons in facilitating US foreign policy toward the Soviet Union was reflected in the considerable (and growing) priority accorded to atomic bombing in US war plans for potential conflict with the Soviet Union. War plan BROILER in 1947 called for 34 bombs to be dropped on 24 cities; TROJAN, approved in 1948, requested 133 bombs be used on 70 cities; while OFFTACKLE in 1949 called for 220 bombs to be dropped on 104 cities.[116] Trachtenberg summarizes the way in which nuclear weapons facilitated US foreign policy toward the Soviet Union:

> What in fact was the situation as it appeared to policymakers at the time? First, it was universally understood that if war broke out, Europe would be overrun; but then the United States would gear up and begin a sustained campaign of atomic bombardment. To be sure, the initial American atomic strike on Russia would have only a limited effect on Soviet war-making capabilities.... [But] Russian industry and war-making power would gradually be destroyed with bombs and bombers produced after the war had started. The United States was sure to win in the end. The Soviets would not start a war because they knew that an American victory would simply be a matter of time.[117]

Nuclear weapons were not a blank check for the United States to do whatever it wanted. The United States had to behave carefully because "even with the nuclear monopoly, American power barely balanced Soviet power in central Europe."[118] As discussed above, any war involving an extended period of US atomic bombing of the Soviet Union would have been unimaginably destructive. Nonetheless, because the United States believed that its nuclear capabilities meant it would ultimately win such a war, the United States was able to resist Soviet encroachments and escalate crises at considerably lower risk: ultimately, it was unlikely that the Soviet Union would risk the atomic bombardment that would come if a crisis escalated to war. Events that occurred reinforced this logic for US policymakers, providing evidence of the bargaining advantages that nuclear weapons granted the United States. For example, after leaving office, Truman argued that it was the threat of nuclear use that coerced the Soviet Union into withdrawing its forces from Iran.

More broadly, however, US officials were aware that this sort of muscular diplomacy involved risks given the conventional balance: in the words of a State Department memo, US policies had to be conducted with "full realization of our military ineffectiveness" and cognizant of the dangers of "Soviet miscalculation of American intentions and potentialities."[119] Nuclear weapons allowed the United States to limit the risks of such behavior even though the conventional balance was unfavorable. Secretary of Defense Forrestal laid out the logic explicitly in 1947. He wrote in a letter to the Senate Armed Services Committee: "At the present time we are keeping our military expenditures below the levels which our military leaders must in good conscience estimate as the minimum which would in themselves ensure national security. . . . In other words, we are taking a calculated risk." He went on to argue that "certain military advantages . . . go far toward covering the risk," which he listed as the "predominance of American sea power; our exclusive possession of the atomic bomb; [and] American productive capacity. As long as we can outproduce the world, can control the sea, and strike inland with the atomic bomb, we can assume certain risks otherwise unacceptable. . . . The years before any possible power can achieve the capability effectively to attack us with weapons of mass destruction are our years of opportunity."[120] The result of the military balance, Forrestal argued in 1948, was that "it is inconceivable that even the gang who run Russia would be willing to take on war."[121] In short, nuclear weapons allowed the United States to escalate disputes with the Soviet Union with reasonable confidence that such actions would not lead to war. And while the United States did not have the conventional capabilities to engage in a large-scale offensive against the Soviet Union, US nuclear weapons meant that there was little to prevent the United States from pursuing low-cost covert actions to undermine the Soviet position. Further evidence for the role of nuclear weapons in facilitating this behavior, and in line with Forrestal's argument, is provided by the modifications made to US policy once the Soviet Union acquired high-yield nuclear weapons capable of being delivered to the United States. For example, the United States constrained some of the covert activities in which it was engaged in Eastern Europe in response to rising Soviet nuclear capabilities.[122]

Other US policymakers were also clear that US nuclear weapons granted the United States significant advantages in its dealings with the Soviet Union, even if they did not lay out the logic as fully as Forrestal. Secretary of War Stimson wrote in his diary in May 1945 about a conversation with Assistant Secretary of War John McCloy in which he recalled: "We have talked too much and been too lavish with our beneficences to them [the Russians]. I told him this was a place where we really held all the cards. I called it a royal straight flush and we mustn't be a fool about the way we play it. They can't get along without our help and industries and we have coming into action a weapon which will be unique."[123] General Carl Spaatz stated: "Our mono-poly of the bomb, even though it is transitory, may well prove to be a critical factor in our efforts to achieve first a stabilized condition and eventually a lasting peace" on American terms.[124] Secretary of State Byrnes had argued that nuclear weapons "might well put us in a position to dictate our own terms at the end of the war," and that US nuclear weapons might make the Russians "more manageable" on the question of Eastern Europe.[125]

Overall, therefore, US nuclear weapons underpinned US foreign policy toward the Soviet Union in important ways. Regardless of the particular la-bel one attaches to this aspect of US foreign policy, the role played by nu-clear weapons is significant.

ECONOMIC DIPLOMACY

Economic diplomacy—the use of the United States' enormous economic power to achieve political ends—was at the core of US foreign policy in the aftermath of World War II. Indeed, Robert Pollard argues that "American leaders used foreign economic power as the chief instrument of U.S. secu-rity from 1945 until the outbreak of the conflict in Korea."[126] Whether or not one goes as far as Pollard, there is little question that the Marshall Plan and creation of the Bretton Woods institutions were prominent parts of US ef-forts to achieve political ends in the immediate aftermath of World War II.[127] Again, in the highly fluid circumstances of the immediate postwar period, one could make a reasonable case that these policies constituted examples of expansion, aggression, or steadfastness. For example, one could see US foreign economic policy as "the first major attempt by the United States to restructure the world economy," or as a more status quo policy aiming sim-ply to reduce the likelihood of another spiral into economic nationalism, pro-tectionism, and war.[128] Instead of trying to resolve such debates, I aim to simply show that nuclear weapons facilitated these policies. Consistent with the story told above, it was the United States' ability to use nuclear weap-ons as a substitute for conventional forces that freed up resources to rebuild Western Europe economically while retaining the ability to deter Soviet mil-itary actions against Western Europe.

The experience of the 1930s had convinced US policymakers that economic nationalism and rivalry were destabilizing forces and causes of interstate conflict, and US policymakers feared a potential postwar economic depres-sion.[129] During the war, US officials were planning for agreements that would ensure a more economically liberal international order, which was not only to the strategic and economic advantage of the United States but without which, a 1944 State Department report argued, the postwar world would "witness a revival, in more intense form, of the international economic warfare which characterized the twenties and thirties."[130] US worries were legitimate: Europe's economies suffered serious balance-of-payment difficulties and production shortfalls, while the inflow of dollars resulting from increased private US foreign investment into Europe in 1946 and 1947 was canceled out by similarly increasing European investments in the United States, culminating in a severe recession in the winter of 1946–1947.[131]

The Bretton Woods agreements in 1944 (which created the International Monetary Fund [IMF] and World Bank) and the Marshall Plan (which aimed to rebuild Western Europe) were the most prominent features of this policy in the immediate postwar period. The Marshall Plan, in particular, involved enormous expenditures: $130 billion in 2016 dollars.[132] Even for an "economic giant," as Truman described the United States, these costs were significant, and congressional approval was not automatic.[133] As Acheson noted in 1947, more foreign aid requests were unlikely to be well received, since it "was understood when the British loan was made last year that no further requests for direct loans to foreign governments would be asked of Congress."[134] Indeed, achieving congressional support for the Marshall Plan ultimately required emphasizing the looming Soviet danger rather than the economic benefits for the United States, and in 1949, spending on the Marshall Plan, military aid, and other international programs was cut significantly, alongside further cuts in the US armed forces.[135]

The considerable resources that the United States wished to dedicate to economic diplomacy therefore required choices to be made.[136] That choice was essentially between rebuilding the US military and rebuilding the economies of Western Europe. US policymakers framed this choice explicitly. As Forrestal argued: by keeping defense expenditure low, "we are able to increase our expenditure on European recovery." This represented a "calculated risk in order to follow a course which offers a prospect of eventually achieving national security and also long-term world stability."[137]

Nuclear weapons, as described above, facilitated this choice between guns and butter in Western Europe by making the consequences of choosing butter less militarily worrisome. Nuclear weapons allowed the United States to retain the ability to deter the Soviet Union with only a "tripwire" of conventional forces. In short, "the Truman administration remained confident that American economic power, backed by the deterrent power of the atomic bomb as a weapon of last resort, could almost single-handedly prevent a return to the economic isolationism of the interwar years and stabilize vital regions and countries."[138] But this trade-off was fragile and dependent on the credibility of US nuclear use: as Paul Nitze pointed out in a meeting of the State Department Policy Planning Staff, if the United States could not use nuclear weapons in response to a Russian conventional assault, it would be necessary to make greater investments in "conventional armaments and their possession by the Western European nations," and that this would necessarily lead to reduced economic investment in these countries, "lower[ing] rather than rais[ing] civilian standards of living in order to produce arms as against consumer goods."[139]

Again, therefore, nuclear weapons played an important role in facilitating a key pillar of US postwar foreign policy: the use of economic power to achieve political ends.

INDEPENDENCE AND COMPROMISE

Despite the ambiguity surrounding many of the foreign policies above, it is relatively clear that the United States did not use nuclear weapons to facilitate two behaviors in the typology: independence and compromise.

The United States did not use its nuclear weapons to facilitate independence—taking actions that allies oppose. As discussed above, the United States sought to use its nuclear weapons to strengthen its alliances and draw new states into its own alliance portfolio. But the United States did not seek to use nuclear weapons to gain independence from allies. The United States did move swiftly to extract itself from the constraints of the Anglo-American wartime agreements. But US nuclear weapons played no role in the United States doing so. After all, the United States was by some distance the world's most powerful country, and the United Kingdom was dependent on US economic support to recover in the aftermath of World War II. The United States was thus able to set an independent course in its foreign policy with or without nuclear weapons, including with respect to the United Kingdom. If anything, nuclear weapons—and their prominence within US war plans— may have increased the reliance of the United States on certain allies due to the need for overseas bases to deliver them. During the Korean War, for example, Dean Acheson remarked that the United States had to pay attention to British concerns about the conduct of the war because the United States would require British bases if it wanted to use nuclear weapons: "We can bring U.S. [atomic] power into play only with the cooperation of the British."[140]

Finally, the United States did not seem to use its nuclear weapons to engage in compromise—accepting less in ongoing disputes. Certainly, the United States was not equally belligerent in all cases and could in many instances have taken more escalatory actions. However, this was a reflection of American perceptions of the limits of its conventional power rather than the result of its nuclear weapons. As George Marshall argued, US military power had to be employed selectively, and thus he was "obliged to resist pressures, however justifiable and understandable," to send US forces on missions that were beyond their capabilities. Instead, "it was necessary to conserve our very limited strength and apply it only where it was likely to be most effective."[141] Similarly, as the Joint Chiefs of Staff argued, "every effort should be made to avoid military commitment" unless it was preceded by a substantial military mobilization.[142] The United States often avoided escalation not because nuclear weapons granted it security but because of the precarious conventional military balance.

Instead, US policymakers seem to have consistently believed that US nuclear weapons granted the United States bargaining advantages that would allow it to achieve better outcomes in international politics rather than guaranteeing it the security that would facilitate it accepting less. Indeed, it is notable how *insecure* US policymakers felt in the aftermath of World War II. Despite the enormously favorable geopolitical position that the United States held at the end of World War II, US elites—perhaps unsurprisingly, given the nature of the conflict that had just concluded—remained deeply concerned about potential adversaries and the possibility of future wars. In fact, the advent of the nuclear age exacerbated these concerns, as the United States now had to consider the possibility of other states acquiring nuclear weapons and potential future nuclear attack. Nuclear weapons did not, therefore, make US policymakers feel sufficiently secure that they felt inclined to use them to facilitate compromise.

Overall, despite the difficulty in distinguishing between the various foreign policy behaviors in the complex international environment that characterized the aftermath of World War II, the theory of nuclear opportunism sheds light on the behavior of the United States. The theory correctly anticipates that US foreign policy would be profoundly affected by nuclear weapons. More specifically, as the theory of nuclear opportunism would anticipate, the United States used nuclear weapons to engage in behaviors that can be reasonably characterized as bolstering, expansion, and steadfastness and did not use nuclear weapons to facilitate independence or compromise. Nonetheless, and against the expectations of the theory, the United States also used nuclear weapons to engage in behaviors that could be reasonably characterized as aggression.

Other Explanations

How do other theories fare in explaining the US response to nuclear acquisition? The theory of the nuclear revolution predicts that nuclear weapons would make the United States more secure and that the United States would have less need to engage in aggression, expansion, or bolstering—all of which are behaviors driven by insecurity. However, the theory of the nuclear revolution predicts that states may use nuclear weapons to facilitate steadfastness, independence, and compromise both during and after the war. The theory does make some correct predictions. For example, as discussed, the United States did use nuclear weapons to facilitate compromise during the war (albeit in a limited way). However, the theory of the nuclear revolution performs particularly poorly in predicting US behavior after World War II.[143] The theory predicts that the United States would use nuclear weapons to facilitate steadfastness, independence, and compromise in the aftermath of nuclear acquisition but would not use them to facilitate aggression, expansion, or bolstering. It is hard to argue that these predictions are realized in US conduct in the aftermath of World War II. Overall, the theory of the nuclear revolution makes fewer correct predictions than the theory of nuclear opportunism and does not anticipate the profound ways in which nuclear weapons facilitated a range of US policies that can reasonably be classified as instances of aggression, expansion, or bolstering.

S. Paul Kapur's theory of emboldenment anticipates that the United States would not have used nuclear weapons to facilitate aggression during (or after) the war. For Kapur, only conventionally weak and revisionist states use nuclear weapons to engage in aggression. While the United States was certainly a revisionist actor in World War II at the point of acquisition—seeking the overthrow and replacement of the Japanese regime—it was also an extremely conventionally powerful state that had developed unprecedented military capabilities during the war. Kapur's theory therefore performs less well than the theory of nuclear opportunism in this case. Crucially, both Kapur's theory of nuclear emboldenment and the theory of the nuclear revolution fail to anticipate the change in the way that nuclear weapons affected US foreign policy with the end of World War II.

US Grand Strategy and Nuclear Weapons through the Cold War and Beyond

Nuclear weapons thus underpinned US grand strategy in the early days of the Cold War. But did these effects endure? Did the United States continue to use nuclear weapons to support a more expansive position in the world, as the theory of nuclear opportunism anticipates? Or did these effects dissipate as other countries acquired nuclear weapons?

It is certainly true that using nuclear weapons as the foundation for an expansive US grand strategy became more complicated as the Soviet Union and other countries began to acquire nuclear weapons, threatening to neutralize America's nuclear advantage. Maintaining the credibility of US nuclear deterrence and, especially, extended deterrence in a world of multiple nuclear-armed powers became an increasingly challenging problem for US policymakers. However, the United States did not respond to these constraints by retrenching or abandoning its more expansive ambitions, or by accepting the constraints of operating in a world characterized by mutual assured destruction among the great powers. Instead, successive administrations concluded that US security demanded a more expansive grand strategy, and an expansive nuclear posture to underpin it. As Francis Gavin notes, there is a great irony in the fact that "rarely has a state had less need for the bomb to guarantee its immediate territorial integrity, sovereignty, and security [than the United States]. Yet no state has invested greater resources in developing and deploying nuclear weapons, nor has any other state relied more heavily on nuclear weapons to implement its grand strategy."[144]

Instead of accepting the condition of mutual assured destruction and the strategic stability it implies, the United States continued to strive for the nuclear superiority necessary to support its expansive ambitions in international politics.

First, at least until the mid-1960s, the United States sought to maintain *quantitative* nuclear superiority over its rivals and particularly the Soviet Union, building up an enormous nuclear arsenal and threatening massive retaliation in response to adversary actions that the United States could not deter with purely conventional means.[145] The Soviet Union, of course, was also capable of building large numbers of nuclear weapons, and by the 1970s, the United States had begun to reluctantly accept quantitative parity with the Soviet Union. Although President Richard Nixon "hated MAD, [and] believed its logic was defeatist and naive," he ultimately signed arms control treaties with the Soviet Union that acknowledged that the United States would never again possess quantitative superiority over its rival.[146]

Instead of abandoning the goal of nuclear superiority, however, the United States shifted to the pursuit of *qualitative* superiority, which, it was hoped, would play more to American advantages in technological development and scientific innovation.[147] Prominent components of this effort included designing, producing, and deploying the Pershing II, MX, and Trident D-5 missiles, while simultaneously investing heavily in missile defense and the capabilities needed to hunt and threaten Soviet nuclear submarines.[148] None of these capabilities would have been necessary had the United States merely wanted a second-strike capability or the ability to deter a nuclear attack.

Second, beyond the numbers and quality of weapons, the United States also pursued a nuclear posture that aimed to make its expansive geopolitical position credible. In an effort to maintain the credibility of US nuclear commitments, the United States invested in highly aggressive and counterforce-oriented US nuclear postures and quixotic efforts to design and build reliable missile defense systems that advocates of the nuclear revolution viewed as destabilizing and doomed to failure.[149] Such efforts, it was believed, could underpin America's ambitious geopolitical goals. For example, the only way to persuade European (or other) allies that the United States might risk its own cities to defend those of its allies was if the US nuclear posture was sufficiently powerful that it could limit its own vulnerability to retaliation: that the United States would not, in fact, have to swap Boston for Bonn. As Earl Ravenal argued during the 1980s, "America's willingness to protect its allies rises or falls with the prospective viability of counterforce and, more generally, with the United States' ability to protect its own society from nuclear attack."[150] The US desire to make nuclear use, and nuclear use on behalf of allies, credible even in a world in which such use might trigger nuclear retaliation provides at least part of the explanation for the fact that US nuclear war plans became dominated by counterforce considerations by the early 1960s.[151]

Counterforce targeting was not the only aspect of US nuclear strategy driven by a desire to maintain the credibility of nuclear use. The United States also deployed nuclear weapons on the territory of a host of allies, including Belgium, Canada, Denmark, Greece, Italy, Morocco, the Netherlands, the Philippines, South Korea, Spain, Taiwan, Turkey, the United Kingdom, and West Germany, to make nuclear use on behalf of allies more feasible and plausible.[152]

Third, the desire to maintain the credibility of US nuclear use and US freedom of action more broadly has motivated the United States to direct military, economic, and diplomatic power to prevent both allies and adversaries from acquiring nuclear weapons and to limit the consequences of proliferation when those efforts failed.[153] Indeed, nonproliferation has frequently taken priority over other important political goals. For example, the United States was willing to work cooperatively with its sworn adversary, the Soviet Union, to prevent the spread of nuclear weapons, partly on the assumption that other countries acquiring nuclear weapons would itself stimulate further proliferation, constrain the United States' freedom of action, and reduce the credibility of the United States' own threats to use nuclear weapons.[154] Again, it was the United States' broad and expansive geopolitical ambitions that made these "strategies of inhibition" both desirable and viable.[155]

Indeed, the belief that nuclear weapons play a crucial role in sustaining America's alliances and expansive grand strategy continues to this day. The United States stations fewer nuclear forces on the territory of allies and has reduced the number of nuclear weapons it possesses. Nonetheless, even in a unipolar world in which the United States faces no peer competitor and possesses by far the most conventional military power of any state in the world, the US government continues to describe nuclear weapons as a "foundational capabilit[y]" critical for reassuring America's allies around the world and underpinning the US role in the world.[156] Similarly, US administrations from both political parties have often sought nuclear solutions to counter perceived military threats to allies, such as a potential Russian threat to hard-to-defend NATO allies in the Baltics and Eastern Europe. As the 2018 *Nuclear Posture Review* states, for example, "Expanding flexible U.S. nuclear options now, to include low-yield options, is important for the preservation of credible deterrence against regional aggression."[157] In short, the strategic thinking that emerged in the aftermath of World War II, that nuclear weapons could facilitate a far more expansive grand strategy and network of alliance commitments than the United States had ever previously considered, has continued well into the twenty-first century. Even as the international system has changed dramatically—including the collapse of the United States' only superpower rival—the United States has continued to view nuclear weapons as being a crucial component of America's position at the apex of the international system.

The evidence shows that nuclear acquisition substantially affected US foreign policy, but did so differently during World War II and in its aftermath. As a state in the midst of a brutal war, the United States first used nuclear weapons to escalate the conflict and try to win the war against the Japanese. In the aftermath of World War II, the United States faced no serious threats or challenges to its military preponderance and used nuclear weapons to substitute for conventional forces, facilitating a mix of foreign policy behaviors that contained elements of bolstering, expansion, aggression, and steadfastness. Overall, despite the difficulty in distinguishing between the various foreign policy behaviors in the complex international environment that characterized the aftermath of World War II, the theory of nuclear opportunism sheds light on the behavior of the United States and correctly anticipates that US foreign policy would be profoundly affected by nuclear weapons. Nuclear weapons thus underpinned crucial portions of US grand strategy in the postwar era, and this role persisted throughout the Cold War. The international order that the United States put in place was in crucial ways built on atomic foundations. Ultimately, nuclear weapons allowed the United States to take on a vastly more ambitious role in international politics without the expense and domestic political challenges that maintaining enormous conventional military capabilities would have entailed.

Past and Future Proliferators

The theory of nuclear opportunism performs well (though not perfectly) in explaining the way in which Britain, South Africa, and the United States thought about and used their nuclear weapons to advance their political goals. But how does the theory perform in explaining the behavior of other states that have acquired nuclear weapons? Further, what does the theory predict for potential future cases of proliferation?

Limited primary sources for many of the cases of nuclear acquisition means that drawing strong conclusions is difficult: without access to evidence about the internal deliberations of senior policymakers, it can be hard to definitively assess the role that nuclear weapons play. Nonetheless, it is worth making an initial assessment of whether the theory of nuclear opportunism appears to offer a plausible explanation for the way in which other states have changed their foreign policies after acquiring nuclear weapons. In this chapter, I examine whether Pakistan, India, France, Israel, and China appear to have responded to nuclear acquisition in the way the theory of nuclear opportunism suggests, and use the theory to make predictions for how Iran, Japan, and South Korea would behave if they acquired nuclear weapons. I do not try to use the case of the Soviet Union to test the theory: as discussed in chapter 4 with respect to the United States, the lack of a clear pre-nuclear baseline for behavior and the considerable flux of the international system in the early days of the Cold War make testing the predictions of the theory more difficult, especially given the much more limited availability of primary documents than for the United States.[1] Similarly, because of substantial uncertainty about North Korea's nuclear posture (and thus, when North Korea acquired the theoretically relevant capabilities), I do not attempt to test the theory using the North Korean case. Depending on how North Korea has conceived of the utility of its nuclear weapons, acquisition could have occurred as early as 1993, or as late as 2017, when North Korea successfully tested a high-yield nuclear weapon and missiles with the ability to target the United States.[2]

As would be expected, the theory of nuclear opportunism performs better in some cases than others. The theory performs well in explaining Pakistani,

Indian, and French behavior in the aftermath of acquiring nuclear weapons. However, the theory performs less well in explaining Israeli behavior and gets the Chinese case largely wrong. Nonetheless, overall, the theory receives significant validation and outperforms the alternative explanations.

Pakistan

Ever since the partition of British India in 1947, Pakistan has faced a serious territorial threat from India. India possesses considerably greater conventional military power than Pakistan, and a far larger economy, population, and territory. Moreover, India's military superiority over Pakistan has been repeatedly demonstrated, with India besting Pakistan in each of the wars they have fought (in 1947, 1965, 1971, and 1999). Most dramatically, in the 1971 war, India dismembered Pakistan, creating the new state of Bangladesh out of East Pakistan, and what remains of Pakistan's territory (previously West Pakistan) is geographically vulnerable to an Indian conventional assault. It is not surprising that in the aftermath of the 1971 humiliation, Pakistani leaders vowed to acquire nuclear weapons: to "eat grass" if necessary in order to acquire the capabilities that might deter India from taking similar actions in the future.[3] Although Pakistan did not test nuclear weapons publicly until 1998, it acquired a nuclear capability by the mid-to-late 1980s.[4]

The theory of nuclear opportunism predicts that Pakistan, facing a severe territorial threat, would use nuclear weapons to facilitate aggression and steadfastness. The theory predicts that pursuing independence from its allies such as China or expanding its interests in South Asia or beyond would be impractical and unattractive goals for Pakistan even *with* nuclear weapons because of Pakistan's overwhelming need to focus on the Indian threat and its need for assistance from any and all sources. According to the theory, Pakistan would choose to use its nuclear weapons to improve its position vis-à-vis India, and would therefore use nuclear weapons to facilitate aggression and steadfastness.

These predictions are realized: Pakistan began using nuclear weapons to advance its political interests by standing more firmly when provoked and in pushing harder to revise the status quo. In the Brasstacks Crisis of 1986–1987, triggered by a large-scale Indian military exercise that Pakistani leaders feared might be a prelude to an invasion, Pakistan engaged in at least some degree of nuclear signaling to deter Indian aggression. Most notably, A. Q. Khan, the "father" of the Pakistani bomb program, gave an interview in which he stated that "nobody can undo Pakistan or take us for granted. . . . Let it be clear that we shall use the bomb if our existence is threatened."[5] However, the interview was not published for several weeks, and it remains unclear whether his threats were officially sanctioned by the government or whether they affected Indian behavior.[6]

Future crises between India and Pakistan would see more overt Pakistani nuclear signaling. In 1990, believing that India might respond to Pakistani support for insurgents in Indian-controlled Jammu and Kashmir, Pakistani leaders met and determined the need to "deter this impending threat."[7] The way in which Pakistan chose to do so had a clear nuclear dimension. Pakistani Army Chief General Aslam Beg stated that "a squadron of [nuclear-capable] F-16s was moved . . . and we pulled out our devices and all to arm the aircraft. . . . Movement was made in a way that is visible, because the purpose was not to precipitate a crisis but to deter."[8] Other acts of nuclear signaling also took place: Pakistan sent Foreign Minister Shahabzada Yaqub-Khan to Delhi to convey that Pakistan would hold India responsible for any attack, a message understood to have a nuclear dimension and with Beg confirming that "Yaqub-Khan did a good job frightening them."[9]

In 1999, in the aftermath of India's and Pakistan's nuclear tests, the Pakistani military took action across the Line of Control to seize territory in Indian-controlled Kashmir. Pakistan's actions triggered Indian retaliation and led to the Kargil War, with Pakistan ultimately forced back to the pre-war status quo.[10] However, India's retaliation was extremely measured, with Indian leaders careful to avoid crossing the Line of Control. This restraint stands in stark contrast to Indian actions in response to prior acts of Pakistani aggression: in response to a similar Pakistani operation in 1965, India had retaliated across the Line of Control and the international border into core Pakistani territory.[11] In 1999, Pakistani nuclear weapons deterred an Indian response of this sort. Pakistan brandished its nuclear weapons during the crisis, with Pakistani foreign secretary Shamshad Ahmad publicly threatening to "use any weapon in our arsenal to defend our territorial integrity."[12] This rhetoric was backed up by action: the evidence suggests that the Pakistani military moved and readied nuclear assets for potential use (possibly without the knowledge of the civilian leadership).[13] The evidence—including statements from Indian officials with every incentive to deny the deterrent effects of Pakistan's nuclear weapons—suggests that it was Pakistani nuclear weapons that restrained India's response. When Indian prime minister Atal Bihari Vajpayee was told that opening a second front against Pakistan across the border might be militarily necessary, Vajpayee reportedly looked shocked and responded, "But General Sahib, they have a nuclear bomb!"[14] The Indian national security advisor Brajesh Mishra confirmed this fear, stating that the use of "nuclear weapons would have been risked if we did [cross the Line of Control]."[15] And in a report by the Kargil Review Committee, analysts commissioned by the Indian government concluded that "Pakistan was convinced that its nuclear weapons capability would deter India's superior conventional forces."[16]

Since the Kargil War, Pakistani leaders have continued to engage in aggression against India, notably by using Pakistani-sponsored insurgents and terrorists against Indian cities. The December 2001 attack on the Indian

Parliament by Jaish-e-Mohammed and Lashkar-e-Taiba (two Pakistani-supported militant organizations), the November 2008 attacks by Lashkar-e-Taiba militants against Mumbai, and the February 2019 Jaish-e-Mohammed suicide attack against Indian security forces in Kashmir are the most prominent examples, but Pakistani support for militants operating on Indian territory has been an increasingly prominent feature of Pakistani foreign policy. In each case, Indian leaders have been deterred from taking large-scale conventional military action in response.[17] Scholars have typically concluded that Pakistani nuclear weapons enable this aggression against India, much as the theory of nuclear opportunism expects. C. Christine Fair argues that nuclear weapons "increase the cost of Indian action" against Pakistan, which facilitates "risk-seeking behavior . . . to change the status quo."[18] For Vipin Narang, Pakistan's nuclear weapons—and the aggressive nuclear posture it has adopted—have "enabled Pakistan to more aggressively pursue long-standing, limited revisionist objectives against India."[19] For Paul Kapur, "nuclear weapons . . . encouraged aggressive Pakistani behavior."[20] There is now a broad scholarly consensus that Pakistan uses nuclear weapons in this way.[21] Regular statements by Pakistani elites reinforce the conclusion that Pakistan's nuclear weapons have inhibited Indian responses to Pakistani aggression. Jalil Jilani, a high-ranking official within the Ministry of Foreign Affairs, stated that "since Pakistan's acquisition [of a nuclear capacity], Pakistan has felt much less threatened" by Indian conventional capabilities.[22] Prime Minister Benazir Bhutto stated that Pakistani decision makers had concluded that Pakistan's "nuclear capability would ensure that India could not launch a conventional war, knowing that it if did, it would turn nuclear."[23] Feroz Khan, a brigadier general (retired) in the Pakistani Army and a former director in the Strategic Plans Division that formulated Pakistan's nuclear policy and strategy, has written that Pakistan's "nuclear capability ensures defense against physical external aggression and coercion from adversaries, and deters infringement of national sovereignty."[24]

Overall, Pakistan appears to conceive of the utility of its nuclear weapons in exactly the way the theory of nuclear opportunism expects: as a tool for advancing its interests against the serious territorial threat posed by India. Pakistani behavior since acquiring nuclear weapons also seems consistent with the theory of nuclear opportunism: it is widely accepted that Pakistan uses nuclear weapons to facilitate both aggression and steadfastness, enabling Pakistan to both push harder in pursuit of long-held revisionist goals and to stand firmer when challenged.

India

India's decades-long path to nuclear acquisition stands in marked contrast to Pakistan's dash to acquire nuclear weapons. India first began pursuing nuclear technologies in the late 1940s and accelerated its interest in nuclear explosives in the 1960s in the aftermath of its defeat in the 1962 Sino-Indian war and China's 1964 nuclear test. Domestic political dynamics, however, prevented a firm decision to acquire nuclear weapons, and the 1974 test of a "Peaceful Nuclear Explosive" did not lead to an all-out effort to weaponize India's nuclear capability. India ultimately remained a threshold nuclear state until the late 1980s. At this point, Pakistan's acquisition of nuclear weapons provided the final impetus for Prime Minister Rajiv Gandhi, a supporter of multilateral nuclear disarmament, to push India's nuclear program over the finish line and acquire a fully fledged nuclear weapons capability. Although India would not publicly test its nuclear weapons until 1998, it had a functional nuclear weapons capability from the late 1980s.[25]

Because India faced a relatively benign security environment, and with domestic politics driving many key decisions in India's slow development of nuclear capabilities, it is far from obvious that nuclear weapons would have any significant effect on India's foreign policy. Despite this, the theory of nuclear opportunism does seem to shed some light on the ways in which Indian foreign policy changed after India acquired nuclear weapons.

What predictions does the theory of nuclear opportunism make? First, India did not face serious territorial threats when it weaponized its nuclear capabilities in the late 1980s. Not only does India possess a large territory and considerable strategic depth, but its plausible opponents would face serious challenges if they attempted to attack India: Pakistan is conventionally much weaker than India, while China would have to cross the formidable geographic barrier of the Himalayas.[26]

Second, India did not have a senior ally providing for its security when it acquired nuclear weapons: although India had signed the Indo-Soviet Treaty of Friendship and Cooperation with the Soviet Union in 1971, it did not commit the Soviet Union to India's defense. In any case, India's relationship with the Soviet Union had been deteriorating since the early 1980s, and Soviet leader Mikhail Gorbachev's "New Thinking" foreign policy indicated that the Soviet Union's global ambitions and commitments were being wound down by the time India acquired nuclear weapons.[27] India was, however, rising in relative power by the late 1980s. For example, India's Correlates of War CINC score had been rising consistently since 1980. The theory of nuclear opportunism would therefore predict that Indian elites would see nuclear weapons as a tool for expanding Indian influence in the world and bolstering any existing junior allies.

In line with these predictions, the desire to expand India's position and status in the world is widely regarded to have been an important driver of Indian nuclear acquisition. T. V. Paul and Baldev Raj Nayar argue that "a key underlying reason for the acquisition of nuclear capabilities . . . is the enduring and deep-rooted aspiration of India for the role of a major power, and the related belief that the possession of an independent nuclear capability is an essential prerequisite for achieving that status."[28] George Perkovich makes a similar argument that Indian leaders were not driven toward nuclear acquisition by narrow security threats. Instead, Indian leaders as early as Prime Minister Jawarharlal Nehru and his chief nuclear scientist Homi Bhabha recognized that a "nuclear weapon capability could enhance India's status and power in the Western-dominated world" and offered a "shortcut" to major power status.[29] Vipin Narang concurs, arguing that Bhabha "had a keen interest in India being viewed as a modern scientific state and, like many nuclear scientists of that era, saw the ability to develop nuclear weapons as the pinnacle of scientific achievement."[30] Relatedly, Jacques Hymans argues that Indian leaders have consistently possessed a "nationalist" NIC and have thus held high conceptions of Indian status, with these beliefs shaping India's nuclear decision making in profound ways.[31]

While a desire to improve its status and standing in the world was certainly a driver of India's nuclear weapons program, did India actually change its foreign policy in a manner consistent with these desires after acquiring nuclear weapons? Overall, India's foreign policies did change in a manner consistent with the predictions of the theory, although it is unclear whether nuclear weapons played a key role in causing the changes.

Consistent with the predictions, Indian foreign policy became dramatically more ambitious and outward looking as India emerged in the post–Cold War world as a nuclear-armed state. This expansion occurred despite the considerable political and economic turmoil that characterized India at the end of the Cold War, the fact that India emerged from the Cold War facing a more assertive (and newly nuclear armed) Pakistan on its border, and fears that the end of the Cold War would be particularly damaging for India's geopolitical position given the collapse of the Soviet Union, its partner since the 1971 treaty. Ross Munro, for example, argued in 1993 that "India's reach for great power status is in shambles. The keystone of Indian power and pretence in the 1980s, the Indo-Soviet link, is history."[32] Despite this potentially challenging strategic environment, India's foreign policy became substantially more ambitious.

The shift to a more expansive, ambitious foreign policy had a number of components. First, India initiated the Look East policy—a broad effort to "develop political contacts, increas[e] economic integration and forg[e] security co-operation with countries of Southeast Asia"—which "marked a shift in India's perspective of the world."[33] Second, India built diplomatic and military relationships with new allies, including Israel (after diplomatic relations were established in 1992), Turkey, and Iran.[34] Third, India aggressively pursued economic liberalization and foreign investment, reversing decades of socialist economic policy.[35] This included devaluing the rupee, raising the ceiling on foreign ownership, removing import and export controls, and reducing business tax rates.[36] Fourth, India increased its investment in defense. Defense expenditure grew slowly during the 1980s: from 15.9 percent of government spending in 1980–1981 to 16.9 percent in 1987–1988, but jumped to 19 percent by 1990–1991 despite a severe balance-of-payment crisis.[37] Fifth, Indian participation in international organizations became more vigorous: increasing engagement and participation in the Association of Southeast Asian Nations (ASEAN), making more prominent demands for a permanent seat on the UN Security Council, and playing a considerably larger role in international peacekeeping efforts. India had not participated in any UN peacekeeping missions since sending two infantry brigades to the Congo in the 1960s, but during the 1990s, India sent forces to Cambodia (1992–1993), Mozambique (1992–1994), Somalia (1993–1994), Rwanda (1994–1996), Angola (1989–1999), and Sierra Leone (1999–2001). Overall, it seems fair to say that India "regained some of its self-confidence in the 1990s," seeking to expand its international position and status.[38]

These changes were not, however, obviously driven by nuclear acquisition. Indeed, the massive shift in the international system that occurred close to the same time that India acquired nuclear weapons makes it hard to firmly attribute any change in behavior to Indian nuclear weapons. However, India has frequently used its "responsible" stewardship of nuclear weapons as a core component of its efforts to be taken seriously as a legitimate great power that contributes to global public goods.[39] These claims were ultimately rewarded and legitimized by the 2005 US-India nuclear deal that future secretary of defense Ashton Carter described as having "openly acknowledged India as a legitimate nuclear power, ending New Delhi's 30-year quest for such recognition."[40] More broadly, it seems plausible that nuclear weapons—through the psychology- and identity-based mechanisms discussed in chapter 1—may have changed the way in which Indian leaders conceived of India's role in international politics, and thus facilitated the more expansive and ambitious Indian foreign policies of the 1990s. After all, and as discussed above, the desire for greater status and a more prominent position in international politics was a core driver of Indian pursuit of nuclear weapons and technologies.

France

France acquired nuclear weapons in a period of considerable uncertainty about its future status in the world. A previously great power with a large empire, France suffered the humiliation of defeat and occupation by Nazi forces during World War II and required liberation by foreign forces at its conclusion. France entered the Cold War economically weak, politically and geographically sandwiched between the two superpowers, and fearful of a revived and potentially nuclear-armed Germany. In this environment, France made a determined effort to acquire nuclear weapons.[41] France established the French Atomic Energy Commission in the aftermath of the war, tested its first nuclear weapon in 1960, and in 1964 acquired the Mirage IV bombers, which offered the delivery capabilities that would allow France to use nuclear weapons militarily.[42]

What effects does the theory of nuclear opportunism predict that nuclear weapons would have on French foreign policy? First, France did not face immediate and severe territorial threats in 1964: while the Soviet Union was certainly a threat, France was sufficiently geographically removed from the Soviet threat and was protected from the Soviet Union by large numbers of NATO forces (and nuclear weapons) in Germany.[43] Second, France had a senior ally—the United States—committed to its security. Third, France was in long-run political decline. Much as Britain was in the same period, France was in the process of adjusting to its status as a medium-ranked power. This is confirmed by the Correlates of War Project: France's Correlates of War CINC score had been declining since the mid-1950s and would continue to do so after France acquired nuclear weapons. The theory would therefore predict that France would see nuclear weapons as serving a foreign policy role similar to that of Britain's nuclear weapons: as a tool to avoid dependence on the United States and to maintain its position in international politics. In terms of French behavior, the theory anticipates that France would use its nuclear weapons to facilitate independence from the United States and maintain its status in the world: standing more firmly in defense of the status quo and bolstering its junior allies. However, given that France had given up its major colonial possessions prior to 1964 and was not a state on NATO's front line, core French interests were not being regularly challenged in a way that would allow us to assess whether France used nuclear weapons to facilitate steadfastness. Similarly, because France lacked junior allies (France itself, of course, was a junior ally in NATO), we should not expect to see France use nuclear weapons to facilitate bolstering. The theory of nuclear opportunism, therefore, anticipates that France would primarily use nuclear weapons to facilitate independence from the United States.

This is what we see in the historical record. Scholars have consistently identified a desire for both independence and status as key drivers of the French nuclear program. David Yost begins his analysis of France's nuclear program with the statement that "rank and independence have been enduring occupations of French statecraft."[44] Wolf Mendl agrees that French elites believed that nuclear weapons would allow France "to reassert its independence and position in the world."[45] Pierre Gallois argues that for France, nuclear weapons were "the instrument . . . for attaining true national military independence."[46] And as Wilfred Kohl writes, "The nuclear force was intrinsically related to [French prime minister Charles de Gaulle's] political goals of ensuring France's independence and augmenting France's freedom of action in world affairs."[47]

This scholarly consensus is unsurprising given the many public and private statements by Charles de Gaulle, the French prime minister from 1958 to 1959 and president from 1959 to 1969, that articulated the need for nuclear weapons to ensure French independence. De Gaulle stated that "American nuclear power does not necessarily and immediately meet all the eventualities concerning France," meaning that France needed to "equip herself with an atomic force of her own."[48] In 1958, in conversation with John Foster Dulles, de Gaulle argued that "only in this way [through the possession of French nuclear weapons] can our defence and foreign policy be independent, which is something we prize above everything else."[49] In public speeches he argued that a state "which does not possess [nuclear weapons] . . . does not command its own destiny" and that "the countries which do not have an atomic arsenal . . . have to accept a strategic and consequently a political dependency."[50] It was not only the United States from which France sought independence, but Britain as well: de Gaulle could not accept a situation in which "only the Americans and the British could in fact loose atomic war whenever they wanted."[51] In terms of status, de Gaulle explicitly argued that the equalizing effect of nuclear weapons would allow France to maintain its status even in a world dominated by the superpowers: "While the megatons that we could launch would not equal in number those which Americans and Russians are in a position to unleash, once a certain level of nuclear strength is reached, the proportion of the respective military resources is no longer absolute. . . . That is why France's modern armaments not only provide it with incomparable security but inject into a dangerous world a new and powerful factor for prudence and circumspection."[52] Even receiving US assistance that might have imposed conditions on the development of the program was judged unacceptable: in de Gaulle's words, such assistance would be "incompatible with [French] sovereignty."[53] However, the belief that nuclear weapons would serve these functions was not limited to de Gaulle and was more widely held among French political elites. After all, France had taken substantial steps toward acquiring nuclear weapons well before de Gaulle came to power.[54] In the words of Defense Minister Jacques Chaban-Delmas, for example, "We intend to be able to make modern weapons in order to maintain an equitable balance within NATO."[55] Or as the military chief of staff told Premier Pierre Mendès-France in 1954, nuclear weapons would give France "the possibility of recovering a role [in international politics] of first rank."[56]

Did France use nuclear weapons to facilitate a more independent foreign policy? France had long been uncomfortable with its subordinate position to the United States and Germany within NATO and took steps to preserve some element of independence. France pressured the United States for greater influence in NATO decision making and announced that its Mediterranean fleet would not be subject to NATO command in the event of war. France also demanded that US intermediate range ballistic missile (IRBM) deployments could not occur on French territory and that tactical nuclear weapons could not be kept in France.[57] However, as its nuclear program achieved a full deliverable capability, French independence increased: the French "became less inclined to accept what it saw as the infringements on sovereign choice implied by its role in a U.S.-dominated alliance."[58] And, in line with these concerns, shortly after acquiring a deliverable nuclear capability, France withdrew from NATO's command structure. France's willingness to take this dramatic step—in spite of the American anger that resulted—was directly motivated by a desire for greater independence within NATO. Furthermore, French leaders saw their ability to take this step as intimately tied to France's newly developed nuclear capabilities: in Yost's words, "Membership in NATO's integrated institutions was portrayed as a subjugation to foreign decisions. . . . Strategic nuclear forces would give France the means of self-reliance and the option of non-belligerency in conflicts."[59]

Withdrawal from NATO's command structure was not the only action that France took after acquiring nuclear weapons. For example, France criticized the Bretton Woods monetary system, actively pursued détente with the Soviet Union, and recognized the status of the PRC: all actions opposed by the United States.[60] By the 1970s, French officials were even prepared to make provocative statements about their ability to harm the United States with nuclear weapons. General Guy Méry, the chief of staff of the armed forces, stated that the "damage that we could cause to either superpower would immediately place it in such a situation of imbalance regarding the other superpower that it is doubtful that either could afford to tolerate suffering that damage at any time."[61]

Overall, the way in which nuclear weapons affected French foreign policy appears consistent with the theory of nuclear opportunism: French elites saw nuclear weapons as a tool to facilitate independence and, consistent with these views, behaved more independently after acquiring nuclear weapons.

Israel

Israel's desire for nuclear weapons emerged from its strategic environment. Since its founding in 1948, Israel has been a geographically vulnerable state with a small territory and population, surrounded by more populous neighbors with which it has fought numerous wars and which have regularly challenged the legitimacy of Israel's existence. For a country formed in response to the Holocaust and the historical persecution of the Jewish people, such vulnerability has added political salience. It is therefore unsurprising that Israel has sought to overcome its vulnerabilities through technological advancement and would seek the protection of nuclear weapons.[62]

As Israel's first prime minister David Ben-Gurion stated, "Science can provide us with the weapons that are needed to deter our enemies from waging war against us. I am confident that science is able to provide us with the weapon that will secure the peace, and deter our enemies."[63] When Ben-

Gurion made this statement, Israel was already close to acquiring a nuclear weapon. Israel had been pursuing nuclear technologies since the 1950s and ultimately assembled its first nuclear weapons (deliverable by existing Israeli Vautour aircraft) on the eve of the 1967 war.[64]

Although it is widely understood that Israel possesses nuclear weapons, Israel has never officially acknowledged the existence of its nuclear program or status as a nuclear-armed power. This policy of "opacity" has had multiple drivers: to avoid forcing the United States to pick between its commitment to nonproliferation and its alliance with Israel, to reduce the domestic pressures pushing neighboring Arab states to respond by pursuing their own nuclear weapons, to reduce international pressure and sanctions, and to retain a source of diplomatic leverage over the United States by being able to threaten the public declaration of its nuclear capabilities.

What does the theory of nuclear opportunism predict in the case of Israel? The theory is clear because Israel faces severe territorial threats. Although Israel has triumphed in the wars it has fought against its Arab neighbors, it nonetheless faced serious threats when it acquired nuclear weapons on the eve of the 1967 war. Although the outcome of the 1967 war—a decisive victory in which Israel seized the Golan Heights, West Bank, Gaza Strip, and Sinai Peninsula—may suggest that the threats Israel faced were limited, the war could have unfolded very differently. Most notably, Israel's preemptive attack against the Egyptian army and air force had a profound effect on the way the conflict unfolded.[65] Similarly, the manner in which the 1973 war unfolded, in which core Israeli territory was conquered before Israel was able to repel the invaders after being resupplied by the United States, demonstrates the vulnerabilities that Israel faced. The theory therefore predicts that Israel would use nuclear weapons to facilitate both aggression and steadfastness toward the threats it faced.

Whether we see this in the historical record is not entirely clear. While the secrecy surrounding Israel's nuclear program would make a definitive assessment of how nuclear weapons affected Israeli foreign policy extremely challenging, it is not clear that nuclear acquisition marked a clear discontinuity in Israeli foreign policy. It is possible that Israel's nuclear weapons emboldened the state to take aggressive and preemptive military actions that began the 1967 war, but it is equally plausible that it would have taken such actions regardless of its nuclear status. Ultimately, Israel's decisive victory with conventional forces meant that nuclear weapons did not play an obvious role in the conflict. As Avner Cohen argues, "Ideas [of seeking to gain political leverage from their nuclear weapons], to the extent that some individuals entertained them, apparently never reached discussions at the highest political forum."[66] Indeed, in some ways, Israel's decision to pursue a preemptive conventional military strategy rather than take the gamble of conducting a nuclear test or unsheathing its nuclear capabilities may have indicated a lack of faith in the political power of nuclear weapons.

There is stronger evidence that nuclear weapons provided Israel with political benefits in the 1973 Yom Kippur war, facilitating Israeli steadfastness
in defense of the status quo. Israeli forces were caught off guard by a joint
Egyptian and Syrian attack seeking to reclaim the Arab territories lost in the
1967 war, and Israeli forces suffered significant losses of territory and materiel in the opening days of the war. An Israeli defeat, previously considered
unthinkable, appeared plausible, and Israeli officials feared that Syrian and
Egyptian aims might not be limited to merely reclaiming the territory previously lost in the 1967 war. While Prime Minister Golda Meir rejected suggestions to explicitly threaten invading forces with nuclear weapons, Minister of Defense Moshe Dayan nonetheless ordered an increase in Israel's
nuclear alert level, including operational checks on Israel's nuclear-capable
Jericho missiles that would be observable by US intelligence.[67] These checks
played an important role in triggering US efforts to resupply Israel with conventional materiel and may have encouraged Syrian and Egyptian restraint,
with the Syrian front line retreating rather than seeking to solidify its gains,
especially in the northern sector where Syria could plausibly have achieved
full control over the Golan Heights.[68] Thus, both by restraining the behavior
of Israel's opponents and by compelling greater assistance from the United
States, nuclear weapons allowed Israel to stand more firmly in defense of
the status quo.

Since the 1973 war, Israel's grand strategy has emphasized maintaining
conventional military superiority, a policy supported by successive US administrations that have committed to maintaining Israel's "qualitative military edge."[69] Conventional superiority has allowed Israel to stand more
firmly in defense of the status quo, and, of course, is intimately related to
Israel's nuclear weapons. Specifically, Israel's continued and implicit threat
to unsheathe its nuclear capabilities provides additional motivation for
Washington to ensure that Israel's conventional military superiority be maintained.[70] Israel, therefore, clearly receives political benefits from its nuclear
weapons. Nonetheless, it is not clear that Israel has used its nuclear weapons to facilitate anything other than steadfastness.

While using nuclear weapons to facilitate steadfastness would be predicted by the theory of nuclear opportunism, the theory would also predict
Israel using nuclear weapons to facilitate aggression, which we do not see
clear evidence for in the historical record. Why might the theory perform
less well in this case? It is plausible that factors left out of the theory play an
important role in the case of Israel. For example, it is possible that the Israeli
desire to maintain its relationship with the United States and to avoid provoking reactive proliferation by adversaries in the region leads Israel to avoid
brandishing its nuclear weapons too overtly, or using its nuclear weapons
to facilitate aggression. These two factors would not necessarily be expected
to generalize to other cases, and it is reasonable to leave them out of a theory that seeks a balance between parsimony and explanatory richness. None-

theless, the theory of nuclear opportunism receives only mixed and limited support from the case of Israel.

China

China first tested a nuclear weapon in October 1964 but did not follow the United States and Soviet Union in developing a large nuclear arsenal.[71] Although China's desire for nuclear weapons emerged in the aftermath of attempted nuclear coercion from the United States during the Korean War and in the 1954 crisis over Quemoy and Matsu, China has never sought to match the nuclear capabilities of either superpower.[72] Instead, China's nuclear arsenal has remained limited in both qualitative and quantitative terms, or, in the words of Taylor Fravel and Even Medeiros, "small, unsophisticated, and, arguably, highly vulnerable."[73] Chinese leaders have consistently believed that even a small arsenal can threaten sufficiently devastating nuclear retaliation to deter nuclear coercion and attack, and that a larger and more diverse arsenal was therefore unnecessary.[74]

What does the theory of nuclear opportunism predict in the case of China? First, China did not face severe territorial threats when it acquired nuclear weapons. China possessed an enormous territory granting it considerable strategic depth, and an impressive army: even against the might of the Soviet Red Army, China maintained a considerable conventional military advantage along the Sino-Soviet border throughout the 1960s and 1970s that was sufficient to deter and resist any invasion or aggression.[75] Second, China did not have an ally committed to its protection: the Sino-Soviet alliance had fractured well before China acquired nuclear weapons. Third, China was rising in power. China's Correlates of War Project CINC score, for example, has been on an upward trajectory since the 1950s. The theory of nuclear opportunism would therefore anticipate that China would use nuclear weapons to facilitate the expansion of its influence in international politics, steadfastness in defense of the status quo, and bolstering of junior allies.

It does not appear, however, that Chinese strategic thinkers have ever thought that nuclear weapons offered China the ability to do much more than deter nuclear coercion by the superpowers (that is, anything beyond facilitating steadfastness).[76] As Fravel and Medeiros write, "Mao Zedong and Deng Zioping, [who] had a consistently dominant influence on Chinese nuclear strategy . . . viewed nuclear weapons, primarily and probably exclusively, as tools for deterring nuclear aggression and countering coercion."[77] In Mao's words, "If we don't want to be bullied, then we cannot do without this thing."[78] Chinese leaders recognized that China required nuclear weapons to ensure its security and resist intimidation in an international environment dominated by two nuclear-armed superpowers, but believed that the number of nuclear weapons they needed was small. This view emerged directly from Mao's view of the importance of manpower rather than technology in determining the outcome of wars. Even as China has sought to modernize its arsenal, this has not reflected a fundamental shift in its understanding of the utility of nuclear weapons. Rather, Chinese modernization has aimed to maintain the ability to assure retaliation even as adversary capabilities have improved.[79]

These views are not consistent with the theory of nuclear opportunism and accord much more closely with the predictions of the theory of the nuclear revolution. Chinese leaders do not appear to have viewed nuclear weapons as a broadly useful political tool, but rather as a capability with very narrow political utility: resisting nuclear coercion and deterring nuclear attack. As with the case of Israel, it is plausible that factors left out of the theory of nuclear opportunism for reasons of parsimony play an important role in this case. Specifically, the distinctive ideational beliefs about the limited utility of nuclear weapons held by Mao and other Chinese leaders may have led both to China's relatively small and vulnerable nuclear force and to a reluctance to use nuclear weapons to achieve broader foreign policy goals. This factor does not appear to influence the effects of nuclear acquisition across a wide range of cases (and is therefore reasonably left out of a theory that aspires to retain parsimony and generalizability) but does appear to play a powerful role in the Chinese case.

How Might Future Proliferators Behave?

Although there are cases that the theory of nuclear opportunism does not explain well, the theory performs well overall. The theory offers a plausible explanation for the way in which the majority of states that have acquired nuclear weapons have both thought about the utility of their nuclear weapons and behaved after acquiring them.

It is thus reasonable to ask what the theory has to say about the ways in which future proliferators might behave. Specifically, I make predictions for how Iran, South Korea, and Japan would behave if they acquired nuclear weapons. Using the theory in this way demonstrates that it has the potential to offer policy-relevant insights into the potential behavior of future nuclear-armed states. While such predictions could prove to be wrong, the ability to make *ex ante* predictions that offer the possibility of falsification is a virtue of the theory. Thus, in addition to being relevant to ongoing policy debates, making such predictions also offers a test of the theory—for example, if Japan were to acquire nuclear weapons and engage in different behaviors than those predicted, that would provide an indication that the theory may be incorrect or require adjustment.

Of course, making these predictions requires some assumptions to be made. The theory makes predictions about the ways in which *states that ac-*

quire nuclear weapons change their behavior after acquiring nuclear weapons.[80] This means that one has to be cautious about using the theory to make predictions about countries that currently lack nuclear weapons: such predictions would apply only *if* that country were to acquire nuclear weapons. For example, in the context of Iran, the theory would apply only in a world in which Iran has acquired nuclear weapons. Envisaging such a world requires additional assumption—for example, that the United States has not taken military action to prevent Iranian nuclear acquisition.

If Iran were to acquire nuclear weapons, how does the theory of nuclear opportunism anticipate that Iranian foreign policy would change? The first variable is the existence of serious territorial threats or an ongoing war. Iran does not currently face such threats. The US invasion of Iraq in 2003 removed Iran's primary threat—Saddam Hussein's Iraq. Of course, the large numbers of US forces on Iran's borders with Iraq and Afghanistan posed a significant territorial threat to Iran, but the subsequent drawdown of US forces in both countries has reduced such dangers. Today, Iran faces weak and internally unstable neighbors that lack power projection capabilities and pose little territorial threat.[81] In addition, despite a long history of intervention by outside powers that have substantially influenced the outlook of the Iranian regime and its military forces, Iran retains "extensive natural defenses" including mountain ranges that encircle much of the country and ensure that "Iran's periphery favors the defender and is ill-suited to maneuver warfare."[82] Similarly, while either the United States or Israel could conduct damaging air strikes against Iran, the possibility of either state invading and holding substantial portions of Iranian territory seems remote.[83] Because Iran does not face such threats, the theory does not predict that Iran would find it attractive to use nuclear weapons as a shield behind which to facilitate aggression.[84]

The second variable is whether Iran possesses a senior ally that partially provides for its security. Iran lacks such an ally. While Russia and China have offered Iran some diplomatic protection in the face of US sanctions and threats, that diplomatic protection has not been absolute and neither country has the power projection capability to defend Iran militarily in a sustained way. It is unlikely that Iran views either country as a patron committed to its security.[85] Nonetheless, to the extent that Iran does view Russia or China as providing for its military security, the theory anticipates that Iran would use nuclear weapons to facilitate independence from those patrons. The final variable is whether Iran is currently rising in power relative to its primary rivals in the region. Although power trends in the Middle East are notoriously fickle, it seems hard to argue that Iran is significantly rising in power at the present point in time. While the US withdrawals from Iraq and Afghanistan have removed a source of threat on Iran's borders and increased Iran's relative position in the region, Iran has also suffered unwelcome changes in the balance of power over the past few years (notably, the civil war threatening ally Bashar al-Assad in Syria, the ongoing effect of multilateral sanctions on the Iranian economy, and the rise of the Islamic State). Iran's economy remains hamstrung by sanctions, high inflation, and unemployment and is likely to remain poorly performing even in the event that some portion of the multilateral sanctions currently in place are lifted.[86] Iran's military forces are outdated and poorly maintained. Further, Iran's defense budget is small compared with those of its rivals, with Iranian defense expenditure amounting to only a quarter of Saudi Arabia's.[87]

The theory of nuclear opportunism therefore anticipates that if Iran were to acquire nuclear weapons, it would use them to facilitate the bolstering of its allies and steadfastness in the face of threats. The theory does not predict the precise form such bolstering would take, but it would be reasonable to assume that it might involve increased resource transfers to existing allies such as Syria and Iraq, greater Iranian efforts to penetrate their domestic politics, and, perhaps, an implicit Iranian offer of extended deterrence to those states. In addition, Iranian bolstering need not only seek to boost other states. Given Iran's history of using proxies throughout the Middle East, such behavior might also be observed to a greater extent in its relationships with proxies than in its relationships with other states. Iran could seek to provide additional resources to Hizbullah, increase its influence over Hamas, or provide additional support to the Houthis in Yemen, as well as seeking greater influence over the governments in Baghdad, Damascus, and Sana'a. This prediction aligns with the expectations of Erica Borghard and Mira Rapp-Hooper, who predict that a "nuclear armed Iran may increase its support of proxies."[88]

The theory of nuclear opportunism thus offers mixed news to those concerned about how Iran would behave if it acquired nuclear weapons. While the theory suggests that Iran using nuclear weapons to facilitate territorial aggression against its neighbors such as Saudi Arabia or Iraq in the way that Pakistan has is unlikely, the prospect of greater Iranian bolstering of existing allies is not an outcome that most US policymakers would find reassuring. Greater Iranian steadfastness, while not actively threatening US interests, would nonetheless reduce US freedom of action in the region. The theory of nuclear opportunism thus offers something of a middle ground between pessimists and optimists when it comes to Iranian nuclear acquisition.[89]

What would the theory predict in the case of US allies such as Japan and South Korea? North Korea's nuclear advances—specifically, its demonstration in the summer of 2017 of both an intercontinental ballistic missile (ICBM) capable of hitting the continental United States and a high-yield nuclear weapon (either a two-stage thermonuclear device or a boosted fission weapon)—have raised doubts about the continued reliability of American extended deterrence. Japanese and South Korean statesmen might reasonably question whether they should rely on American protection in the face of potential North Korean aggression when North Korea can threaten to hold

US cities at risk of devastating retaliation. Just as European allies doubted America's willingness to sacrifice Boston or New York for Bonn or Paris during the Cold War, US allies in Asia may well become increasingly skeptical of US commitments to sacrifice Seattle or Los Angeles to protect Tokyo or Seoul. If so, just as US allies such as Germany, Taiwan, and Sweden considered pursuing nuclear weapons during the Cold War, US allies may again begin to find nuclear weapons an attractive option.

For Japan, the predictions are similar to those made for the United Kingdom in chapter 2. Japan is protected by highly defensible sea borders, with a substantial buffer between its territory and that of its adversary. While both North Korea and China are seen as adversaries by Japanese leaders, they do not rise to the level of severe territorial threats. Japan does possess an ally dedicated to its protection (the United States) and is in long-run geopolitical decline thanks to an aging population and vigorously rising powers in the region. The theory of nuclear opportunism therefore predicts that if Japan acquired nuclear weapons, it would use them to facilitate independence from the United States and steadfastness in responding to threats (the theory would also predict Japan using nuclear weapons to facilitate bolstering of junior allies, but Japan does not currently have any alliances in which it is the senior partner).

For South Korea, the more severe threat posed by North Korea's military capabilities results in the theory of nuclear opportunism making different predictions. Much as with the case of Pakistan or Israel, the theory of nuclear opportunism predicts that South Korea would not seek to use its nuclear weapons to facilitate independence from the United States. Rather, South Korea would be more inclined to see nuclear weapons as a tool for improving its position on the Korean peninsula, and to use nuclear weapons to facilitate both aggression and steadfastness against North Korea. South Korea would likely respond more vigorously to North Korean provocations and might be more tempted to engage in aggression against North Korea itself, judging that its nuclear arsenal would restrain North Korean retaliation.

The theory thus anticipates different challenges for US foreign policy if Japan or South Korea were to acquire independent nuclear weapons. In the South Korean case, restraining South Korean aggression or retaliation after North Korean provocations may become a key task of US foreign policy, and South Korean nuclear weapons would be expected to lead to a more volatile and violent Korean peninsula. Japan, on the other hand, may be less likely to use nuclear weapons to facilitate aggression, but may become a less consistent ally of the United States and more inclined to chart its own course in international politics. In both cases, therefore, the theory of nuclear opportunism provides clear reasons why US policymakers would be concerned about the possibility of proliferation to either Japan or South Korea.

Conclusion

Nuclear Revolution or Nuclear Revolutions?

The theory of nuclear opportunism offers an explanation for the way in which states think about and use nuclear weapons in international politics. Nuclear weapons are useful tools that allow a state to pursue a range of foreign policy goals, and states that acquire nuclear weapons use them in a variety of ways that reflect the differing political priorities and goals that different states have. These political priorities, in turn, reflect the different strategic circumstances that states find themselves in. The evidence from Britain, South Africa, and the United States, as well as the additional cases examined in chapter 5, largely supports the theory. This chapter summarizes the findings of the book and outlines implications both for our theoretical understanding of nuclear weapons and international politics and for policymakers.

Summary of the Findings

The small number of cases of nuclear acquisition means that there is inevitably uncertainty regarding the interpretation of individual cases and in the strength of the conclusions we can draw about the way in which nuclear weapons affect the foreign policies of the states that acquire them. This uncertainty is exacerbated by the extent to which statesmen (wisely) seek to maintain secrecy around their nuclear weapons and the strategic goals they hope to achieve with them. Nonetheless, the weight of the evidence examined here supports the theory of nuclear opportunism. The theory of nuclear opportunism performs well (though certainly not perfectly) across the cases, and performs better than the alternative explanations.

In the case of the United Kingdom, from the immediate aftermath of World War II, British elites viewed nuclear weapons as a solution to two fundamental political problems they faced: the problem of dependence on the United

States, and the problem of maintaining Britain's position in the world despite Britain facing long-run economic (and thus political) decline. Britain therefore found pursuing independence from the United States, bolstering its junior allies, and standing more firmly in the face of challenges to its position to be attractive, and Britain used nuclear weapons to facilitate those behaviors. After acquiring a deliverable nuclear capability in 1955, Britain was able to bolster its allies in Asia, the Middle East, and Europe, and responded to challenges to its position more steadfastly and independently of the preferences of the United States, despite simultaneously cutting back on its conventional forces over the same period. These outcomes are consistent with the predictions of nuclear opportunism for a state in Britain's position: not facing severe territorial threats or involved in a war but constrained by a senior ally and declining in power.

The way in which South African elites thought about and used their nuclear weapons was dramatically different from the way in which the British had done some twenty years earlier. South African elites viewed nuclear weapons as a partial solution to the constraints posed by fears of escalation in South Africa's conduct of the Border War in Angola. South African elites were deeply fearful of escalation and the potential for further Soviet involvement in the conflict, and saw nuclear weapons as a tool that allowed them to reduce those risks. As a result, after acquiring nuclear weapons, South African tolerance for escalation in the Border War increased and South Africa became more willing to act aggressively in the conflict, taking actions that South African elites had previously avoided due to the risk of escalation that they posed. South Africa did not use nuclear weapons to engage in the other foreign policy behaviors that nuclear weapons facilitate, an outcome largely consistent with the theory of nuclear opportunism for a state facing serious threats and involved in an ongoing war.

The United States offers the most complex case, and the one in which the precise predictions of the theory of nuclear opportunism are hardest to validate. In part this is because the enormously complex and changing international environment in the aftermath of World War II makes distinguishing between the different foreign policy behaviors in the typology more challenging than in the other two cases. Even in this case, however, the theory of nuclear opportunism outperforms the alternative explanations. Nuclear acquisition substantially affected US foreign policy, but did so differently during World War II and in its aftermath. As a state in the midst of a brutal war, the United States first used nuclear weapons to escalate the conflict and win the war against Japan. Within the typology advanced by this book, this is best characterized as aggression, although there are also ways in which US nuclear weapons facilitated compromise over the terms of Japanese surrender and independence from the Soviet Union in the final days of the war. In the aftermath of World War II, the United States did not face severe territorial threats and was rising in power. The United States placed nuclear weapons at the heart of its foreign policy in the immediate aftermath of World War II, using nuclear weapons to facilitate behaviors that combined expansion, aggression, and steadfastness, as well as bolstering its allies. Nuclear weapons allowed the United States to engage in a rapid conventional demobilization while pursuing an ambitious grand strategy: maintaining a forward posture, seeking to bolster existing allies and take on new ones, resisting and deterring Soviet encroachments, and going beyond a purely defensive model of containment in its dealings with the Soviet Union.

The theory thus receives validation, performing well in explaining these cases in absolute terms and relative to the alternative explanations. Chapter 5 also shows the theory's ability to shed light on the behavior of many (though not all) of the other states to have acquired nuclear weapons, and makes clear predictions for how potential future proliferators would behave if they were to acquire nuclear weapons. The empirical evidence validates the broader view of nuclear weapons envisaged by the theory of nuclear opportunism. Political and military elites have generally viewed nuclear weapons as tools that enable them to pursue and protect their preexisting political interests and ambitions. Nuclear weapons were employed pragmatically in the service of those political priorities.

Avenues for Future Research

The book opens a number of avenues for future research.

First, the argument made here is in many ways a simple one: states are viewed as unitary actors and only three binary variables (of which none incorporates features of the domestic politics of the state) are used to explain variation in outcomes. This is obviously a simplification of a much more complex reality. There may be ways to add additional explanatory power to the theory by adding additional complexity that future research could explore. For example, there may be ways to incorporate the role of individual leaders' ideas about nuclear weapons, a factor that—as discussed in chapter 5—clearly appears to be important in explaining the way in which Chinese leaders have thought about the utility of nuclear weapons.[1] Similarly, norms about the acceptability of nuclear use have changed dramatically over the nuclear era and may have influenced the effects that nuclear weapons have had in different eras.[2] Last, different domestic political arrangements may influence the effects that nuclear weapons have. For example, nuclear weapons may have different effects in cases where the military controls the state's nuclear weapons compared with states in which civilians retain control of nuclear weapons.[3]

Similarly, the theory ignores the possibility of strategic interaction, and particularly, the possibility that other states can take actions to reduce the benefits that states receive from acquiring nuclear weapons. As it stands, the theory is choice theoretic rather than game theoretic or strategic: according to the theory, states that acquire nuclear weapons make decisions about how to use nuclear weapons without considering the actions that other states may take.[4] As discussed in chapter 1, this is a justifiable simplification that should bias us against observing evidence of the effect of nuclear weapons (if other states can take actions to mitigate the effects that nuclear weapons have, we should be less likely to observe a change in foreign policy behavior at the point of nuclear acquisition). Nonetheless, it ignores a potentially important dynamic that future work could incorporate. In short, the theory described here provides a baseline that future research can add qualifications and nuance to in order to enhance its ability to explain the full range of variation we observe.

Second, there may be opportunities to generalize the argument made here. Do other military capabilities facilitate the same range of foreign policy behaviors as nuclear weapons? If not, what are the characteristics of military technologies that lead them to facilitate particular behaviors? Similarly, does the theory shed light on the way in which states respond to other endogenous increases (that is, increases that the state chooses to invest in) in their power and military capabilities? Both the typology and the theory may have broader applicability, and the extent to which the theory travels to other circumstances may have important insights for exactly what is special or unusual about nuclear weapons.

Finally, the research design that this study employed focused on the effects of nuclear weapons at the point of acquisition and offered only relatively brief evidence in each case to suggest that these effects have endured over time. This was justified given the lack of existing work on the question of how nuclear weapons affect state foreign policy, the research design advantages of focusing on the point of nuclear acquisition, and the fact that policymakers care particularly about the immediate effects of nuclear acquisition. Nonetheless, it represents an important opportunity for future research. It would be productive for future research to examine in more detail why and to what extent the effects of nuclear weapons do indeed endure over time, and what, if anything, can cause states to fundamentally reevaluate the way in which they use their nuclear weapons to support their foreign policy goals.

Implications for Scholars

The book offers a number of implications for scholars of international politics and nuclear weapons.

The argument made here offers a new way of thinking about nuclear weapons that is at odds with the dominant theory of the nuclear revolution, and thus contributes to a growing body of work challenging various aspects of the theory of the nuclear revolution.[5] While the theory of the nuclear revolution offers a powerful explanation for the absence of great power war since 1945, the political judgment within it about how states respond to the security provided by nuclear weapons appears flawed. The theory of the nuclear revolution is correct that nuclear weapons are a revolutionary capability in terms of the destructive power that they offer to states, and that they are therefore a powerful deterrent against aggression. However, the theory of the nuclear revolution errs in its political judgment about how states respond to those capabilities. Nuclear weapons do not cause states to worry less about their own security, do not reduce states' inclination to compete vigorously with each other, and do not tamp down states' ambitions in international politics. Instead, states use nuclear weapons in service of their preexisting political goals, and nuclear weapons are often useful in pursuit of those goals. Statesmen appear to view nuclear weapons in a political, pragmatic, and opportunistic manner: nuclear weapons can facilitate a range of foreign policy behaviors, and states seek to take advantage of this to pursue their political goals.

This vision of nuclear weapons is in some ways both more and less revolutionary than that implied by the theory of the nuclear revolution. It is less revolutionary in that it suggests nuclear weapons transform international politics or the preferences of states to a lesser degree than advocates of the theory of the nuclear revolution believe. Instead, nuclear weapons are incorporated into the practice of international politics and are used by states to pursue the political goals and aspirations that they found attractive before nuclear acquisition. Politics remains king, even in a nuclear-armed world. In other ways, however, the theory of nuclear opportunism views nuclear weapons as more revolutionary than the theory of the nuclear revolution. Specifically, the theory of nuclear opportunism views nuclear weapons as having much broader political utility than the theory of the nuclear revolution suggests. While the theory of the nuclear revolution views nuclear weapons as being primarily useful for deterring nuclear attack or resisting nuclear coercion, the theory of nuclear opportunism views nuclear weapons as facilitating a wide range of foreign policy goals that a range of states may find attractive. Nuclear weapons, in short, may transform a state's foreign policy in a more profound way than the theory of the nuclear revolution anticipates, but transform international politics less than the theory of the nuclear revolution expects.

Similarly, the book therefore offers a way for scholars to make sense of the heterogeneity in the way in which states have responded to nuclear acquisition. This heterogeneity has largely been missed or assumed away by the theory of the nuclear revolution, which argues that nuclear weapons should have a consistent effect across all states because of the technological characteristics of the weapons which make nuclear weapons easy to hide and protect, hard to defend against, and enormously destructive. However, because states occupy profoundly different positions in international politics and have profoundly different political priorities, the ways in which nuclear acquisition affects the foreign policies of acquiring states vary tremendously. There has not been one nuclear revolution. Instead, each nuclear-armed state has discovered the revolutionary capabilities that nuclear weapons offer and used them to pursue its own interests: each state, in short, has experienced its own nuclear revolution. The typology and theory offered here allow scholars to identify and understand the different effects that nuclear weapons have, and thus to make sense of the variety and nuance that we see in the historical record.[6]

The argument also has implications for other scholarly debates about nuclear weapons.

First, the book has implications for debates about the causes of proliferation. In particular, it suggests we should expand our assessment of the range of states that may find nuclear weapons attractive. For example, since the end of the Cold War, it has become increasingly common for scholars to think of nuclear weapons as "weapons of the weak" or "the great equalizer," implying that nuclear weapons are only useful for conventionally weak states seeking to deter the United States.[7] It is certainly true that conventionally weak states gain from the acquisition of nuclear weapons because of their limited conventional capabilities. But it is not just weak or "rogue" states that may find nuclear weapons attractive. Since the dawn of the nuclear age, powerful states have regularly sought and benefited from the acquisition of nuclear weapons. The typology and theory offered in this book shed light on why this is and why it may continue in the future. Nuclear weapons can facilitate foreign policy behaviors that conventionally powerful states are likely to find extremely attractive, such as expansion or the bolstering of allies. It should not, therefore, be surprising that states have sometimes seen nuclear weapons as "status symbols," or that powerful states have often sought to acquire them, or that conventionally powerful and nuclear-armed states today show little interest in relinquishing their nuclear arsenals. Nuclear weapons are not simply a relic of the Cold War, and many states today continue to find nuclear weapons useful for pursuing their goals in international politics.

However, if we expand our assessment of the states that may find nuclear acquisition attractive, the book also points to the reasons why few states have acquired nuclear weapons despite their utility. In particular, the book offers a theoretical foundation for scholarship that emphasizes the role of the United States in preventing proliferation to both allies and adversaries.[8] The argument here provides a theoretical justification for *why* the United States would place significant priority on the goal of nonproliferation. While the theory of the nuclear revolution suggests that proliferation should not be especially concerning to the United States,[9] the theory of nuclear opportunism recognizes that proliferation—whether to adversaries or to states with which the United States has alliances—has the potential to harm the interests of the United States. Indeed, it is US policymakers' recognition of the benefits that nuclear weapons offer to states that has led the United States to seek to prevent proliferation. Adversaries of the United States can use nuclear weapons in a variety of ways that would harm the interests of the United States: to facilitate aggression against the United States or its allies, to better resist challenges from the United States, or to bolster their own allies. Further, even allies of the United States can use nuclear weapons in a range of ways that are inimical to US interests: allies can use nuclear weapons to become more independent from the United States and thus harder for the United States to control, to engage in aggression, or to pursue other behaviors that may draw the United States into conflicts it would rather avoid. The argument here, therefore, provides a theoretical justification for the United States' relative consistency in pursuing nonproliferation, and the importance that nonproliferation has historically played within US grand strategy.

Second, the argument here in some way reinforces, but also challenges, the notion of the "stability-instability paradox." As traditionally conceived, the stability-instability paradox provides an addendum to the theory of the nuclear revolution. The paradox points out that the high levels of strategic stability created by mutual assured destruction may lead to reduced stability at lower levels: if escalation to nuclear war is unthinkable, it paradoxically becomes safer to engage in lower-level conflict.[10] In some ways, the argument here is consistent with the paradox: mutual assured destruction is not necessarily an impediment to lower-level conflict because states do not respond to nuclear weapons in the way the theory of the nuclear revolution expects. However, the logic is different from that which underpins the stability-instability paradox: states can compete at lower levels even in the shadow of nuclear weapons in the same way that they compete in a non-nuclear world, because nuclear weapons do not fundamentally change the nature of international politics. In an anarchic system in which states have differing and competing interests, conflict is always possible, even if nuclear weapons make such conflict deeply dangerous. The low-level conflict and crises that we see between nuclear-armed states, and that the stability-instability paradox identifies as an anomaly for the theory of the nuclear revolution, may simply be standard international politics between states competing for influence, territory, and security.

Third, the argument here offers a way to move beyond debates about whether nuclear weapons are "useful" to states in international crises, and the simple dichotomy between whether nuclear weapons are useful for compellence and whether they are useful solely for deterrence.[11] The argument offered here clearly views nuclear weapons as politically useful weapons, and thus is not consistent with arguments that view nuclear weapons as being of limited use to states beyond offering the ability to deter.[12] However, the theory also offers a more complex interpretation of the role nuclear weapons play in both the instigation and the resolution of crises than that offered by scholars who argue that nuclear weapons offer states clear advantages in crises.[13] By shifting the analytic focus to foreign policy, and demonstrating the different foreign policy behaviors that nuclear weapons can facilitate, the argument here shows the ways in which nuclear weapons may affect how crises occur and play out in complex ways. For example, nuclear weapons have may have encouraged Britain to instigate crises that it was not well equipped to prevail in. Such a position would be hard to capture in a simple debate over whether nuclear weapons are helpful in crises.

Similarly, the argument here allows analysts to make sense of episodes that contain elements of both deterrence and compellence. For example, the way in which nuclear weapons facilitated US behavior in the postwar period is hard to capture within the compellence-deterrence dichotomy. Was the US decision to extend nuclear deterrence to states in Europe, Asia, and Australasia an effort to deter attacks against these allies? An effort to compel adversaries of these states to back down? An effort to deter allies from acquiring their own nuclear weapons? An effort to compel others to accept US dominance of the postwar world order? By focusing on the ways in which nuclear weapons facilitate particular behaviors, rather than compellence or deterrence, the argument here allows for a more nuanced assessment of the ways in which states use nuclear weapons to achieve their goals in international politics.

Fourth, the analysis demonstrates the importance of looking beyond the possession of nuclear weapons in understanding their political effects. Instead, it is the state's nuclear posture that determines the technological threshold at which nuclear weapons begin to affect state calculations about foreign policy. For example, although Britain first tested a nuclear weapon in 1952, it was only with the acquisition of a deliverable capability in 1955 that nuclear weapons began to influence British foreign policy. Despite this, political scientists tend to emphasize a country's first nuclear test as indicating the point at which the effects of nuclear weapons should be observed.[14] This approach may generate misleading inferences, because nuclear weapons may not necessarily begin to influence a state's foreign policy at the point at which a country first tests a device.

Implications for Policymakers

The argument also has implications for policymakers thinking about nuclear proliferation and disarmament.

First, substantial traction on the effects of nuclear weapons can be gained by using a more discriminating conceptual language. "Emboldenment" is a convenient catch-all term, but it conflates conceptually distinct behaviors and misses other effects that nuclear weapons may have. Policymakers through-out the nuclear age have often expressed broad and generic concerns about the emboldening effects of nuclear weapons, but have often failed to think in detail about the precise behaviors that nuclear weapons may facilitate.[15] These distinctions are important because not all emboldening effects are equally concerning to policymakers. Both aggression and steadfastness may be considered emboldening effects, but, for example, a nuclear-armed Iran that displays greater steadfastness is likely less concerning to US policy-makers than a nuclear-armed Iran that pursues aggression. The typology offered here provides policymakers with a conceptual language with which to more precisely specify the concerns associated with particular potential proliferants.

Second, the theory offers policymakers a tool with which to make an ini-tial assessment of the relative likelihood of different outcomes that may oc-cur if particular states acquire nuclear weapons. The theory suggests, for example, that different US allies might respond to nuclear acquisition in different ways that would have different implications for US foreign policy. The theory suggests, for example, that the United States should be more wor-ried by South Korea acquiring nuclear weapons than by Japan doing so. Similarly, the theory suggests that Iranian nuclear acquisition is more likely to lead to certain behaviors (such as bolstering of allies) than others (such as aggression). This is not to suggest that policymakers should not prepare for the possibility of Iranian aggression in the aftermath of nuclear acquisition—policymakers correctly prepare for a wide range of unlikely contingencies. Nonetheless, the theory has the potential to guide policymakers as they as-sess which outcomes are more likely, and help policymakers as they decide how to dedicate finite military and political resources to different contingen-cies. In this way, the theory can potentially help to refine, adjust, or provide a more solid intellectual foundation for policymakers' prior beliefs about the likelihood of different outcomes in a given case of proliferation.

Finally, the argument suggests that making substantial progress toward nuclear disarmament is likely to be difficult, and sheds light on the limited progress that the nuclear-armed states have made toward that goal. If nu-clear weapons were merely vestiges of the Cold War, or if states simply wanted to possess nuclear weapons out of a misplaced belief that nuclear weapons confer great power status, then nuclear abolition would seem an achievable task: statesmen would simply need to be educated about the dis-utility of nuclear weapons. This book suggests, by contrast, that states that acquire nuclear weapons view them as useful for achieving foreign policy goals that they deem important and do in fact use nuclear weapons to fa-cilitate a wide range of foreign policy behaviors. If so, nuclear-armed states will generally be less inclined to relinquish an important source of political power. Just as states do not typically give up other tools with which they can achieve their foreign policy goals—their militaries, intelligence services, diplomatic corps, and so on—nuclear-armed states will also be generally disinclined to give up their nuclear weapons. The argument of this book is that nuclear weapons facilitate foreign policy behaviors that a range of states find attractive, and help states achieve foreign policy goals that they value. If so, nuclear weapons are likely here to stay. Managing the risks that they pose will continue to be a central challenge for policymakers for some time to come.

Notes

Acknowledgments

1. Mark S. Bell, "Beyond Emboldenment: How Acquiring Nuclear Weapons Can Change Foreign Policy," *International Security* 40, no. 1 (2015): 87–119; Mark S. Bell, "Nuclear Opportunism: A Theory of How States Use Nuclear Weapons in International Politics," *Journal of Strategic Studies* 42, no. 1 (2019): 3–28; Noel Anderson and Mark S. Bell, "The Limits of Regional Power: South Africa's Security Strategy, 1975–1989," *Journal of Strategic Studies*, forthcoming.

Introduction

1. "Likelihood and Consequences of a Proliferation of Nuclear Weapons Systems (National Intelligence Estimate 4–63)," June 28, 1963, National Security Archive (NSA) Electronic Briefing Book 155, document 8.

2. Matthew Kroenig, *A Time to Attack: The Looming Iranian Nuclear Threat* (New York: Palgrave Macmillan, 2014), 133–134.

3. Barry R. Posen, *A Nuclear-Armed Iran: A Difficult but Not Impossible Policy Problem* (New York: Century Foundation, 2006), 12–13.

4. For example, S. Paul Kapur, *Dangerous Deterrent: Nuclear Weapons Proliferation and Conflict in South Asia* (Stanford, CA: Stanford University Press, 2007); Vipin Narang, "Posturing for Peace? Pakistan's Nuclear Postures and South Asian Stability," *International Security* 34, no. 3 (2009–2010): 38–78.

5. Important works articulating or reinforcing the theory of the nuclear revolution include Bernard Brodie, ed., *The Absolute Weapon: Atomic Power and World Order* (New York: Harcourt Brace, 1946); Bernard Brodie, *Strategy in the Missile Age* (Princeton, NJ: Princeton University Press, 1959); Bernard Brodie, "The Development of Nuclear Strategy," *International Security* 2, no. 4 (1978): 65–83; Robert Jervis, "Why Nuclear Superiority Doesn't Matter," *Political Science Quarterly* 94, no. 4 (1979): 617–633; Kenneth N. Waltz, "The Spread of Nuclear Weapons: More May Be Better," *Adelphi Papers* 21, no. 171 (1981): 1–32; Shai Feldman, *Israeli Nuclear Deterrence: A Strategy for the 1980s* (New York: Columbia University Press, 1982); Charles L. Glaser, "Why Even Good Defenses May Be Bad," *International Security* 9, no. 2 (1984): 92–123; Robert Jervis, *The Meaning of the Nuclear Revolution: Statecraft and the Prospects of Armageddon* (Ithaca, NY: Cornell

175

University Press, 1989); Charles L. Glaser, "Why Do Strategists Disagree about the Requirements of Strategic Nuclear Deterrence?," in *Nuclear Arguments: Understanding the Strategic Nuclear Arms and Arms Control Debates*, ed. Lynn Eden and Steven E. Miller (Ithaca, NY: Cornell University Press, 1989): 109–171; Charles L. Glaser, *Analyzing Strategic Nuclear Policy* (Princeton, NJ: Princeton University Press, 1990); Kenneth N. Waltz, "Nuclear Myths and Political Realities," *American Political Science Review* 84, no. 3 (1990): 730–745; Stephen Van Evera, *Causes of War: Power and the Roots of Conflict* (Ithaca, NY: Cornell University Press, 1999); Charles L. Glaser and Steve Fetter, "National Missile Defense and the Future of U.S. Nuclear Weapons Policy," *International Security* 26, no. 1 (2001): 40–92.

6. For example, Brodie, *Absolute Weapon*, 24; Waltz, "Nuclear Myths and Political Realities," 732.

7. Van Evera, *Causes of War*, 246.

8. Charles L. Glaser, "When Are Arms Races Dangerous? Rational versus Suboptimal Arming," *International Security* 28, no. 4 (2004): 75.

9. In the language of international relations theory, the theory of the nuclear revolution builds on defensive realist assumptions. For broader theoretical arguments by proponents of the theory of the nuclear revolution who argue that security is the first goal of states, see Robert Jervis, "Cooperation under the Security Dilemma," *World Politics* 30, no. 2 (1978): 167–214; Kenneth N. Waltz, *Theory of International Politics* (Long Grove, IL: Waveland Press, 1979); Van Evera, *Causes of War*; Charles L. Glaser, *Rational Theory of International Politics: The Logic of Competition and Cooperation* (Princeton, NJ: Princeton University Press, 2010).

10. Feldman, *Israeli Nuclear Deterrence*, 45.

11. Barry R. Posen and Stephen Van Evera, "Defense Policy and the Reagan Administration: Departure from Containment," *International Security* 8, no. 1 (1983): 33; Van Evera, *Causes of War*, 245.

12. Jervis, *Meaning of the Nuclear Revolution*, 35–36; Kenneth N. Waltz, "The Emerging Structure of International Politics," *International Security* 18, no. 2 (1993): 73.

13. Glaser, *Analyzing Strategic Nuclear Policy*, 361.

14. Waltz, "Nuclear Myths and Political Realities," 739.

15. Jervis, *Meaning of the Nuclear Revolution*, 45.

16. Jervis, *Meaning of the Nuclear Revolution*, 42; Waltz, "Emerging Structure of International Politics," 73.

17. Van Evera, *Causes of War*, 244.

18. Scott D. Sagan and Kenneth N. Waltz, *The Spread of Nuclear Weapons: A Debate Renewed* (New York: W. W. Norton, 2003), 39.

19. Robert Jervis, *The Illogic of American Nuclear Strategy* (Ithaca, NY: Cornell University Press, 1984), 13, 147; Charles L. Glaser and Steve Fetter, "Should the United States Reject MAD? Damage Limitation and U.S. Nuclear Strategy toward China," *International Security* 41, no. 1 (2016): 50.

20. S. Paul Kapur, "India and Pakistan's Unstable Peace: Why Nuclear South Asia Is Not Like Cold War Europe," *International Security* 30, no. 2 (2005): 127–152; Kapur, *Dangerous Deterrent*; S. Paul Kapur, "Ten Years of Instability in a Nuclear South Asia," *International Security* 33, no. 2 (2008): 71–94. For other accounts of the circumstances in which nuclear acquisition leads to aggression, see T. Negeen Pegahi, "Dangerous Deterrent? Assessing the Risk That Nuclear Acquisition Will Embolden Weak States" (PhD diss., University of Chicago, 2013); Michael D. Cohen, *When Proliferation Causes Peace: The Psychology of Nuclear Crises* (Washington, DC: Georgetown University Press, 2017); Christopher J. Watterson, "Armed and Insecure: Explaining Foreign Policy Aggression after Nuclear Weapons Acquisition" (PhD diss., University of Sydney, 2017).

21. This label mirrors Keir Lieber's theory of "technological opportunism," which similarly emphasizes the primacy of politics in conditioning the effects of technologies on international politics. Keir A. Lieber, *War and the Engineers: The Primacy of Politics over Technology* (Ithaca, NY: Cornell University Press, 2005).

1. Nuclear Opportunism

1. This definition of grand strategy comes from Barry R. Posen, *The Sources of Military Doctrine: France, Britain, and Germany between the World Wars* (Ithaca, NY: Cornell University Press, 1984), 7. See also Hal Brands, *What Good Is Grand Strategy? Power and Purpose in American Statecraft from Harry S. Truman to George W. Bush* (Ithaca, NY: Cornell University Press, 2014), 1.

2. Thomas C. Schelling, *Arms and Influence* (New Haven, CT: Yale University Press, 1966), 19–20.

3. Thomas C. Schelling, *The Strategy of Conflict* (Cambridge, MA: Harvard University Press, 1960), chap. 8.

4. For example, Vipin Narang argues that a "catalytic" nuclear posture is particularly well suited to encouraging interventions by friendly third parties. Vipin Narang, *Nuclear Strategy in the Modern Era: Regional Powers and International Conflict* (Princeton, NJ: Princeton University Press, 2014).

5. For analyses of how institutional and bureaucratic dynamics affect whether states acquire nuclear weapons, see James J. Walsh, "Bombs Unbuilt: Power, Ideas and Institutions in International Politics" (PhD diss., Massachusetts Institute of Technology, 2001); Jacques E. C. Hymans, "Veto Players, Nuclear Energy, and Nonproliferation: Domestic Institutional Barriers to a Japanese Bomb," *International Security* 36, no. 2 (2011): 154–189; Jacques E. C. Hymans, *Achieving Nuclear Ambitions: Scientists, Politicians, and Proliferation* (New York: Cambridge University Press, 2012).

6. For example, Timothy D. Hoyt, "Kargil: The Nuclear Dimension," in *Asymmetric Warfare in South Asia: The Causes and Consequences of the Kargil Conflict*, ed. Peter R. Lavoy (New York: Cambridge University Press, 2009), 153.

7. For example, Jacques E. C. Hymans, *The Psychology of Nuclear Proliferation: Identity, Emotions and Foreign Policy* (Cambridge: Cambridge University Press, 2006).

8. Memo on Atomic Research from Lord Cherwell to Mr. Churchill, August 6, 1950, Churchill Archives, Cambridge, United Kingdom (CHUR) 2/28/45–51.

9. On selection effects in international relations, see, for example, James Fearon, "Selection Effects and Deterrence," *International Interactions* 28, no. 1 (2002): 5–29.

10. The most obvious would be the presence of a "nuclear taboo," which should make nuclear use less credible and thus lead nuclear weapons to have a limited effect on a state's foreign policy. See Nina Tannenwald, *The Nuclear Taboo: The United States and the Non-use of Nuclear Weapons since 1945* (Cambridge: Cambridge University Press, 2008).

11. Hymans, *Psychology of Nuclear Proliferation*, 2. For a similar argument that it is a highly unusual group of states that ultimately acquire nuclear weapons, see Maria Rost Rublee, *Nonproliferation Norms: Why States Choose Nuclear Restraint* (Athens: University of Georgia Press, 2009).

12. It is worth clarifying that the typology identifies *behaviors* rather than the *goals* that a state may be aiming to achieve by engaging in the behavior. This is important because foreign policy behaviors are far easier to observe than the goals or motivations underlying them. For example, the typology avoids the need for difficult assessments of whether a state is ultimately security seeking or revisionist in order to identify whether it is engaging in aggression. The typology distinguishes between different behaviors and is agnostic about the goals that states may ultimately have in pursuing those behaviors. Nonetheless, this is worth emphasizing because the language of the typology has the potential to cause confusion; for example, a state may engage in aggression but nonetheless ultimately have status quo preferences (that is, the state may not have what might be called "aggressive" preferences or goals). Equally, a state may engage in expansion or bolstering for "aggressive" reasons but not engage in the behavior that I label as "aggression."

13. S. Paul Kapur, *Dangerous Deterrent: Nuclear Weapons Proliferation and Conflict in South Asia* (Stanford, CA: Stanford University Press, 2007); Vipin Narang, "Posturing for Peace? Pakistan's Nuclear Postures and South Asian Stability," *International Security* 34, no. 3 (2009–2010): 38–78;

C. Christine Fair, *Fighting to the End: The Pakistan Army's Way of War* (Oxford: Oxford University Press, 2014).

14. Fair, *Fighting to the End*, 203.

15. Hal Brands and David Palkki, "Saddam, Israel, and the Bomb: Nuclear Alarmism Justified?," *International Security* 36, no. 1 (2011): 133–166.

16. For example, Jack Snyder, *Myths of Empire: Domestic Politics and International Ambition* (Ithaca, NY: Cornell University Press, 1991), 1.

17. While it may sometimes be challenging to empirically distinguish expansion from aggression, this does not affect the importance of the conceptual distinction between the two behaviors.

18. The role of nuclear weapons in facilitating postwar US grand strategy is discussed in detail in chapter 4.

19. David Holloway, *Stalin and the Bomb: The Soviet Union and Atomic Energy, 1939–1956* (New Haven, CT: Yale University Press, 1996), 276.

20. Mark S. Bell and Nicholas L. Miller, "Questioning the Effect of Nuclear Weapons on Conflict," *Journal of Conflict Resolution* 59, no. 1 (2015): 74–92.

21. On the distinction between internal and external forms of balancing, see Kenneth N. Waltz, *Theory of International Politics* (Long Grove, IL: Waveland Press, 1979), 168. While I use the language of "alliance," this theoretical mechanism is not dependent on the alliance being formal or codified in any way: a state may implicitly provide for the security of another state, and the value of that security may be changed by nuclear acquisition, even if the relationship is not codified in an alliance.

22. This is not to say that the alliance becomes of no value to the state; indeed, it may still be extremely valuable for a range of reasons. It is just to say that its value is reduced upon nuclear acquisition.

23. Philip H. Gordon, "Charles de Gaulle and the Nuclear Revolution," in *Cold War Statesmen Confront the Bomb: Nuclear Diplomacy since 1945*, ed. John Lewis Gaddis (Oxford: Oxford University Press, 1999), 234; Wilfrid L. Kohl, *French Nuclear Diplomacy* (Princeton, NJ: Princeton University Press, 1971).

24. Dick K. Nanto and Mark E. Manyin, "China–North Korea Relations," *North Korean Review* 7, no. 2 (2011): 97; Jonathan D. Pollack, "China's North Korea Conundrum: How to Balance a Three Legged Stool," *Yale Global Online*, 2009, https://yaleglobal.yale.edu/content/chinas-north-korea-conundrum-how-balance-three-legged-stool; Jonathan D. Pollack, *No Exit: North Korea, Nuclear Weapons, and International Security* (London: International Institute for Strategic Studies, 2011), 105.

25. As in the discussion of independence, the alliance does not need to be formalized or codified. Nuclear weapons can facilitate the bolstering of another state even if that state is not a formal ally.

26. Matthew Kroenig, *Exporting the Bomb: Technology Transfer and the Spread of Nuclear Weapons* (Ithaca, NY: Cornell University Press, 2010).

27. Feroz Hassan Khan, *Eating Grass: The Making of the Pakistani Bomb* (Stanford, CA: Stanford University Press, 2012), 188.

28. Kroenig, *Exporting the Bomb*.

29. Khan, *Eating Grass*, 207. See also Fair, *Fighting to the End*, 221.

30. See, for example, Kenneth A. Oye, "Explaining the End of the Cold War: Morphological and Behavioral Adaptations to the Nuclear Peace," in *International Relations Theory and the End of the Cold War*, ed. Richard Ned Lebow and Thomas Risse-Kappen (Cambridge: Cambridge University Press, 1995), 78.

31. Shai Feldman, *Israeli Nuclear Deterrence: A Strategy for the 1980s* (New York: Columbia University Press, 1982).

32. For similarly structured theories, see Narang, *Nuclear Strategy in the Modern Era*; Vipin Narang, "Strategies of Nuclear Proliferation: How States Pursue the Bomb," *International Security* 41, no. 3 (2017): 110–150.

33. The theory thus leaves aside a range of factors, including international norms, domestic political institutions, and features of individual leaders. This is not to suggest that such factors

are of no importance, just that any theory is necessarily a simplification of a more complex reality.

34. The theory therefore predicts that states facing severe territorial threats or involved in an ongoing war are likely to use nuclear weapons to facilitate both aggression and steadfastness. That is to say, it anticipates that states would seek to use nuclear weapons *both* to stand firmer when challenged *and* to find opportunities to revise the status quo more attractively in their favor. It does not, however, indicate which is likely to be the more obvious or dramatic effect: the precise balance between aggression and steadfastness that should be observed will likely depend on a range of factors, such as the conventional balance of power, revisionism, or geographic proximity.

35. Stephen M. Walt, *The Origins of Alliances* (Ithaca, NY: Cornell University Press, 1987), 21–26; Narang, *Nuclear Strategy in the Modern Era*.

36. Narang, *Nuclear Strategy in the Modern Era*, 44.

37. This is another difference between the theory of nuclear opportunism and the theory of the nuclear revolution. While the theory of the nuclear revolution is about how pairs of nuclear-armed states should behave toward each other, the theory of nuclear opportunism aims to make predictions about how nuclear-armed states behave toward nuclear and nonnuclear states.

38. Avery Goldstein, *Deterrence and Security in the 21st Century: China, Britain, France, and the Enduring Legacy of the Nuclear Revolution* (Stanford, CA: Stanford University Press, 2000), 21.

39. John J. Mearsheimer, *The Tragedy of Great Power Politics* (New York: W. W. Norton, 2001), 31.

40. Goldstein, *Deterrence and Security in the 21st Century*, 25–26.

41. Mancur Olson and Richard Zeckhauser, "An Economic Theory of Alliances," *Review of Economics and Statistics* 48, no. 3 (1966): 266–279.

42. Fareed Zakaria, *From Wealth to Power: The Unusual Origins of America's World Role* (Princeton, NJ: Princeton University Press, 1998), 38; Robert Jervis, "Do Leaders Matter and How Would We Know?," *Security Studies* 22, no. 2 (2013): 176.

43. Walt, *Origins of Alliances*.

44. This prediction only applies to the acquiring state's relationships with its junior allies. As previously discussed, independence is still incentivized for the acquiring state's relationships with its senior allies. Even for declining states, senior allies can be a constraint on their foreign policy, and nuclear acquisition thus makes independence from the senior ally politically attractive.

45. Both of these measures are regularly used in quantitative studies of international politics to assess changing power.

46. On potential differences between perceptions and reality of power trajectories, see William C. Wohlforth, "The Perception of Power: Russia in the Pre-1914 Balance," *World Politics* 39, no. 3 (1987): 353–381. However, in the case of the states that have acquired nuclear weapons, the two approaches generally yield similar conclusions at the point at which the state acquired nuclear weapons.

47. For example, Joseph S. Nye, "Nuclear Learning and US-Soviet Security Regimes," *International Organization* 41, no. 3 (1987): 371–402; Michael Horowitz, "The Spread of Nuclear Weapons and International Conflict: Does Experience Matter?," *Journal of Conflict Resolution* 53, no. 2 (2009): 234–257; Cohen, *When Proliferation Causes Peace*.

48. Posen, *Sources of Military Doctrine*.

49. For example, Lynn Eden, *Whole World on Fire: Organizations, Knowledge, and Nuclear Weapons Devastation* (Ithaca, NY: Cornell University Press, 2004). For a similar argument about path dependence in a different military domain, see Austin Long, *The Soul of Armies: Counterinsurgency Doctrine and Military Culture in the US and UK* (Ithaca, NY: Cornell University Press, 2016).

50. Ronald R. Krebs, "How Dominant Narratives Rise and Fall: Military Conflict, Politics, and the Cold War Consensus," *International Organization* 69, no. 4 (2015): 809–845.

51. To take an analogy, if an individual buys a lawnmower because he or she wants the grass to be shorter, and then uses the lawnmower to facilitate shorter grass, the lawnmower is still having an effect on grass length. And, indeed, assessing how grass length changes after the

individual acquires a lawnmower provides a way to assess the effect of the lawnmower, even if the desire for shorter grass motivated the lawnmower purchase.

52. For overviews of the literature on the causes of proliferation, see Scott D. Sagan, "The Causes of Nuclear Weapons Proliferation," *Annual Review of Political Science* 14 (2011): 225–244; Mark S. Bell, "Examining Explanations for Nuclear Proliferation," *International Studies Quarterly* 60, no. 3 (2016): 520–529.

53. Robert Jervis, *The Meaning of the Nuclear Revolution: Statecraft and the Prospects of Armageddon* (Ithaca, NY: Cornell University Press, 1989), 3. As discussed above, this is also why the theory does not make predictions about which states will seek to acquire nuclear weapons: the theory does not make any claims about which states will find that the benefits that nuclear weapons offer outweigh the costs associated with them.

54. M. Taylor Fravel and Evan S. Medeiros, "China's Search for Assured Retaliation: The Evolution of Chinese Nuclear Strategy and Force Structure," *International Security* 35, no. 2 (2010): 48–87.

55. Gary King, Robert O. Keohane, and Sidney Verba, *Designing Social Inquiry: Scientific Inference in Qualitative Research* (Princeton, NJ: Princeton University Press, 1994), 118–122.

56. Kapur, *Dangerous Deterrent*.

57. This approach therefore allows us to rule out a range of alternative explanations through research design rather than through modeling assumptions, as most large-*n* work typically does. For more on the difference between design-based and model-based approaches, see Donald B. Rubin, "For Objective Causal Inference, Design Trumps Analysis," *Annals of Applied Statistics* 2, no. 3 (2008): 808–840. This approach is also similar to the interrupted time series analysis originally proposed by Donald T. Campbell and Julian C. Stanley, *Experimental and Quasi-Experimental Designs for Research* (Boston: Houghton Mifflin, 1966). This approach is of particular use where (a) the outcome occurs over time, (b) the treatment occurs at a specific point in time, and (c) a small number of units receive the treatment, all of which apply to analyzing the effects of nuclear acquisition on foreign policy.

58. On the perils of using datasets and variables that are not "tightly coupled" with the precise theoretical questions being tested, see Alexander H. Montgomery and Scott D. Sagan, "The Perils of Predicting Proliferation," *Journal of Conflict Resolution* 53, no. 2 (2009): 302–328.

59. The extent to which this is possible is debatable. For example, India has consistently sought to undermine the strategic benefits that Pakistan gains from its nuclear weapons, but it is not clear that these efforts have reduced Pakistan's ability to aggress against India and use nuclear weapons to deter retaliation. See Walter C. Ladwig III, "A Cold Start for Hot Wars? The Indian Army's New Limited War Doctrine," *International Security* 32, no. 3 (2008): 158–190; Shashank Joshi, "India's Military Instrument: A Doctrine Stillborn," *Journal of Strategic Studies* 36, no. 4 (2013): 512–540; Christopher Clary and Vipin Narang, "India's Counterforce Temptations: Strategic Dilemmas, Doctrine, and Capabilities," *International Security* 43, no. 3 (2019): 7–52.

60. Tristan A. Volpe, "Atomic Leverage: Compellence with Nuclear Latency," *Security Studies* 26, no. 3 (2017): 517–544.

61. On reactive proliferation, see Nicholas L. Miller, "Nuclear Dominoes: A Self-Defeating Prophecy?," *Security Studies* 23, no. 1 (2014): 33–73.

62. Aaron Rapport, "Hard Thinking about Hard and Easy Cases in Security Studies," *Security Studies* 24, no. 3 (2015): 431–465.

63. There are also important challenges associated with the case of the United States, which I discuss in detail in chapter 4.

64. Narang, *Nuclear Strategy in the Modern Era*.

65. Narang, *Nuclear Strategy in the Modern Era*, chap. 8.

66. Feldman, *Israeli Nuclear Deterrence*.

67. Walt, *Origins of Alliances*.

68. Kapur, *Dangerous Deterrent*.

2. Independence and Status

1. Initially, British targeting was focused on counterforce operations aimed at Soviet air bases from which nuclear attacks against the United Kingdom would be launched, but this shifted over time as nuclear weapons became more powerful and the doctrine of massive retaliation increasingly prioritized countervalue targeting of Soviet cities. See Matthew Jones, *The Official History of the UK Strategic Nuclear Deterrent*, vol. 1, *From the V-Bomber Era to the Arrival of Polaris, 1945–1964* (Abingdon: Routledge, 2017), 34–35.

2. A. J. R. Groom, *British Thinking about Nuclear Weapons* (London: Pinter, 1974), 36.

3. Jones, *Official History of the UK Strategic Nuclear Deterrent*, 1:25.

4. Jones, *Official History of the UK Strategic Nuclear Deterrent*, 1:9.

5. Winston Churchill, "Note on Tube Alloys," December 12, 1954, Churchill Archives, Cambridge, United Kingdom (CHUR) 2/217/15 (emphasis added).

6. Anthony Eden, *Full Circle: The Memoirs of Sir Anthony Eden* (London: Cassell, 1960), 414 (emphasis added).

7. John Slessor, *Strategy for the West* (New York: William Morrow, 1954), 114.

8. "The RAF Strategic Nuclear Deterrent Forces: Their Origins, Roles and Deployment 1946–1969," 1991, United Kingdom National Archives, Kew, United Kingdom (UKNA) AIR 41/87, 41–42, 62; Christopher J. Bartlett, *The Long Retreat: A Short History of British Defence Policy, 1945–70* (Basingstoke: Macmillan, 1972), 99; Robert S. Norris, Andrew S. Burrows, and Richard W. Fieldhouse, *Nuclear Weapons Databook*, vol. 5, *British, French, and Chinese Nuclear Weapons* (Boulder, CO: Westview Press, 1994), chaps. 2–3; John Baylis and Kristan Stoddart, *The British Nuclear Experience: The Role of Beliefs, Culture, and Identity* (Oxford: Oxford University Press, 2015), 62; Jones, *Official History of the UK Strategic Nuclear Deterrent*, 1:25.

9. "The RAF Strategic Nuclear Deterrent Forces," 1991, UKNA AIR 41/87, 64, 68, 100–101; George C. Peden, *Arms, Economics and British Strategy: From Dreadnoughts to Hydrogen Bombs* (Cambridge: Cambridge University Press, 2007), 238.

10. "Command Directive to Air Marshal Sir George H. Mills," May 31, 1955, UKNA AIR 2/15917.

11. For a 1955 discussion of the capabilities of the different V-bombers, see "The Size of the V-Bomber Force," March 23, 1955, UKNA DEFE 11/101. See also Andrew Pierre, *Nuclear Politics: The British Experience with an Independent Strategic Force, 1939–1970* (Oxford: Oxford University Press, 1972), 155; Groom, *British Thinking about Nuclear Weapons*, 122; William P. Snyder, *The Politics of British Defense Policy, 1945–1962* (Columbus: Ohio State University Press, 1964), 26; Peden, *Arms, Economics and British Strategy*, 238; Baylis and Stoddart, *British Nuclear Experience*, 62.

12. "The RAF Strategic Nuclear Deterrent Forces," UKNA AIR 41/87, 98.

13. Sebastian Rosato, *Europe United: Power Politics and the Making of the European Community* (Ithaca, NY: Cornell University Press, 2011), 83–87.

14. John Darwin, *The Empire Project: The Rise and Fall of the British World-System, 1830–1970* (Cambridge: Cambridge University Press, 2009), 574.

15. Tore T. Petersen, *The Middle East between the Great Powers: Anglo-American Conflict and Cooperation, 1952–7* (Basingstoke: Macmillan Press, 2000), xi.

16. John Dumbrell, *A Special Relationship: Anglo-American Relations in the Cold War and After* (Basingstoke: Macmillan Press, 2001), 6.

17. John Baylis, *Anglo-American Relations since 1939: The Enduring Alliance* (Manchester: Manchester University Press, 1997), 18.

18. Baylis, *Anglo-American Relations since 1939*, 38–39.

19. For a thorough analysis of Britain's power trajectory in the twentieth century, see Joshua R. Itzkowitz Shifrinson, *Rising Titans, Falling Giants: How Great Powers Exploit Power Shifts* (Ithaca, NY: Cornell University Press, 2018), chap. 2.

20. Pierre, *Nuclear Politics*, 69; Peden, *Arms, Economics and British Strategy*, 245–249.

21. Anthony Adamthwaite, "Britain and the World, 1945–9: The View from the Foreign Office," *International Affairs* 61, no. 2 (1985): 231; Paul C. Avey, "Confronting Soviet Power: U.S. Policy during the Early Cold War," *International Security* 36, no. 4 (2012): 162–163.

22. Itzkowitz Shifrinson, *Rising Titans, Falling Giants*, 44.

23. Adamthwaite, "Britain and the World, 1945–9," 231.

24. Quoted in Avey, "Confronting Soviet Power," 163.

25. Throughout this book I use version 4.0 of the National Material Capabilities Dataset, released in 2010. The original data is described in David J. Singer, "Reconstructing the Correlates of War Dataset on Material Capabilities of States, 1816–1985," *International Interactions* 14, no. 2 (1988): 115–132.

26. "The Size of the V-Bomber Force," March 23, 1955, UKNA DEFE 11/101.

27. Avery Goldstein, *Deterrence and Security in the 21st Century: China, Britain, France, and the Enduring Legacy of the Nuclear Revolution* (Stanford, CA: Stanford University Press, 2000), 21.

28. Memorandum for the Secretary of State from R. G. Arneson, February 3, 1949, Truman Presidential Library, Independence, Missouri (TRUM), Truman Papers, National Security Council File, box 12, File on Atomic Energy Policy vis-a-vis the United Kingdom and Canada, 1943–1949.

29. Memorandum on the Properties of a Radioactive Superbomb, March 1940, UKNA AB 1/210.

30. "Report by M.A.U.D. Committee on the Use of Uranium for a Bomb," March 1941, UKNA CAB 104/227. On the impact of the MAUD Committee, see Margaret Gowing, *Britain and Atomic Energy, 1939–1945* (London: Macmillan, 1964), chap. 2.

31. Roosevelt to Churchill, October 11, 1941, UKNA PREM 3/139/8A.

32. Pierre, *Nuclear Politics*, 27–29; Gowing, *Britain and Atomic Energy, 1939–1945*, 123; Graham Farmelo, *Churchill's Bomb: A Hidden History of Science, War and Politics* (London: Faber & Faber, 2013), 203.

33. Pierre, *Nuclear Politics*, 27, 29.

34. Lindemann (Lord Cherwell) to Churchill, August 27, 1941, UKNA CAB 126/330.

35. Churchill to Hastings Ismay, August 30, 1941, UKNA PREM 3/139/8A.

36. Gowing, *Britain and Atomic Energy, 1939–1945*, 128.

37. Quoted in Pierre, *Nuclear Politics*, 33.

38. Farmelo, *Churchill's Bomb*, 241; Jones, *Official History of the UK Strategic Nuclear Deterrent*, 1:1.

39. Quoted in Martin J. Sherwin, "The Atomic Bomb and the Origins of the Cold War: U.S. Atomic-Energy Policy and Diplomacy, 1941–45," *American Historical Review* 78, no. 4 (1973): 949.

40. Quoted in Roger Ruston, *A Say in the End of the World: Morals and British Nuclear Weapons Policy, 1941–1987* (Oxford: Oxford University Press, 1989), 85.

41. Pierre, *Nuclear Politics*, 40; Groom, *British Thinking about Nuclear Weapons*, 8; Wilson D. Miscamble, *The Most Controversial Decision: Truman, the Atomic Bombs, and the Defeat of Japan* (Cambridge: Cambridge University Press, 2011), 11.

42. Quoted in Richard N. Rosecrance, *Defence of the Realm: British Strategy in the Nuclear Epoch* (New York: Columbia University Press, 1968), 40.

43. Thomas J. Christensen, *Useful Adversaries: Grand Strategy, Domestic Mobilization, and Sino-American Conflict, 1947–1958* (Princeton, NJ: Princeton University Press, 1996), 39; Goldstein, *Deterrence and Security in the 21st Century*, 142; Margaret Gowing and Laura Arnold, *Independence and Deterrence: Britain and Atomic Energy, 1945–1952*, vol. 1, *Policy Making* (London: Macmillan, 1974), 93–94.

44. Aide-Memoire of Conversation between Roosevelt and Churchill, September 19, 1944, in *Foreign Relations of the United States (FRUS), Conference at Quebec, 1944*, document 299, *FRUS* documents available at https://history.state.gov/historicaldocuments. See also Gowing and Arnold, *Independence and Deterrence*, 1:95–123.

45. "The Prime Minister," March 1, 1955, Records of the United Kingdom Houses of Parliament (Hansard) (UKHoP), vol. 537, column 1897. See also "The Size of the V-Bomber Force," March 23, 1955, UKNA DEFE 11/101.

46. Goldstein, *Deterrence and Security in the 21st Century*, 146.

47. "Mr. Churchill," February 15, 1951, UKHoP, vol. 484, column 630.

48. Quoted in Ruston, *A Say in the End of the World*, 90.

49. Quoted in Ruston, *A Say in the End of the World*, 90.

50. Quoted in Baylis and Stoddart, *British Nuclear Experience*, 32.

51. Christopher J. Bowie and Alan Platt, *British Nuclear Policymaking* (Santa Monica, CA: RAND Corporation, 1984), 8.

52. "Defence Policy and Global Strategy: Report by the Chiefs of Staff," June 17, 1952, UKNA CAB 131/12, D(52) 26; Ruston, *A Say in the End of the World*, 95.

53. Quoted in Snyder, *Politics of British Defense Policy*, 233.

54. "Confidential Annex," January 10, 1956, UKNA DEFE 32/5.

55. Jones, *Official History of the UK Strategic Nuclear Deterrent*, 1:2.

56. Memo on Atomic Research from Lord Cherwell to Mr. Churchill, August 6, 1950, CHUR 2/28/45–51, 1–2.

57. For example, "COS(56)451," December 31, 1956, UKNA AIR 20/12508.

58. For a theoretical treatment of these dynamics, see Albert O. Hirschman, *Exit, Voice, and Loyalty: Responses to Decline in Firms, Organizations, and States* (Cambridge, MA: Harvard University Press, 1970).

59. Gowing and Arnold, *Independence and Deterrence*, 1:184. See also Groom, *British Thinking about Nuclear Weapons*, 2.

60. Memo on Atomic Research from Lord Cherwell to Mr. Churchill, August 6, 1950, CHUR 2/28/45–51.

61. "Draft Command Directive to Air Marshal Sir George H. Mills," 1954, UKNA AIR 2/15917.

62. Quoted in Snyder, *Politics of British Defense Policy*, 233.

63. Quoted in George C. Peden, "Suez and Britain's Decline as a World Power," *Historical Journal* 55, no. 4 (2012): 1081.

64. "Britain and the Western Alliance," August 26, 1959, U.S. Central Intelligence Agency Archives (CIAA) CREST, General CIA Records, document RDP79R01012A014700050017–8.

65. "Note of a Meeting of Ministers," August 29, 1945, UKNA CAB 130/2, GEN 75/2nd Meeting.

66. "Cabinet Defence Committee," September 13, 1946, UKNA CAB 21/2086, DO(46) 107.

67. Rosecrance, *Defence of the Realm*, 188.

68. "Defence Policy and the Royal Air Force 1956–1963," 1987, UKNA AIR 41/86, 11.

69. "Defense Policy in Economic Crisis," October 20, 1952, Private Papers of Sir John Slessor, UKNA AIR 75/119.

70. "Defence Policy and Global Strategy," June 17, 1952, UKNA CAB 131/12.

71. Martin S. Navias, *Nuclear Weapons and British Strategic Planning, 1955–1958* (Oxford: Clarendon Press, 1991), 4; Bartlett, *Long Retreat*, 97; Jones, *Official History of the UK Strategic Nuclear Deterrent*, 1:46.

72. Groom, *British Thinking about Nuclear Weapons*, 62–63; Navias, *Nuclear Weapons and British Strategic Planning*, 5.

73. I use version 4.0 of the National Material Capabilities Dataset, released in 2010. The original data is described in Singer, "Reconstructing the Correlates of War Dataset on Material Capabilities of States."

74. Rosecrance, *Defence of the Realm*, 190.

75. Quoted in John Baylis, *Ambiguity and Deterrence: British Nuclear Strategy, 1945–1964* (Oxford: Clarendon Press, 1995), 206.

76. Bartlett, *Long Retreat*, 129; Lawrence Freedman, *Britain and Nuclear Weapons* (Basingstoke: Macmillan Press, 1980), 4; Navias, *Nuclear Weapons and British Strategic Planning*, 139.

77. Lewis Betts, *Duncan Sandys and British Nuclear Policy-Making* (London: Palgrave Macmillan, 2016).

78. "The Prime Minister," April 17, 1957, UKHoP, vol. 568, column 2040.

79. "Defence Policy and the Royal Air Force 1956–1963," 1987, UKNA AIR 41/86, xv–xiv.

80. This uses the latest MID 4.0 codings. Glenn Palmer, Vito D'Orazio, Michael Kenwick, and Matthew Lane, "The MID4 Dataset, 2002–2010: Procedures, Coding Rules and Description," *Conflict Management and Peace Science* 32, no. 2 (2015): 222–242.

81. William R. Thompson, "Identifying Rivals and Rivalries in World Politics," *International Studies Quarterly* 45, no. 4 (2001): 557–586.

82. Thompson, "Identifying Rivals and Rivalries in World Politics."

83. Navias, *Nuclear Weapons and British Strategic Planning*, 37.

84. Navias, *Nuclear Weapons and British Strategic Planning*, 47–48.

85. Matthew Jones, "The Radford Bombshell: Anglo-Australian-US Relations, Nuclear Weapons and the Defence of South East Asia, 1954–57," *Journal of Strategic Studies* 27, no. 4 (2004): 643; Baylis, *Ambiguity and Deterrence*, 228.

86. "Annex to COS(56)76," February 16, 1956, UKNA DEFE 5/65.

87. Letter from the Acting Director of Central Intelligence to the Secretary of State, September 12, 1955, in *FRUS 1955–1957*, vol. 21, document 67.

88. Matthew Jones, "Up the Garden Path? Britain's Nuclear History in the Far East, 1954–1962," *International History Review* 25, no. 2 (2003): 310.

89. For detailed discussions of British nuclear commitments to SEATO, see Jones, "Up the Garden Path?"; Jones, "Radford Bombshell"; Navias, *Nuclear Weapons and British Strategic Planning*, 47–51.

90. Jones, "Radford Bombshell," 653.

91. "JP(56)104," June 5, 1956, UKNA DEFE 4/87.

92. Wayne Reynolds, "The Wars That Were Planned: Australia's Forward Defence Posture in Asia and the Role of Tactical Nuclear Weapons, 1945–1967," *Australian Journal of International Affairs* 53, no. 3 (1999): 305.

93. "Annex to COS(57)40," 1957, UKNA DEFE 5/73; Jones, "Radford Bombshell," 637, 653; Wayne Reynolds, *Australia's Bid for the Atomic Bomb* (Melbourne: Melbourne University Press, 2000), 169–170.

94. "Annex to COS(57)40," 1957, UKNA DEFE 5/73.

95. Jones, "Radford Bombshell," 655. See also Reynolds, *Australia's Bid for the Atomic Bomb*, 169.

96. "Review of Middle East Policy and Strategy: Report by the Chiefs of Staff," September 15, 1950, UKNA CAB 21/2088, COS(50) 363.

97. "Defence Policy and Global Strategy: Report by the Chiefs of Staff," June 17, 1952, UKNA CAB 131/12, D(52) 26.

98. Nigel John Ashton, *Eisenhower, Macmillan and the Problem of Nasser: Anglo-American Relations and Arab Nationalism, 1955–59* (Basingstoke: MacMillan, 1996), 59; Simon C. Smith, *Ending Empire in the Middle East: Britain, the United States and Post-War Decolonization* (New York: Routledge, 2012), 39; John Darwin, *Britain and Decolonisation: The Retreat from Empire in the Post-War World* (New York: St. Martin's Press, 1988), 210; Stephen M. Walt, *The Origins of Alliances* (Ithaca, NY: Cornell University Press, 1987), 58–62.

99. Memorandum of a Telephone Conversation between the President and the Secretary of State, Washington, April 7, 1956, in *FRUS 1955–1957*, vol. 12, document 111.

100. "JP(56)193: Baghdad Pact National Comments on Nuclear Study Brief for United Kingdom Deputy," December 20, 1956, UKNA DEFE 4/94.

101. Quoted in Navias, *Nuclear Weapons and British Strategic Planning*, 45.

102. "COS(56)79," February 21, 1956, UKNA DEFE 5/65.

103. "COS(55)49," March 4, 1955, UKNA DEFE 5/57.

104. "DC(56)17," July 3, 1956, UKNA CAB 131/17.

105. "The Minister of Defence," March 2, 1955, UKHoP, vol. 537, column 2182.

106. Reynolds, *Australia's Bid for the Atomic Bomb*, 168n37; "JP(56)54: Facilities Required by H.M. Forces in Cyprus in Peace and War: Report by the Joint Planning Staff," May 26, 1956, UKNA DEFE 4/87.

107. "Annex to JP(56)97," May 25, 1956, UKNA DEFE 4/87; "Annex to COS 131(56)," December 7, 1956, UKNA DEFE 4/91, British Documents on the End of Empire (BDEE) Series B, vol. 4, document 648.

108. Navias, *Nuclear Weapons and British Strategic Planning*, 39–51; Baylis, *Ambiguity and Deterrence*, 229.

109. "Defence Policy and the Royal Air Force 1956–1963," 1987, UKNA AIR 41/86, xiv, 20.

110. "The RAF Strategic Nuclear Deterrent Forces: Their Origins, Roles and Deployment 1946–1969," 1991, UKNA AIR 41/87, 125–126.

111. "The Most Effective Pattern of NATO Military Strength for the Next Few Years," November 22, 1954, NATO Strategy Documents (NATOSD) 1949–1969, MC 48/1.

112. "CC(54)," March 10, 1954, UKNA CAB 128/27/17.

113. Eden, *Full Circle*, 372–373; Baylis, *Ambiguity and Deterrence*, 230. See also "Annex to JP(56)120," June 27, 1956, UKNA DEFE 4/88.

114. "COS(56)271: Long Term Defence Review," July 13, 1956, UKNA DEFE 32/5.

115. "Annex II to COS(56)271: Military Brief by the Chief of the Air Staff," July 13, 1956, UKNA DEFE 32/5.

116. Baylis, *Ambiguity and Deterrence*, 231.

117. Memorandum from the Secretary of State to the President, October 1, 1956, in *FRUS 1955–1957*, vol. 4, document 37.

118. Memorandum of a Conversation, Paris, December 11, 1956, in *FRUS 1955–1957*, vol. 4, document 44. In his memo to Eisenhower summarizing the meeting, he acknowledged "the reality of the British predicament." Message from the Secretary of State to the President, December 11, 1956, in *FRUS 1955–1957*, vol. 4, document 45.

119. Baylis, *Ambiguity and Deterrence*, 231.

120. Navias, *Nuclear Weapons and British Strategic Planning*, 184.

121. "Defence Policy and the Royal Air Force, 1956–1963" 1987, UKNA AIR 41/86, 1.

122. "Defence Policy and the Royal Air Force, 1956–1963," 1987, UKNA AIR 41/86, 44.

123. Petersen, *Middle East between the Great Powers*, xi.

124. S. Paul Kapur, *Dangerous Deterrent: Nuclear Weapons Proliferation and Conflict in South Asia* (Stanford, CA: Stanford University Press, 2007).

125. Steven G. Galpern, *Money, Oil, and Empire in the Middle East: Sterling and Postwar Imperialism, 1944–1971* (Cambridge: Cambridge University Press, 2009), 84.

126. Galpern, *Money, Oil, and Empire in the Middle East*, 87–88.

127. Galpern, *Money, Oil, and Empire in the Middle East*, 91.

128. Daniel Yergin, *The Prize: The Epic Quest for Oil, Money & Power* (New York: Free Press, 2009), 435.

129. Yergin, *The Prize*, 437; Galpern, *Money, Oil, and Empire in the Middle East*, 97.

130. H. W. Brands, "The Cairo-Tehran Connection in Anglo-American Rivalry in the Middle East, 1951–1953," *International History Review* 11, no. 3 (1989): 437–438.

131. Darwin, *Britain and Decolonisation*, 161; Smith, *Ending Empire in the Middle East*, 29; Stephen Kinzer, *All the Shah's Men: An American Coup and the Roots of Middle East Terror* (Hoboken, NJ: Wiley & Sons, 2008), 3; Yergin, *The Prize*, 440.

132. CP(51)212: Memorandum by the Secretary of State for Foreign Affairs, July 20, 1951, UKNA CAB 129/46.

133. Walter to State Department, May 16, 1951, in *FRUS 1952–1954*, vol. 10, document 22.

134. "CM(51)," September 27, 1951, UKNA CAB 128/20/10.

135. Melvyn P. Leffler, *A Preponderance of Power: National Security, the Truman Administration, and the Cold War* (Stanford, CA: Stanford University Press, 1992), 77; Galpern, *Money, Oil, and Empire in the Middle East*, 1; Darwin, *Empire Project*, 525; Petersen, *Middle East between the Great Powers*, 19.

136. CP(51)212: Memorandum by the Secretary of State for Foreign Affairs, July 20, 1951, UKNA CAB 129/46.

137. Darwin, *Empire Project*, 556–557; Galpern, *Money, Oil, and Empire in the Middle East*, 2.

138. Galpern, *Money, Oil, and Empire in the Middle East*, 71.

139. Galpern, *Money, Oil, and Empire in the Middle East*, 107.

140. Galpern, *Money, Oil, and Empire in the Middle East*, 19, 67, 81.

141. Minutes of meeting, November 1, 1951, UKNA FO 371/91608.

142. Memorandum of Conversation, April 18, 1951, in *FRUS 1952–1954*, vol. 10, document 13.

143. Brands, "Cairo-Tehran Connection in Anglo-American Rivalry," 440.

144. Statement of Policy Proposed by the National Security Council, June 27, 1951, in *FRUS 1952–1954*, vol. 10, document 32. See also Francis J. Gavin, "Politics, Power, and U.S. Policy in Iran, 1950–1953," *Journal of Cold War Studies* 1, no. 1 (1999): 65–68.

145. Truman to Attlee, May 31, 1951, in *FRUS 1952–1954*, vol. 10, document 25.

146. Acheson to Iranian embassy, May 11, 1951, in *FRUS 1952–1954*, vol. 10, document 21.

147. "Paper prepared in the Department of State," n.d., in *FRUS 1952–1954*, vol. 10, document 12. The document was presented to the British ambassador at a meeting on April 17, 1951. See Memorandum of Conversation, April 17, 1951, in *FRUS 1952–1954*, vol. 10, document 12.

148. Acheson to UK Embassy, May 31, 1951, in *FRUS 1952–1954*, vol. 10, document 30.

149. Gifford to State Department, May 16, 1951, in *FRUS 1952–1954*, vol. 10, document 22. Memorandum of Conversation, April 18, 1951, in *FRUS 1952–1954*, vol. 10, document 13.

150. CP(51)114: Memorandum by the Secretary of State for Foreign Affairs, April 20, 1951, UKNA CAB 129/45.

151. CP(51)200: Memorandum by the Secretary of State for Foreign Affairs, July 11, 1951, UKNA CAB 129/46.

152. "CM51(51)2," July 12, 1951, UKNA CAB 128/20, BDEE Series A, vol. 2, document 36.

153. "CM(51)," September 27, 1951, UKNA CAB 128/20/10.

154. "CM(51)," September 27, 1951, UKNA CAB 128/20/10.

155. Petersen, *Middle East between the Great Powers*, 19.

156. Eden, *Full Circle*, 217–225.

157. Henry Byroade to H. Freeman Matthews, November 26, 1952, NSA Electronic Briefing Book 601, document 1; "British Proposal to Organize a Coup d'etat in Iran," December 3, 1952, NSA Electronic Briefing Book 601, document 2; Smith, *Ending Empire in the Middle East*, 30.

158. Kinzer, *All the Shah's Men*, 4; Gavin, "Politics, Power and U.S. Policy in Iran."

159. Smith, *Ending Empire in the Middle East*, 30–31.

160. Darwin, *Britain and Decolonisation*, 113.

161. Galpern, *Money, Oil, and Empire in the Middle East*, 142.

162. Yergin, *The Prize*, 461.

163. Cabinet Memorandum by Eden, July 28, 1952, UKNA C(52)267, CAB 129/54, BDEE Series A, vol. 3, document 31.

164. Julian Amery to Eden, March 16, 1953, UKNA FO 371/102807, BDEE Series B, vol. 4, document 377.

165. Yergin, *The Prize*, 463.

166. Darwin, *Britain and Decolonisation*, 121; Darwin, *Empire Project*, 564.

167. Notes by Robert Hankey on meeting with Churchill, May 22, 1953, UKNA FO 371/102765, BDEE Series B, vol. 4, document 396. See also Petersen, *Middle East between the Great Powers*, 1–3.

168. Letter from Churchill to Eisenhower, February 25, 1953, UKNA PREM 11/704, BDEE Series B, vol. 4, document 373.

169. Telegram from Eden to Roger Makins, March 21, 1953, UKNA PREM 11/486, BDEE Series B, vol. 4, document 380.

170. "CC(17)53," March 9, 1953, UKNA CAB 128/26/1, BDEE Series B, vol. 4, document 374.

171. Christopher Steel to Foreign Office, March 23, 1953, UKNA PREM 11/486, BDEE Series B, vol. 4, document 382; Memo from William Strang, March 24, 1953, UKNA FO 371/102803, BDEE Series B, vol. 4, document 383.

172. Petersen, *Middle East between the Great Powers*, 11.

173. For example, Hankey to Robert Gascoyne-Cecil (Lord Salisbury), July 5, 1953, UKNA FO 371/102811, BDEE Series B, vol. 4, document 413; "CC(53)3," July 6, 1953, UKNA CAB 128/62/2, BDEE Series B, vol. 4, document 415.

174. For example, "CC51(53)2," September 8, 1953, UKNA CAB 128/26/2, BDEE Series B, vol. 4, document 432.

175. Eden to Churchill, December 1, 1953, UKNA PREM 11/484, BDEE Series B, vol. 4, document 454.

176. Petersen, *Middle East between the Great Powers*, 14.

177. Telegram from Eden, December 15, 1953, UKNA FO 371/102822, BDEE Series B, vol. 4, document 458; Churchill to Eisenhower, December 22, 1953, UKNA PREM 11/699, BDEE Series 4, vol. 2, document 461.

178. Draft Memo from Eden to Churchill, December 28, 1953, UKNA FO 371/108413, BDEE Series B, vol. 4, document 465.

179. Churchill to Eisenhower, June 21, 1954, in *FRUS 1952–1954*, vol. 9, part 2, document 1335. Churchill did not explicitly acknowledge that Britain was backing down, instead justifying the change in position with reference to "thermonuclear developments" and the "Tito-Greek-Turco front coming into being" altering the strategic value of the canal zone. Neither of these justifications was fully convincing, and, indeed, Churchill continued to argue for the "political disadvantages of abandoning the position which we had held in Egypt since 1882" in a cabinet meeting the following day. "CC43(54)1," June 22, 1954, UKNA CAB 128/27/1, BDEE Series B, vol. 4, document 525. The most plausible explanation is that Churchill's rationale in his letter to Eisenhower was an effort to preserve some dignity in the midst of a humiliating reversal.

180. Eden to Ralph Stevenson, July 2, 1954, UKNA FO 371/108420, BDEE Series B, vol. 4, document 529.

181. Rosecrance, *Defence of the Realm*, 202; Darwin, *Britain and Decolonisation*, 208.

182. Churchill to Chiefs of Staff, July 21, 1954, UKNA DEFE 7/31, BDEE Series 4, vol. 2, document 537.

183. Petersen, *Middle East between the Great Powers*, 17; Darwin, *Empire Project*, 596.

184. CP(55)153: Memorandum by the Secretary of State for Foreign Affairs, October 15, 1955, UKNA CAB 129/78.

185. For example, Raymond Hare to State Department, March 10, 1952, in *FRUS 1952–1954*, vol. 9, part 2, document 1467.

186. Hare to State Department, September 28, 1952, in *FRUS 1952–1954*, vol. 9, part 2, document 1478.

187. Memorandum of Conversations by Joseph Palmer, April 16, 1953, in *FRUS 1952–1954*, vol. 9, part 2, document 1514.

188. Ashton, *Eisenhower, Macmillan and the Problem of Nasser*, 75; Tore T. Petersen, "Anglo-American Rivalry in the Middle East: The Struggle for the Buraimi Oasis, 1952–1957," *International History Review* 14, no. 1 (1992): 71.

189. Gifford to Acheson, December 11, 1952, in *FRUS 1952–1954*, vol. 9, part 2, document 1495.

190. Petersen, *Middle East between the Great Powers*, 38; Petersen, "Anglo-American Rivalry in the Middle East," 74.

191. For example, Acheson to U.K. Embassy, October 10, 1952, in *FRUS 1952–1954*, vol. 9, part 2, document 1484.

192. Petersen, "Anglo-American Rivalry in the Middle East," 73.

193. The British were eager for the Americans to know that their pursuit of a diplomatic solution and acceptance of the "Standstill Agreement" were due to the United States. See Salisbury to Dulles, July 27, 1953, in *FRUS 1952–1954*, vol. 9, part 2, document 1530.

194. Petersen, "Anglo-American Rivalry in the Middle East," 74.

195. Petersen, *Middle East between the Great Powers*, 42.

196. Dulles to British Embassy, May 22, 1954, in *FRUS 1952–1954*, vol. 9, part 2, document 1563. See also Petersen, "Anglo-American Rivalry in the Middle East," 77.

197. "CM(55)," October 4, 1955, UKNA CAB 128/29/34.

198. "The Prime Minister," October 26, 1955, UKHoP, vol. 545, column 198–202.

199. CP(55)153: Memorandum by the Secretary of State for Foreign Affairs, October 15, 1955, UKNA CAB 129/78.

200. Petersen, *Middle East between the Great Powers*, 53.

201. Petersen, *Middle East between the Great Powers*, 53; Smith, *Ending Empire in the Middle East*, 37.

202. Dulles to Dulles, n.d., in *FRUS 1955–1957*, vol. 13, document 184.

203. Dulles to UK Embassy, December 13, 1955, in *FRUS 1955–1957*, vol. 13, document 145.

204. Quoted in Petersen, "Anglo-American Rivalry in the Middle East," 85. The British were informed that "the best [the United States] could probably do would be to abstain." Hoover to Dulles, December 20, 1955, in *FRUS 1955–1957*, vol. 13, document 199; Petersen, "Anglo-American Rivalry in the Middle East," 85.

205. Memorandum of a Conversation, January 30, 1956, in *FRUS 1955–1957*, vol. 13, document 213.

206. Minutes on letter from Dulles to Macmillan, December 6, 1955, UKNA FO 371/115469, BDEE Series B, vol. 2, document 614; Selwyn Lloyd to Dulles, January 23, 1956, in *FRUS 1955–1957*, vol. 13, document 209.

207. Ashton, *Eisenhower, Macmillan and the Problem of Nasser*, 75.

208. Memorandum of Conversation, January 10, 1956, in *FRUS 1955–1957*, vol. 13, document 207.

209. Galpern, *Money, Oil, and Empire in the Middle East*, 142–143.

210. Yergin, *The Prize*, 467.

211. Yergin makes this comparison explicit, arguing that "a Nasser victory in Egypt might have had the same kind of repercussions as a Mossadegh victory in Iran would have had." Yergin, *The Prize*, 467.

212. For example, Memorandum of a Conference with the President, July 31, 1956, in *FRUS 1955–1957*, vol. 16, document 34.

213. Dulles to UK Embassy, July 30, 1956, in *FRUS 1955–1957*, vol. 16, document 28.

214. Eisenhower to Eden, July 31, 1956, in *FRUS 1955–1957*, vol. 16, document 35.

215. Petersen, *Middle East between the Great Powers*, 82.

216. Memorandum of a Conversation, August 1, 1956, in *FRUS 1955–1957*, vol. 16, document 41.

217. Smith, *Ending Empire in the Middle East*, 46–47; Ashton, *Eisenhower, Macmillan and the Problem of Nasser*, 85.

218. Memorandum of a Conversation, August 1, 1956, in *FRUS 1955–1957*, vol. 16, document 42.

219. Memorandum of a Conversation, August 1, 1956, in *FRUS 1955–1957*, vol. 16, document 46; Dulles to Eisenhower, August 1, 1956, in *FRUS 1955–1957*, vol. 16, document 48.

220. Yergin, *The Prize*, 471.

221. Memorandum of a Conference with the President, October 29, 1956, in *FRUS 1955–1957*, vol. 16, document 411.

222. Eisenhower to Eden, October 30, 1956, in *FRUS 1955–1957*, vol. 16, document 411.

223. Memorandum of Telephone Conversation between Eisenhower and Dulles, October 30, 1956, in *FRUS 1955–1957*, vol. 16, document 411.

224. Yergin, *The Prize*, 472.

225. Conversation between Dulles and Eisenhower, November 7, 1956, in *FRUS 1955–1957*, vol. 16, document 542.

226. Phone Conversation between Eisenhower and Eden, November 7, 1956, in *FRUS 1955–1957*, vol. 16, document 540; Eisenhower to Eden, November 7, 1956, in *FRUS 1955–1957*, vol. 16, document 545.

227. UK Embassy to Department of State, November 19, 1956, in *FRUS 1955–1957*, vol. 16, document 583.

228. UK Embassy to Department of State, November 19, 1956, in *FRUS 1955–1957*, vol. 16, document 593.

229. Memorandum of a Conversation with the President, November 20, 1956, in *FRUS 1955–1957*, vol. 16, document 596.

230. "The Secretary of State for Foreign Affairs," December 3, 1956, UKHoP, vol. 561, column 877–883.

231. CP(57)8: Note by the Prime Minister, January 7, 1957, UKNA 129/84.

232. Quoted in Smith, *Ending Empire in the Middle East*, 67.

233. Rosecrance, *Defence of the Realm*; John Charmley, *Churchill's Grand Alliance: The Anglo-American Special Relationship, 1940–1957* (London: Hodder & Stoughton, 1995); Scott Lucas, *Divided We Stand: Britain, the United States, and the Suez Crisis* (London: Hodder & Stoughton, 1991); Keith Kyle, *Suez: Britain's End of Empire in the Middle East* (London: I. B. Tauris, 2003); Peter L. Hahn, *The United States, Great Britain, and Egypt, 1945–1956: Strategy and Diplomacy in the Early Cold War* (Chapel Hill: University of North Carolina Press, 1991).

234. See, for example, Peden, "Suez and Britain's Decline as a World Power"; Simon C. Smith, "'America in Britain's Place?' Anglo-American Relations and the Middle East in the Aftermath of the Suez Crisis," *Journal of Transatlantic Studies* 10, no. 3 (2012): 252–270.

235. Smith, *Ending Empire in the Middle East*, 67.

236. Ashton, *Eisenhower, Macmillan and the Problem of Nasser*, 112.

237. Petersen, *Middle East between the Great Powers*, 216.

238. Macmillan to Eisenhower, July 19, 1957, in *FRUS 1955–1957*, vol. 13, document 148.

239. John to State Department, July 23, 1957, in *FRUS 1955–1957*, vol. 13, document 149.

240. Smith, *Ending Empire in the Middle East*, 81.

241. Smith, *Ending Empire in the Middle East*, 81.

242. Ashton, *Eisenhower, Macmillan and the Problem of Nasser*, 189.

243. For example, "Special National Intelligence Estimate," June 5, 1958, in *FRUS 1958–1960*, vol. 11, document 60.

244. Phone Conversation between Eisenhower and Macmillan, July 14, 1958, in *FRUS 1958–1960*, vol. 11, document 131.

245. Macmillan to Eisenhower, July 14, 1958, in *FRUS 1958–1960*, vol. 11, document 132.

246. Ashton, *Eisenhower, Macmillan and the Problem of Nasser*, 9, 189.

247. Memorandum of Conversation between Dulles and Samuel Hood, July 14, 1958, in *FRUS 1958–1960*, vol. 11, document 134; Memorandum of Conversation between Dulles and Hood, July 15, 1958, in *FRUS 1958–1960*, vol. 11, document 177. For the British enthusiasm for intervention, see Macmillan to Eisenhower, July 14, 1958, in *FRUS 1958–1960*, vol. 11, document 172.

248. Memorandum of a Conference with the President, July 16, 1958, in *FRUS 1958–1960*, vol. 11, document 179; Memorandum of a Conference with the President, July 20, 1958, in *FRUS 1958–1960*, vol. 11, document 205.

249. Memorandum of a Conference with the President, July 20, 1958, in *FRUS 1958–1960*, vol. 11, document 205.

250. Memorandum of a Conversation between Macmillan and Dulles, July 16, 1958, in *FRUS 1958–1960*, vol. 11, document 182; Memorandum of a Conversation between Macmillan and Dulles, July 16, 1958, in *FRUS 1958–1960*, vol. 11, document 184; Memorandum of a Conversation, July 17, 1958, in *FRUS 1958–1960*, vol. 11, document 187; Memorandum of a Conversation, July 17, 1958, in *FRUS 1958–1960*, vol. 11, document 188.

251. Memorandum of Discussion at the 292nd Meeting of the National Security Council, Washington, August 9, 1956, in *FRUS 1955–1957*, vol. 16, document 72.

252. Memorandum of a Conversation, August 1, 1956, in *FRUS 1955–1957*, vol. 16, document 46.

253. Bulganin Message to Eden, November 5, 1956, CIAA CREST, General CIA Records, document RDP79R01012A006900020011-4.

254. Memorandum of a Conversation, November 6, 1956, in *FRUS 1955–1957*, vol. 16, document 524.

255. Quoted in Groom, *British Thinking about Nuclear Weapons*, 190; Richard K. Betts, *Nuclear Blackmail and Nuclear Balance* (Washington, DC: Brookings Institution Press, 1987), 64. See also Jonathan Pearson, *Sir Anthony Eden and the Suez Crisis: Reluctant Gamble* (Basingstoke: Palgrave Macmillan, 2003), 161; Diane B. Kunz, *The Economic Diplomacy of the Suez Crisis* (Chapel Hill: University of North Carolina Press, 1991), 131; Jonathan Kirshner, *Currency and Coercion: The Political Economy of International Monetary Power* (Princeton, NJ: Princeton University Press, 1997), 72–73.

256. Groom, *British Thinking about Nuclear Weapons*, 190–191.

257. Hymans, *Psychology of Nuclear Proliferation*.

258. For analyses of Eden's personality, background, and political beliefs, see John T. Henderson, "Leadership Personality and War: The Cases of Richard Nixon and Anthony Eden," *Political Science* 28, no. 2 (1976): 141–164; David Carlton, *Anthony Eden* (London: Penguin Books, 1981); Pearson, *Sir Anthony Eden and the Suez Crisis*; D. R. Thorpe, *Eden: The Life and Times of Anthony Eden, First Earl of Avon, 1897–1977* (London: Pimlico, 2003); Robert Rhodes-James, *Anthony Eden* (London: Weidenfeld & Nicolson, 1986).

259. Tony Shaw, *Eden, Suez and the Mass Media: Propaganda and Persuasion during the Suez Crisis* (London: I. B. Tauris, 1996), 6; Eden, *Full Circle*, chaps. 9–10.

260. Eden, *Full Circle*, 274.

261. Hymans, *Psychology of Nuclear Proliferation*.

262. Rhodes-James, *Anthony Eden*, 203–204; Carlton, *Anthony Eden*, 295–296; Thorpe, *Eden*, 420–421.

263. Rhodes-James, *Anthony Eden*, 379; Thorpe, *Eden*, 420. For a further example of Eden taking a more restrained position than Churchill, see Matthew Jones, *After Hiroshima: The United States, Race and Nuclear Weapons in Asia, 1945–1965* (New York: Cambridge University Press, 2010), 139.

264. For example, Narang, *Nuclear Strategy in the Modern Era*, 3n3.

265. Matthew Jones, *The Official History of the UK Strategic Nuclear Deterrent*, vol. 2, *The Labour Government and the Polaris Programme, 1964–1970* (Abingdon: Routledge, 2017), xii.

266. Simon J. Ball, "Military Nuclear Relations between the United States and Great Britain under the Terms of the McMahon Act, 1946–1958," *Historical Journal* 38, no. 2 (1995): 453. See also Justin Bronk, "Britain's 'Independent' V-Bomber Force and US Nuclear Weapons, 1957–1962," *Journal of Strategic Studies* 37, nos. 6–7 (2014): 974–997; Matthew Jones, "Prelude to the Skybolt Crisis: The Kennedy Administration's Approach to British and French Strategic Nuclear Policies in 1962," *Journal of Cold War Studies* 21, no. 2 (2019): 58–109.

267. Bundy to Kennedy, April 24, 1962, in *FRUS 1961–1963*, vol. 13, document 392.

268. Minutes of Cabinet Defence Committee Meeting D.(57) 2nd meeting, February 27, 1957, UKNA CAB 131/18.

269. Memorandum of Conversation, December 20, 1962, in *FRUS 1961–1963*, vol. 13, document 406.

270. "Delegation to the Heads of Government Meeting to the Embassy in France," December 20, 1962, in *FRUS 1961–1963*, vol. 13, document 407.

271. See, for example, the exchange of letters between Prime Minister Margaret Thatcher and President Ronald Reagan requesting and confirming Britain's purchase of Trident II missiles "in a manner generally similar to that in which Polaris was supplied" and repeating the "supreme national interests" language guaranteeing Britain's ability to use nuclear weapons independently. Thatcher to Reagan, March 11, 1982, Reagan Presidential Library, Simi Valley, California (REAG), Dennis Blair Files, RAC box 5, folder 8; Reagan to Thatcher, March 11, 1982, REAG, Dennis Blair Files, RAC box 5, folder 8.

272. For example, "Falklands Warships Carried Nuclear Weapons, MoD Admits," *The Guardian*, December 6, 2003. There is also less reliable evidence that Prime Minister Thatcher resorted to more explicit threats of British nuclear use in the conflict to compel French assistance in dealing with Argentina's French-bought Exocet missiles. See "Thatcher Threatened to Nuke Argentina," *The Guardian*, November 21, 2005.

273. The Secretary of State for Defence and the Secretary of State for Foreign and Commonwealth Affairs, *The Future of the United Kingdom's Nuclear Deterrent* (London: Government Stationery Office, 2006), 5.

274. "MPs Vote to Renew Trident," *The Guardian*, March 14, 2007; "Commons Votes for Trident Renewal by Majority of 355," *The Guardian*, July 18, 2016.

275. Nick Ritchie, "Relinquishing Nuclear Weapons: Identities, Networks and the British Bomb," *International Affairs* 86, no. 2 (2010): 469–472.

276. Ritchie, "Relinquishing Nuclear Weapons," 469.

277. For arguments challenging the utility of British nuclear weapons, see, for example, Robert O'Neill, "Britain and the Future of Nuclear Weapons," *International Affairs* 71, no. 4 (1995): 747–761; Michael MccGwire, "Comfort Blanket or Weapon of War: What Is Trident For?," *International Affairs* 82, no. 4 (2006): 639–650; Rebecca Johnson, Nicola Butler, and Stephen Pullinger, *Worse Than Irrelevant? British Nuclear Weapons in the 21st Century* (London: Acronym Institute for Disarmament Diplomacy, 2006); Nick Ritchie, "Deterrence Dogma? Challenging the Relevance of British Nuclear Weapons," *International Affairs* 85, no. 1 (2009): 81–98; Ritchie, "Relinquishing Nuclear Weapons"; Nick Ritchie, *A Nuclear Weapons-Free World? Britain, Trident and the Challenges Ahead* (Basingstoke: Palgrave Macmillan, 2012).

3. Apartheid and Aggression

1. David Steward, interview with the author, Johannesburg, June 6, 2014.

2. Deon Fourie, interview with the author, Pretoria, June 16, 2014.

3. Vipin Narang, *Nuclear Strategy in the Modern Era: Regional Powers and International Conflict* (Princeton, NJ: Princeton University Press, 2014), 207.

4. For example, Mitchell Reiss, *Bridled Ambition: Why Countries Constrain Their Nuclear Capabilities* (Baltimore: Johns Hopkins University Press, 1995); Waldo Stumpf, "South Africa's Nuclear Weapons Program: From Deterrence to Dismantlement," *Arms Control Today* 25, no. 10 (1995/1996): 3–8; Peter Liberman, "The Rise and Fall of the South African Bomb," *International Security* 26, no. 2 (2001): 45–86; Helen E. Purkitt and Stephen F. Burgess, *South Africa's Weapons of Mass Destruction* (Bloomington: Indiana University Press, 2005); Narang, *Nuclear Strategy in the Modern Era*; Or Rabinowitz, *Bargaining on Nuclear Tests: Washington and Its Cold War Deals* (Oxford: Oxford University Press, 2014).

5. André Buys, interview with the author, Pretoria, July 1, 2014; Waldo Stumpf, interview with the author, Pretoria, June 11, 2014; Major General (retired) Gert Opperman, interview with the author, Johannesburg, June 23, 2014; Ambassador Victor Zazeraj, interview with the author, Johannesburg, July 4, 2014.

6. Ambassador Jeremy Shearar, interview with the author, Pretoria, July 1, 2014.

7. Stumpf, interview; Zazeraj, interview.

8. Narang, *Nuclear Strategy in the Modern Era*, 15–17.

9. Buys, interview. See also Liberman, "Rise and Fall of the South African Bomb," 52.

10. Liberman, "Rise and Fall of the South African Bomb," 54–56.

11. Nor were methods of delivering nuclear weapons a constraint. As a UN 1980 report observed, "South Africa already possesses a variety of suitable delivery systems [for nuclear weapons], mostly high-performance aircraft." "Report of the Secretary General on the Implementation of the Declaration on the Denuclearization of Africa," September 9, 1980, South Africa Department of International Relations and Co-operation Archives, Pretoria, South Africa (DIRCO) 137/28, vol. 5.

12. Buys, interview.

13. Buys, interview. See also Nic Von Wielligh and Lydia Von Wielligh-Steyn, *The Bomb: South Africa's Nuclear Weapons Programme* (Pretoria: Litera Publications, 2015), 171.

14. Stumpf, interview.

15. Buys dates the point at which South Africa reached this threshold more precisely to October 1979. Buys, interview.

16. Buys, interview; Liberman, "Rise and Fall of the South African Bomb," 54; Magnus Malan, *My Life with the SA Defence Force* (Pretoria: Protea Book House, 2006), 219. Whether South Africa developed glide bombs is debated. Waldo Stumpf, for example, denies that any glide bombs were manufactured. Stumpf, interview.

17. Buys, interview; Liberman, "Rise and Fall of the South African Bomb," 54; Malan, *My Life with the SA Defence Force*, 219.

18. For example, Leopold Scholtz, *The SADF in the Border War, 1966–1989* (Cape Town: Tafelberg, 2013), chap. 2; Jamie Miller, *An African Volk: The Apartheid Regime and Its Search for Survival* (New York: Oxford University Press, 2016), chap. 6. Operation Savannah is discussed in more detail below.

19. For example, Anna-Mart Van Wyk, "South African Nuclear Development in the 1970s: A Non-proliferation Conundrum?," *International History Review* 40, no. 5 (2018): 1158–1159.

20. Rabinowitz, *Bargaining on Nuclear Tests*, 109.

21. Ronald W. Walters, *South Africa and the Bomb: Responsibility and Deterrence* (Lexington, MA: Lexington Books, 1987), 12.

22. Piero Gleijeses, *Visions of Freedom: Havana, Washington, Pretoria, and the Struggle for Southern Africa, 1976–1991* (Chapel Hill: University of North Carolina Press, 2013), 31.

23. Van Wyk, "South African Nuclear Development in the 1970s," 1159.

24. Gleijeses, *Visions of Freedom*, 31.

25. Walters, *South Africa and the Bomb*, 12; Gleijeses, *Visions of Freedom*, 139–145.

26. The extent to which these Cuban and Soviet actions were themselves triggered by South African provocations and aggression is disputed. Irina Filatova and Apollon Davidson, *The Hidden Thread: Russia and South Africa in the Soviet Union* (Johannesburg: Jonathan Ball, 2013), 272; Scholtz, *SADF in the Border War*, 21–22; Piero Gleijeses, *Conflicting Missions: Havana, Washington, and Africa, 1959–1976* (Chapel Hill: University of North Carolina Press, 2002), 254–262; Edward George, *Cuban Intervention in Angola, 1965–1991: From Che Guevara to Cuito Cuanavale* (New York: Routledge, 2005), chap. 4.

27. Stumpf, "South Africa's Nuclear Weapons Program," 4; Narang, *Nuclear Strategy in the Modern Era*, 209–210.

28. Zazeraj, interview.

29. Fourie, interview.

30. Steward, interview.

31. Colonel Jan Breytenbach (retired), interview with the author, Wilderness, June 20, 2014; Scholtz, *SADF in the Border War*, 7.

32. Malan, *My Life with the SA Defence Force*, 190; Scholtz, *SADF in the Border War*, 52.

33. Jannie Geldenhuys, *We Were There: Winning the War for Southern Africa* (Pretoria: Kraal Publishers, 2012), 19.

34. Narang, *Nuclear Strategy in the Modern Era*, 217.

35. Steward, interview.

36. Opperman, interview.

37. Walters, *South Africa and the Bomb*, 75.

38. Anna-Mart Van Wyk, "The USA and Apartheid South Africa's Nuclear Aspirations, 1949–1980," in *Cold War in Southern Africa: White Power, Black Liberation*, ed. Sue Onslow (New York: Routledge, 2009), 69. See also Chris Alden, *Apartheid's Last Stand: The Rise and Fall of the South African Security State* (Basingstoke: Macmillan Press, 1996), 30, 37.

39. Verne Harris, Sello Hatang, and Peter Liberman, "Unveiling South Africa's Nuclear Past," *Journal of Southern African Studies* 30, no. 3 (2004): 457–475.

40. Major General Johann Dippenaar (retired), interview with the author, Pretoria, June 30, 2014.

41. Opperman, interview.

42. Major General Roland de Vries (retired), phone interview with the author, September 9, 2014.

43. Dippenaar, interview.

44. "Effects of SA Attack on ANC Bases in Maputo," April 3, 1981, DIRCO 1-113-7, vol. 2.

45. Opperman, interview.

46. Breytenbach, interview.

47. de Vries, interview.

48. Opperman, interview.

49. Opperman, interview.

50. Breytenbach, interview.

51. Shearar, interview.

52. Breytenbach, interview.

53. For example, "South African Military Involvement in Angola," January 14, 1976, DIRCO 1/22/3, vol. 8.

54. Zazeraj, interview.

55. Zazeraj, interview.

56. Steward, interview.

57. Opperman, interview.

58. Dippenaar, interview.

59. Breytenbach, interview; Jannie Geldenhuys, *At the Front: A General's Account of South Africa's Border War* (Johannesburg: Jonathan Ball, 1994), 93.

60. Breytenbach, interview; George, *Cuban Intervention in Angola*, 70.

61. Zazeraj, interview.

62. de Vries, interview.
63. Opperman, interview.
64. For example, Shearar, interview.
65. Gleijeses, *Visions of Freedom*, 117.
66. Gleijeses, *Visions of Freedom*, 117.
67. Opperman, interview.
68. "South Africa: Policy Considerations Regarding a Nuclear Test," August 18, 1977, U.S. Central Intelligence Agency Archives (CIAA) CREST, General CIA Records, document RDP-79R00603A002900120001-0.
69. "Trends in South Africa's Nuclear Security Policies and Programs," September 5, 1984, CIAA National Identity Conception (NIC) Collection, document 0000107420.
70. Opperman, interview.
71. de Vries, interview.
72. This strategy is described explicitly in "Meeting of Ad Hoc Cabinet Committee," September 3, 1985, reproduced in Von Wielligh and Von Wielligh-Steyn, *The Bomb*, 480–483.
73. Buys, interview.
74. "A Balanced Approach to the NPT: ARMSCOR/AEC Concerns Viewed from a DFA Standpoint," September 1, 1988, Woodrow Wilson Center Digital Archive (WWCDA), document 114185.
75. Dippenaar, interview.
76. Buys, interview.
77. Buys, interview.
78. Narang, *Nuclear Strategy in the Modern Era*, chap. 8.
79. Stumpf, interview; Zazeraj, interview.
80. Rabinowitz, *Bargaining on Nuclear Tests*, 106.
81. Buys, interview.
82. For example, "Message Conveyed to Minister of Foreign Affairs by U.S. Ambassador W. Bowdler," August 18, 1977, DIRCO 356/2/5/2/1.
83. For example, Memo from South African Embassy in Washington, D.C. to Secretary for Foreign Affairs Regarding the Indian Nuclear Explosion, June 20, 1974, DIRCO 137/10/21, vol. 2.
84. "Trends in South Africa's Nuclear Security Policies and Programs," October 5, 1984, NSA Electronic Briefing Book 181, document 27.
85. Buys, interview.
86. Von Wielligh and Von Wielligh-Steyn, *The Bomb*, 133.
87. Buys, interview.
88. Buys, interview; Stumpf, interview; Liberman, "Rise and Fall of the South African Bomb," 54; Malan, *My Life with the SA Defence Force*, 219; Von Wielligh and Von Wielligh-Steyn, *The Bomb*, 183.
89. "Report of the Secretary General on the Implementation of the Declaration on the Denuclearization of Africa," September 9, 1980, DIRCO 137/28, vol. 5.
90. Von Wielligh and Von Wielligh-Steyn, *The Bomb*, 157.
91. "Trends in South Africa's Nuclear Security Policies and Programs," September 5, 1984, CIAA NIC Collection, document 0000107420.
92. Zazeraj, interview.
93. Quoted in Gleijeses, *Visions of Freedom*, 428.
94. Zazeraj, interview (emphasis added).
95. "The Jericho Weapon System," March 31, 1975, WWCDA document 114145.
96. "Report of the Secretary General on the Implementation of the Declaration on the Denuclearization of Africa," September 9, 1980, DIRCO 137/28, vol. 5.
97. Scholtz, *SADF in the Border War*, 12.
98. Scholtz, *SADF in the Border War*, 13.
99. Scholtz, *SADF in the Border War*, 14.
100. Scholtz, *SADF in the Border War*, 14.
101. Gleijeses, *Conflicting Missions*, 291; George, *Cuban Intervention in Angola*, 70.

102. Steward, interview; Opperman, interview.

103. Zazeraj, interview; Scholtz, *SADF in the Border War*, 17; Willem Steenkamp, *South Africa's Border War, 1966–1989* (Pretoria: Ashanti Publishing, 1989), 43.

104. Chester A. Crocker, *High Noon in Southern Africa: Making Peace in a Rough Neighborhood* (New York: W. W. Norton, 1992), 49.

105. Piero Gleijeses, "From Cassinga to New York: The Struggle for the Independence of Namibia," in *Cold War in Southern Africa: White Power, Black Liberation*, ed. Sue Onslow (New York: Routledge, 2009), 203. For a contrasting account that downplays the role of the United States in shaping South Africa's decision to intervene, see Jamie Miller, "Yes, Minister: Reassessing South Africa's Intervention in the Angolan Civil War, 1975–1976," *Journal of Cold War Studies* 15, no. 3 (2013): 4–33.

106. Memo to the Secretary for Foreign Affairs: Dr. Kissinger on Angola, November 21, 1975, DIRCO 1/22/1, vol. 20.

107. Opperman, interview; Scholtz, *SADF in the Border War*, 17.

108. Quoted in Scholtz, *SADF in the Border War*, 19; Malan, *My Life with the SA Defence Force*, 138.

109. Scholtz, *SADF in the Border War*, 19; Steenkamp, *South Africa's Border War*, 54; Breytenbach, interview.

110. Scholtz, *SADF in the Border War*, 19; Gleijeses, *Visions of Freedom*, 9, 29.

111. Steenkamp, *South Africa's Border War*, 56, 59.

112. Gleijeses, *Visions of Freedom*, 29.

113. Steenkamp, *South Africa's Border War*, 60–61.

114. Malan, *My Life with the SA Defence Force*, 189.

115. Steenkamp, *South Africa's Border War*, 63.

116. Steenkamp, *South Africa's Border War*, 71.

117. Steenkamp, *South Africa's Border War*, 67; Malan, *My Life with the SA Defence Force*, 189.

118. Steenkamp, *South Africa's Border War*, 69.

119. Steenkamp, *South Africa's Border War*, 71; Miller, *An African Volk*, 309.

120. Steenkamp, *South Africa's Border War*, 71.

121. Breytenbach, interview; Steenkamp, *South Africa's Border War*, 74–80; Scholtz, *SADF in the Border War*, chap. 5; Miller, *An African Volk*, 312–314.

122. Gleijeses, *Visions of Freedom*, 60–62; Gleijeses, "From Cassinga to New York," 204–205; Steenkamp, *South Africa's Border War*, 80; Scholtz, *SADF in the Border War*, 82–87; Malan, *My Life with the SA Defence Force*, 192–194; Geldenhuys, *At the Front*, 99–100; George, *Cuban Intervention in Angola*, 133–135; Miller, *An African Volk*, 313–319.

123. Steenkamp, *South Africa's Border War*, 86; Scholtz, *SADF in the Border War*, 99–100; Malan, *My Life with the SA Defence Force*, 194–195.

124. Scholtz, *SADF in the Border War*, 45–49.

125. Quoted in Scholtz, *SADF in the Border War*, 58.

126. Gleijeses, *Visions of Freedom*, 118.

127. Robert Scott Jaster, *The Defence of White Power: South African Foreign Policy under Pressure* (Basingstoke: Macmillan Press, 1988), 93.

128. "Report of the Secretary General on the Implementation of the Declaration on the Denuclearization of Africa," September 9, 1980, DIRCO 137/28, vol. 5.

129. Scholtz, *SADF in the Border War*, 103.

130. Geldenhuys, *At the Front*, 129.

131. Scholtz, *SADF in the Border War*, 114.

132. Steenkamp, *South Africa's Border War*, 92.

133. Opperman, interview; Zazeraj, interview; Gleijeses, *Visions of Freedom*, 186.

134. Steenkamp, *South Africa's Border War*, 97–98; Geldenhuys, *At the Front*, 154–155.

135. Scholtz, *SADF in the Border War*, 120.

136. Scholtz, *SADF in the Border War*, 121; Geldenhuys, *At the Front*, 156.

137. Gleijeses, *Visions of Freedom*, 188. See also George, *Cuban Intervention in Angola*, 141.

138. Scholtz, *SADF in the Border War*, 144, 168; Steenkamp, *South Africa's Border War*, 99.

139. Gleijeses, *Visions of Freedom*, 189.

140. Scholtz, *SADF in the Border War*, 162.

141. Steenkamp, *South Africa's Border War*, 109–110.

142. Steenkamp, *South Africa's Border War*, 112.

143. Scholtz, *SADF in the Border War*, 182.

144. Scholtz, *SADF in the Border War*, 167.

145. Scholtz, *SADF in the Border War*, 184.

146. Scholtz, *SADF in the Border War*, 187–191.

147. Gleijeses, *Visions of Freedom*, 251–252.

148. Gleijeses, *Visions of Freedom*, 181.

149. Gleijeses, "From Cassinga to New York," 207.

150. Gleijeses, *Visions of Freedom*, 181–183.

151. Breytenbach, interview; Zazeraj, interview.

152. Narang, *Nuclear Strategy in the Modern Era*, 216.

153. de Vries, interview.

154. Opperman, interview.

155. Dippenaar, interview.

156. Quoted in Miller, *African Volk*, 201.

157. For example, "Recent Developments in US-SA Relations," n.d., DIRCO 1/33/3, vol. 31.

158. Pieter Snyman, interview with the author, Ruimsig, June 24, 2014.

159. Ambassador Shearar to the Secretary for Foreign Affairs, February 3, 1977, DIRCO 1/33/3, vol. 39A.

160. de Vries, interview.

161. "Impact Upon U.S. Security of a South African Nuclear Weapons Capability," April 1, 1981, CIAA CREST, General CIA Records, document RDP87T00126R001201660002-2.

162. For example, Robert Turner to Hon. Major R. Owens, October 22, 1984, Reagan Presidential Library, Simi Valley, California (REAG), CO141 (South Africa), box 165, folder 247000.

163. Mona Charen to Patrick Buchanan, July 29, 1985, REAG, CO141 (South Africa), box 165, folder 275000.

164. "Political Relations with the Reagan Administration," n.d., DIRCO 1/33/3, vol. 74.

165. Crocker to the Secretary of State, May 1981, DIRCO 1/33/3, vol. 77.

166. Theresa Papenfus, *Pik Botha and His Times* (Pretoria: Litera Publications, 2010), 541.

167. Sasha Polakow-Suransky, *The Unspoken Alliance: Israel's Secret Relationship with Apartheid South Africa* (New York: Pantheon Books, 2010); Peter Liberman, "Israel and the South African Bomb," *Nonproliferation Review* 11, no. 2 (2004): 46–80; Von Wielligh and Von Wielligh-Steyn, *The Bomb*, part 5.

168. Dippenaar, interview.

169. Polakow-Suransky, *Unspoken Alliance*, 6.

170. Scholtz, *SADF in the Border War*, xiv.

171. S. Paul Kapur, *Dangerous Deterrent: Nuclear Weapons Proliferation and Conflict in South Asia* (Stanford, CA: Stanford University Press, 2007).

172. Narang, *Nuclear Strategy in the Modern Era*, 218.

173. Whether South Africa had revisionist preferences is somewhat debatable. South Africa certainly had status quo preferences at a strategic level—it sought to preserve its position in southern Africa and uphold the domestic political institutions of apartheid in the face of increasing international isolation and condemnation. However, South Africa also had some revisionist preferences with respect to its neighbors at a tactical level (for example, seeking the fall of the MPLA government in Angola).

174. Breytenbach, interview.

175. Steward, interview.

176. Military expenditure figures are taken from the Correlates of War Project and are in 2010 US dollars.

177. Figures on South African military expenditure used data from the Correlates of War Project.

178. Breytenbach, interview.
179. Stumpf, interview.
180. Liberman, "Rise and Fall of the South African Bomb," 72.
181. Buys, interview.

4. The Foundations of a New World Order

1. The existence of a vast historiography on the origins of the Cold War that profoundly divides on these questions does not help in resolving these issues. See, for example, Howard Jones and Randall B. Woods, "Origins of the Cold War in Europe and the Near East: Recent Historiography and the National Security Imperative," *Diplomatic History*, 17, no. 2 (1993): 251–276.

2. Lawrence Freedman, *The Evolution of Nuclear Strategy*, 3rd ed. (Basingstoke: Palgrave Macmillan, 2003), 16–20; Wilson D. Miscamble, *The Most Controversial Decision: Truman, the Atomic Bombs, and the Defeat of Japan* (Cambridge: Cambridge University Press, 2011), 14.

3. On the impact that prior thinking about strategic bombing had on the way in which nuclear weapons were initially understood, see Freedman, *Evolution of Nuclear Strategy*, chap. 1; Miscamble, *Most Controversial Decision*, 12–15.

4. Richard Rhodes, *The Making of the Atomic Bomb* (New York: Simon & Schuster, 1995), 405.

5. Aide-Memoire of Conversation between Roosevelt and Churchill, September 19, 1944, in *FRUS, Conference at Quebec, 1944*, document 299, *FRUS* documents available at https://history .state.gov/historicaldocuments.

6. "Notes of the Interim Committee Meeting," June 1, 1945, Truman Presidential Library, Independence, Missouri (TRUM), Papers of R. Gordon Arneson, box 1.

7. The gun-type device was considered sufficiently reliable and thus a full nuclear test was not needed.

8. That both devices would be ready by August 1945 was in line with General Leslie Groves's expectations six months earlier. See Groves to Marshall, December 30, 1945, in *FRUS Diplomatic Papers, Conferences at Malta and Yalta, 1945*, document 262.

9. Paul Kennedy, *The Rise and Fall of the Great Powers: Economic Change and Military Conflict from 1500 to 2000* (London: Harper Collins, 1989), 461–462.

10. Melvyn P. Leffler, *A Preponderance of Power: National Security, the Truman Administration, and the Cold War* (Stanford, CA: Stanford University Press, 1992), 2; Paul C. Avey, "Confronting Soviet Power: U.S. Policy during the Early Cold War," *International Security* 36, no. 4 (2012): 159.

11. Leffler, *Preponderance of Power*, 2.

12. Thomas C. Schelling, *Arms and Influence* (New Haven, CT: Yale University Press, 1966), 19.

13. Richard Smoke, *War: Controlling Escalation* (Cambridge, MA: Harvard University Press, 1978), 32.

14. "The United States Strategic Bombing Survey: The Effects of Atomic Bombs on Hiroshima and Nagasaki," June 30, 1946, TRUM, Papers of Harry S. Truman, Confidential File, box 3, File on "Atomic Bomb and Energy, August 1945–November 1947." These casualty estimates are today regarded as significantly underestimating the numbers of fatalities.

15. "Minutes of Meeting Held at the White House," June 18, 1945, in *FRUS: Diplomatic Papers, The Conference of Berlin (The Potsdam Conference)*, vol. 1, document 598.

16. "The United States Strategic Bombing Survey: The Effects of Atomic Bombs on Hiroshima and Nagasaki (June 30, 1946)," TRUM, Papers of Harry S. Truman, Confidential File, box 3, File on "Atomic Bomb and Energy, August 1945–November 1947."

17. Ward Wilson, "The Winning Weapon? Rethinking Nuclear Weapons in Light of Hiroshima," *International Security* 31, no. 4 (2007): 167–171. It also remains a matter of debate whether the nuclear attacks on Japan did indeed cause Japanese surrender. For a sampling of this literature, see Robert J. C. Butow, *Japan's Decision to Surrender* (Stanford, CA: Stanford University Press, 1954); Gar Alperovitz, *Atomic Diplomacy: Hiroshima and Potsdam; The Use of the Atomic Bomb and the American Confrontation with Soviet Power* (New York: Vintage, 1965); Robert James Maddox, *Weapons for Victory: The Hiroshima Decision* (Columbia: University of Missouri Press, 1995); Robert A. Pape, "Why Japan Surrendered," *International Security* 18, no. 2 (1993):

154–201; Tsuyoshi Hasegawa, *Racing the Enemy: Stalin, Truman, and the Surrender of Japan* (Cambridge, MA: Harvard University Press, 2005); Wilson, "Winning Weapon?"; Miscamble, *Most Controversial Decision*. The effect of nuclear weapons on Japanese behavior, however, is less important here than the effect of nuclear weapons on US calculations and behavior.

18. Wilson, "Winning Weapon?," 167. See also Freedman, *Evolution of Nuclear Strategy*, 16–20.

19. Wilson, "Winning Weapon?," 167–168.

20. Herbert Feis, *The Atomic Bomb and the End of World War II* (Princeton, NJ: Princeton University Press, 1966), 36.

21. "Notes of the Interim Committee Meeting," May 31, 1945, TRUM, R. Gordon Arneson Papers, box 1.

22. "Statement by the President Announcing the Use of the A-Bomb at Hiroshima," August 6, 1945, Public Papers of the Presidents of the United States (PPPUS), Harry S. Truman, 1945, document 93.

23. Webb to Truman, July 22, 1948, TRUM, Papers of Harry S. Truman, President's Secretary's Files, box 175, file 5.

24. For example, J. Samuel Walker, "The Decision to Use the Bomb: A Historiographical Update," in *America in the World: The Historiography of American Foreign Relations since 1945*, ed. Michael J. Hogan (Cambridge: Cambridge University Press, 1995), 216.

25. Henry L. Stimson, "The Decision to Use the Atomic Bomb," *Harper's Magazine* 194, no. 1161 (1947): 98.

26. Martin J. Sherwin, *A World Destroyed: Hiroshima and Its Legacies*, 3rd ed. (Stanford, CA: Stanford University Press, 2003), 194–195.

27. Leslie R. Groves, *Now It Can Be Told: The Story of the Manhattan Project* (New York: De Capo Press, 1975), 49.

28. "Minutes of a Meeting of the Combined Policy Committee," July 4, 1945, in *FRUS: Diplomatic Papers, The Conference of Berlin (The Potsdam Conference)*, vol. 1, document 619.

29. "Radio Report to the American People on the Potsdam Conference," August 9, 1945, PPPUS, Harry S. Truman, 1945, document 97.

30. Stimson, "Decision to Use the Atomic Bomb," 98.

31. Quoted in Rhodes, *Making of the Atomic Bomb*, 406.

32. Quoted in Rhodes, *Making of the Atomic Bomb*, 407.

33. Quoted in Miscamble, *Most Controversial Decision*, 8.

34. For example, Memorandum by Leslie R. Groves, May 5, 1943, NSA Electronic Briefing Book 525, document 3. See also Gregg Herken, *The Winning Weapon: The Atomic Bomb in the Cold War, 1945–1950* (Princeton, NJ: Princeton University Press, 1980), 13; Sherwin, *World Destroyed*, 209.

35. Quoted in Herken, *Winning Weapon*, 13. For an account that acknowledges the racial dimension of the use of nuclear weapons against Japan but concludes that the United States would nonetheless have been prepared to use nuclear weapons against Germany had the bomb been ready in time, see Matthew Jones, *After Hiroshima: The United States, Race and Nuclear Weapons in Asia, 1945–1965* (New York: Cambridge University Press, 2010), 22–23.

36. Quoted in Leffler, *Preponderance of Power*, 37.

37. Quoted in Herken, *Winning Weapon*, 20–21.

38. For discussion of the evolution of the terms of Japanese surrender, see Miscamble, *Most Controversial Decision*, chap. 6.

39. Quoted in Miscamble, *Most Controversial Decision*, 101.

40. Leffler, *Preponderance of Power*, 31, 83, 88.

41. Leffler, *Preponderance of Power*, 81, 83. See also Melvyn P. Leffler, "Adherence to Agreements: Yalta and the Experiences of the Early Cold War," *International Security* 11, no. 1 (1986): 88–123.

42. Quoted in Leffler, *Preponderance of Power*, 33.

43. Wilson D. Miscamble, *From Roosevelt to Truman: Potsdam, Hiroshima, and the Cold War* (Cambridge: Cambridge University Press, 2007), 226. For broader discussion of Soviet reactions to the Hiroshima bombing, see David Holloway, *Stalin and the Bomb: The Soviet Union and Atomic Energy, 1939–1956* (New Haven, CT: Yale University Press, 1996), 127–129.

44. Miscamble, *Most Controversial Decision*, 70.

45. Richard B. Frank, *Downfall: The End of the Imperial Japanese Empire* (New York: Random House, 1999), 323–324; Miscamble, *Most Controversial Decision*, 111.

46. Leffler, *Preponderance of Power*, 34. See also Sherwin, *World Destroyed*, 198–199. For the view that the United States used nuclear weapons primarily to intimidate the Soviet Union rather than to defeat Japan, see Alperovitz, *Atomic Diplomacy*.

47. Rhodes, *Making of the Atomic Bomb*, 405.

48. For an overview of the debate, see Jones and Woods, "Origins of the Cold War in Europe and the Near East."

49. John Lewis Gaddis, "The Emerging Post-Revisionist Synthesis on the Origins of the Cold War," *Diplomatic History* 7, no. 3 (1983): 171–190. For responses to Gaddis, see Lloyd C. Gardner, Lawrence S. Kaplan, Warren F. Kimball, and Bruce R. Kuniholm, "Responses to John Lewis Gaddis, "The Emerging Post-Revisionist Synthesis on the Origins of the Cold War," *Diplomatic History* 7, no. 3 (1983): 191–204.

50. For examples of works that adopt this view, see Marc Trachtenberg, *A Constructed Peace: The Making of the European Settlement, 1945–1963* (Princeton, NJ: Princeton University Press, 1999); Mark S. Sheetz, "Exit Strategies: American Grand Designs for Postwar European Security," *Security Studies* 8, no. 4 (1999): 1–43; James McAllister, *No Exit: America and the German Problem, 1943–1954* (Ithaca, NY: Cornell University Press, 2002); Michael Creswell, *A Question of Balance: How France and the United States Created Cold War Europe* (Cambridge, MA: Harvard University Press, 2006); Brendan Rittenhouse Green, "Two Concepts of Liberty: U.S. Cold War Grand Strategies and the Liberal Tradition," *International Security* 37, no. 2 (2012): 9–43.

51. Sheetz, "Exit Strategies," 4.

52. Green, "Two Concepts of Liberty," 9.

53. For examples of this view, see Leffler, *Preponderance of Power*; Christopher Layne, "The 'Poster Child for Offensive Realism': America as a Global Hegemon," *Security Studies* 12, no. 2 (2002): 120–164; Christopher Layne, *The Peace of Illusions: American Grand Strategy from 1940 to the Present* (Cambridge: Cambridge University Press, 2006).

54. Layne, "'Poster Child for Offensive Realism,'" 152.

55. Francis J. Gavin, "Strategies of Inhibition: U.S. Grand Strategy, the Nuclear Revolution, and Nonproliferation," *International Security* 40, no. 1 (2015): 16n22.

56. Secretary of State to the Acting Secretary of State, September 15, 1950, in *FRUS 1950*, vol. 3, document 573.

57. R. Alton Lee, "The 'Army Mutiny' of 1946," *Journal of American History* 53, no. 3 (1966): 555.

58. Version 4.0 of the National Material Capabilities Dataset.

59. Secretary of State to the Secretary of Defense, March 23, 1948, in *FRUS 1948*, vol. 1, part 2, document 8.

60. Quoted in David Mayers, *George Kennan and the Dilemmas of US Foreign Policy* (Oxford: Oxford University Press, 1988), 304.

61. "Review of the World Situation as It Relates to the Security of the United States," September 26, 1947, TRUM, Papers of Harry S. Truman, President's Secretary's Files, box 177, file 5.

62. "Draft Report by the National Security Council on United States Policy on Atomic Warfare," n.d., in *FRUS 1948*, vol. 1, part 2, document 42.

63. Walter Millis, ed., *The Forrestal Diaries* (New York: Viking Press, 1951), 538.

64. "Minutes of a Meeting of the Policy Planning Staff, Department of State," November 3, 1949, in *FRUS 1949*, vol. 1, document 212.

65. "NSC 68: United States Objectives and Programs for National Security," April 14, 1950, Woodrow Wilson Center Digital Archive (WWCDA), document 116191.

66. "Paper Prepared by Leon W. Fuller of the Policy Planning Staff," September 10, 1954, in *FRUS 1952–1954*, vol. 5, part 2, document 39.

67. For example, Michael Mandelbaum, *The Nuclear Question: The United States and Nuclear Weapons, 1946–1976* (New York: Cambridge University Press, 1979), 55–60.

68. Memorandum for the Chairman, August 15, 1951, TRUM, Papers of Harry S. Truman, President's Secretary's Files, box 177, file 1.

69. Trachtenberg, *Constructed Peace*, 89–90.

70. Wilson D. Miscamble, *George F. Kennan and the Making of American Foreign Policy, 1947–1950* (Princeton, NJ: Princeton University Press, 1992), 298.

71. Quoted in Matthew A. Evangelista, "Stalin's Postwar Army Reappraised," *International Security* 7, no. 3 (1982): 110.

72. "Catalog of Commitments Involving the Use or Possible Use of United States Armed Forces," September 1, 1948, TRUM, Papers of Harry S. Truman, Confidential File, box 170, file 2.

73. Trachtenberg, *Constructed Peace*, 89. See also Herken, *Winning Weapon*, 225–229; David Alan Rosenberg, "The Origins of Overkill: Nuclear Weapons and American Strategy, 1945–1960," *International Security* 7, no. 4 (1983): 12–13.

74. "Evaluation of Effect on Soviet War Effort Resulting from the Strategic Air Offensive," May 11, 1949, in *Containment: Documents on American Policy and Strategy, 1945–1950*, ed. Thomas H. Etzold and John Lewis Gaddis (New York: Columbia University Press, 1978), 360–364.

75. The Secretary of State in Paris to the Acting Secretary of State, November 8, 1948, in *FRUS 1948*, vol. 1, part 2, document 58; The Secretary of State in Paris to the Acting Secretary of State, November 8, 1948, in *FRUS 1948*, vol. 1, part 2, document 59.

76. Melvyn P. Leffler, "The American Conception of National Security and the Beginnings of the Cold War, 1945–1948," *American Historical Review* 89, no. 2 (1984): 371–373.

77. Avi Shlaim, *The United States and the Berlin Blockade, 1948–1949: A Study in Crisis Decision-Making* (Berkeley: University of California Press, 1983), 254.

78. Scott D. Sagan, *Moving Targets: Nuclear Strategy and National Security* (Princeton, NJ: Princeton University Press, 1989), 15.

79. Quoted in Shlaim, *United States and the Berlin Blockade*, 255.

80. The Joint Chiefs of Staff to the Secretary of State, March 29, 1946, in *FRUS 1946*, vol. 1, document 590.

81. "For the Common Defense (July 1, 1943 to June 30, 1945)," in George C. Marshall, *Biennial Reports of the Chief of Staff of the United States Army to the Secretary of War, 1 July 1939–30 June 1945* (Washington, DC: Center of Military History, United States Army, 1996), 210.

82. Quoted in Gabriel Kolko, *The Politics of War: The World and United States Foreign Policy, 1943–1945* (New York: Random House, 1968), 400.

83. Joint Chiefs of Staff to the Secretary of State, November 7, 1945, in *FRUS 1946*, vol. 1, document 580.

84. Leffler, *Preponderance of Power*, 56.

85. Layne, "'Poster Child for Offensive Realism,'" 141.

86. Memorandum by Groves, January 2, 1946, in *FRUS 1946*, vol. 1, document 600.

87. "Statement of Effect of Atomic Weapons on National Security and Military Organization," February 6, 1946, Digital National Security Archive (DNSA), Collection on U.S. Nuclear Non-Proliferation Policy, 1945–1991, NP00019, 46, 48.

88. "Current Strategic Evaluation of the U.S. Security Needs in Japan," June 15, 1949, TRUM, Papers of Harry S. Truman, President's Secretary's Files, box 173, file 2.

89. "Overall Effect of Atomic Bomb on Warfare and Military Organization," October 30, 1945, DNSA, Collection on U.S. Nuclear Non-Proliferation Policy, 1945–1991, NP00007.

90. "Guidance on Military Aspects of United States Policy to Be Adopted in Event of Continuing Impasse in Acceptance of International Control of Atomic Energy," July 14, 1947, DNSA, Collection on U.S. Nuclear Non-Proliferation Policy, 1945–1991, NP00044.

91. Memorandum Prepared by the Joint Chiefs of Staff, March 27, 1946, in *FRUS 1946*, vol. 1, part 1, document 589.

92. John Lewis Gaddis, *Strategies of Containment: A Critical Appraisal of American National Security Policy during the Cold War*, rev. ed (New York: Oxford University Press, 2005), 22.

93. Memorandum Prepared in the Department of State, February 6, 1948, in *FRUS 1948*, vol. 4, document 26.

94. Stephen G. Xydis, "The Truman Doctrine in Perspective," *Balkan Studies* 8, no. 2 (1967): 257.

95. Leffler, *Preponderance of Power*, 124.

96. Howard Jones, *A New Kind of War: America's Global Strategy and the Truman Doctrine in Greece* (Oxford: Oxford University Press, 1989), 36.

97. Trachtenberg, *Constructed Peace*, 38–41.

98. Acting Secretary of State to the Secretary of State, at Paris, August 15, 1946, in *FRUS 1946*, vol. 8, document 655.

99. Leffler, *Preponderance of Power*, 124; Eduard Mark, "The War Scare of 1946 and Its Consequences," *Diplomatic History* 21, no. 3 (1997): 385–386.

100. "Address of the President of the United States," March 12, 1947, TRUM Papers of George M. Elsey, box 11.

101. Quoted in Trachtenberg, *Constructed Peace*, 81.

102. "Address of the President of the United States," March 12, 1947, TRUM Papers of George M. Elsey, box 11.

103. Gaddis, *Strategies of Containment*, 57–58; Trachtenberg, *Constructed Peace*, 87–88.

104. "A Report to the President Pursuant to the President's Directive of January 31, 1950," April 7, 1950, TRUM, Papers of Harry S. Truman, President's Secretary's Files, box 176, file 2.

105. For work on US covert and psychological warfare against the Soviet Union, see Scott Lucas, *Freedom's War: The U.S. Crusade against the Soviet Union, 1945–56* (Manchester: Manchester University Press, 1999); Gregory Mitrovich, *Undermining the Kremlin: America's Strategy to Subvert the Soviet Bloc, 1947–1956* (Ithaca, NY: Cornell University Press, 2000); Kenneth A. Osgood, "Form before Substance: Eisenhower's Commitment to Psychological Warfare and Negotiations with the Enemy," *Diplomatic History* 24, no. 3 (2000): 405–433; Peter Grose, *Operation Rollback: America's Secret War behind the Iron Curtain* (Boston: Houghton Mifflin, 2000).

106. Mitrovich, *Undermining the Kremlin*, 17–18.

107. "Report to the President by the National Security Council," November 23, 1948, in *FRUS 1948*, vol. 1, part 2, document 61.

108. "National Security Council Directive on Office of Special Projects," June 18, 1948, in *FRUS 1945–1950 (Retrospective Volume)*, document 292.

109. Mitrovich, *Undermining the Kremlin*, 182.

110. "National Security Council Progress Report by the Acting Secretary of State on the Implementation of United States Policy toward the Soviet Satellite States in Eastern Europe," May 29, 1950, TRUM, Papers of Harry S. Truman, President's Secretary's Files, box 173, file 3; "A Report to the President Pursuant to the President's Directive of January 31, 1950," April 7, 1950, TRUM, Papers of Harry S. Truman, President's Secretary's Files, box 176, file 2.

111. Quoted in Ronald R. Krebs, *Dueling Visions: U.S. Strategy toward Eastern Europe under Eisenhower* (College Station: Texas A&M University Press, 2001), 12.

112. For a summary of US thinking about preventive war in this period, see Marc Trachtenberg, "A 'Wasting Asset': American Strategy and the Shifting Nuclear Balance, 1949–1954," *International Security* 13, no. 3 (1988): 7–11; Marc Trachtenberg, "Preventive War and U.S. Foreign Policy," *Security Studies* 16, no. 1 (2007): 4–8; Keir A. Lieber, *War and the Engineers: The Primacy of Politics over Technology* (Ithaca, NY: Cornell University Press, 2005), 134–140.

113. Quoted in George H. Quester, *Nuclear Monopoly* (New Brunswick, NJ: Transaction Publishers, 2000), 38.

114. Trachtenberg, "'Wasting Asset,'" 7–11; Trachtenberg, "Preventive War and U.S. Foreign Policy," 4–8.

115. "Relations between the Big Three," May 13, 1946, DNSA, Collection on U.S. Nuclear Non-proliferation Policy, 1945–1991, NP00025, 7.

116. Rosenberg, "Origins of Overkill," 15–16.

117. Trachtenberg, *Constructed Peace*, 89.

118. Trachtenberg, *Constructed Peace*, 91.

119. Memorandum by the Acting Department of State Member (Matthews) to the State–War–Navy Coordinating Committee, April 1, 1946, in *FRUS 1946*, vol. 1, document 591. See also Leffler, *Preponderance of Power*, 111–112.

120. Quoted in Millis, *Forrestal Diaries*, 350–351.

121. Herken, *Winning Weapon*, 247. Forrestal did qualify that apparently confident assertion with an acknowledgment that "one always has to remember that there seemed to be no reason in 1939 for Hitler to start war, and yet he did." Millis, *Forrestal Diaries*, 395.

122. Mitrovich, *Undermining the Kremlin*, 155–171.

123. Stimson Diary Entries, May 14–15, 1945, NSA Electronic Briefing Book 525, document 12.

124. Quoted in Leffler, *Preponderance of Power*, 116.

125. Quoted in Herken, *Winning Weapon*, 43.

126. Robert A. Pollard, "Economic Security and the Origins of the Cold War: Bretton Woods, the Marshall Plan, and American Rearmament, 1944–50," *Diplomatic History* 9, no. 3 (1985): 271–272.

127. Gaddis, "Emerging Post-Revisionist Synthesis on the Origins of the Cold War," 1983.

128. Pollard, "Economic Security and the Origins of the Cold War," 273.

129. Jones and Woods, "Origins of the Cold War in Europe and the Near East," 238; Gavin, "Strategies of Inhibition," 14.

130. Quoted in Pollard, "Economic Security and the Origins of the Cold War," 273.

131. Pollard, "Economic Security and the Origins of the Cold War," 276–277.

132. On the Marshall Plan, see John Gimbel, *The Origins of the Marshall Plan* (Stanford, CA: Stanford University Press, 1976); Michael J. Hogan, *The Marshall Plan: America, Britain and the Reconstruction of Western Europe, 1947–1952* (Cambridge: Cambridge University Press, 1989); Gabriel Kolko and Joyce Kolko, *The Limits of Power: The World and United States Foreign Policy, 1945–1954* (New York: Harper & Row, 1972), chaps. 13, 16–17.

133. Pollard, "Economic Security and the Origins of the Cold War," 279; Layne, *Peace of Illusions*, 78–79.

134. Acheson to the Secretary of State, February 21, 1947, in *FRUS 1947*, vol. 5, document 23.

135. Pollard, "Economic Security and the Origins of the Cold War," 283–285; Layne, *Peace of Illusions*, 79–80.

136. Gaddis, "Emerging Post-Revisionist Synthesis on the Origins of the Cold War," 180.

137. Millis, *Forrestal Diaries*, 350. Ultimately, rebuilding Europe's economy took priority over redressing the conventional imbalance that the West faced. Trachtenberg, *Constructed Peace*, 90.

138. Pollard, "Economic Security and the Origins of the Cold War," 288.

139. "Minutes of the 148th Meeting of the Policy Planning Staff," October 11, 1949, in *FRUS 1949*, vol. 4, document 148.

140. Quoted in Marc Trachtenberg, *History and Strategy* (Princeton, NJ: Princeton University Press, 1991), 120n70.

141. Loy Henderson to Karl Rankin, March 25, 1948, in *FRUS 1948*, vol. 4, document 47.

142. "Report to the National Security Council by the Executive Secretary of the Council," May 25, 1948, in *FRUS 1948*, vol. 4, document 67.

143. For a broader discussion of the theory of the nuclear revolution and US postwar grand strategy, see Francis J. Gavin, "Rethinking the Bomb: Nuclear Weapons and American Grand Strategy," *Texas National Security Review* 2, no. 1 (2018): 74–100.

144. Gavin, "Rethinking the Bomb," 79.

145. Rosenberg, "Origins of Overkill"; James Cameron, *The Double Game: The Demise of America's First Missile Defense System and the Rise of Strategic Arms Limitation* (New York: Oxford University Press, 2017), chaps. 1–3; Gavin, "Rethinking the Bomb," 80.

146. Cameron, *Double Game*, 5.

147. Indeed, arms control efforts may have contributed to the value of qualitative superiority by reducing the quantity of missiles that both sides possessed. See John D. Maurer, "The Purposes of Arms Control," *Texas National Security Review* 2, no. 1 (2018): 8–27.

148. Brendan Rittenhouse Green and Austin Long, "The MAD Who Wasn't There: Soviet Reactions to the Late Cold War Strategic Balance," *Security Studies* 26, no. 4 (2017): 606–641; Niccolo Petrelli and Giordana Pulcini, "Nuclear Superiority in the Age of Parity: US Planning, Intelligence Analysis, Weapons Innovation and the Search for a Qualitative Edge 1969–1976," *International History Review* 40, no. 5 (2018): 1191–1209.

149. For example, Charles L. Glaser, "Why Even Good Defenses May Be Bad," *International Security* 9, no. 2 (1984): 92–123.

150. Earl C. Ravenal, "Counterforce and Alliance: The Ultimate Connection," *International Security* 6, no. 4 (1982): 34. See also R. Harrison Wagner, "Nuclear Deterrence, Counterforce Strategies, and the Incentive to Strike First," *American Political Science Review* 85, no. 3 (1991): 727–749.

151. Desmond Ball, "U.S. Strategic Forces: How Would They Be Used?," *International Security* 7, no. 3 (1982): 34; Lieber, *War and the Engineers*, 142.

152. Matthew Fuhrmann and Todd S. Sechser, "Nuclear Strategy, Nonproliferation, and the Causes of Foreign Nuclear Deployments," *Journal of Conflict Resolution* 58, no. 3 (2014): 466.

153. See, for example, Nicholas L. Miller, "Nuclear Dominoes: A Self-Defeating Prophecy?," *Security Studies* 23, no. 1 (2014): 33–73; Nicholas L. Miller, "The Secret Success of Nonproliferation Sanctions," *International Organization* 68, no. 4 (2014): 913–944; Nicholas L. Miller, *Stopping the Bomb: The Sources and Effectiveness of U.S. Nonproliferation Policy* (Ithaca, NY: Cornell University Press, 2018); Or Rabinowitz, *Bargaining on Nuclear Tests: Washington and Its Cold War Deals* (Oxford: Oxford University Press, 2014); Matthew Kroenig, "Force or Friendship? Explaining Great Power Nonproliferation Policy," *Security Studies* 23, no. 1 (2014): 1–32; Gene Gerzhoy, "Alliance Coercion and Nuclear Restraint: How the United States Thwarted West Germany's Nuclear Ambitions," *International Security* 39, no. 4 (2015): 91–129; Gavin, "Strategies of Inhibition"; Andrew Coe and Jane Vaynman, "Superpower Collusion and the Nuclear Nonproliferation Treaty," *Journal of Politics* 77, no. 4 (2015): 983–997; Or Rabinowitz and Nicholas L. Miller, "Keeping the Bombs in the Basement: U.S. Nonproliferation Policy toward Israel, South Africa, and Pakistan," *International Security* 40, no. 1 (2015): 47–86. For the counterargument that US nonproliferation policy has been less consistent, see, for example, Thomas P. Cavanna, "Geopolitics over Proliferation: The Origins of US Grand Strategy and Their Implications for the Spread of Nuclear Weapons in South Asia," *Journal of Strategic Studies* 41, no. 4 (2018): 576–603; Galen Jackson, "The United States, the Israeli Nuclear Program, and Nonproliferation, 1961–69," *Security Studies* 28, no. 2 (2019): 360–393.

154. On US-Soviet cooperation, see Gavin, "Strategies of Inhibition," 17–18; Coe and Vaynman, "Superpower Collusion and the Nuclear Nonproliferation Treaty."

155. Gavin, "Strategies of Inhibition."

156. White House, *National Security Strategy* (Washington, DC: The White House, 2015), 8.

157. Department of Defense, *Nuclear Posture Review* (Arlington, VA: Department of Defense, 2018), xii.

5. Past and Future Proliferators

1. Nonetheless, it is at least plausible that the Soviet Union engaged in more expansive foreign policies after acquiring nuclear weapons, as the theory of nuclear opportunism would predict. In the aftermath of acquiring nuclear weapons, the Soviet Union expanded its interests in Asia, most notably by reversing its cautious attitude toward the Chinese revolution and signing an alliance with the PRC, approving the transfer of substantial military capabilities to North Korea and ultimately approving Kim Il Sung's attack on South Korea. See, for example, David Holloway, *Stalin and the Bomb: The Soviet Union and Atomic Energy, 1939–1956* (New Haven, CT: Yale University Press, 1996), chap. 13. Similarly, after acquiring the ability to target the United States in the late 1950s, the Soviet Union engaged in a second round of expansive and assertive foreign policies, triggering both the Berlin Crisis and the Cuban Missile Crisis. See, for example, Marc Trachtenberg, *History and Strategy* (Princeton, NJ: Princeton University Press, 1991), chaps. 5–6; Michael D. Cohen, *When Proliferation Causes Peace: The Psychology of Nuclear Crises* (Washington, DC: Georgetown University Press, 2017), chap. 3.

2. On North Korean capabilities, see, for example, Jacques E. C. Hymans, "When Does a State Become a 'Nuclear Weapon State'? An Exercise in Measurement Validation," *Nonproliferation Review* 17, no. 1 (2010): 162–163; Vipin Narang, "Nuclear Strategies of Emerging Nuclear Powers: North Korea and Iran," *Washington Quarterly* 38, no. 1 (2015): 73–91; Nicholas L. Miller

and Vipin Narang, "North Korea Defied the Theoretical Odds: What Can We Learn from Its Successful Nuclearization?," *Texas National Security Review* 1, no. 2 (2018): 58–75.

3. This quote is attributed to Pakistani president Zulfikar Ali Bhutto.

4. For discussions of when Pakistan acquired the relevant capabilities, see Feroz Hassan Khan, *Eating Grass: The Making of the Pakistani Bomb* (Stanford, CA: Stanford University Press, 2012); Vipin Narang, *Nuclear Strategy in the Modern Era: Regional Powers and International Conflict* (Princeton, NJ: Princeton University Press, 2014), chaps. 3, 10; S. Paul Kapur, *Dangerous Deterrent: Nuclear Weapons Proliferation and Conflict in South Asia* (Stanford, CA: Stanford University Press, 2007).

5. Quoted in Narang, *Nuclear Strategy in the Modern Era*, 264. For more on the Brasstacks crisis, see Narang, *Nuclear Strategy in the Modern Era*, 260–265; Sumit Ganguly and Devin T. Hagerty, *Fearful Symmetry: India-Pakistan Crises in the Shadow of Nuclear Weapons* (Seattle: University of Washington Press, 2005), chap. 4; P. R. Chari, Pervaiz Iqbal, and Stephen P. Cohen, *Four Crises and a Peace Process: American Engagement in South Asia* (Washington, DC: Brookings Institution Press, 2007), chap. 3.

6. Narang, *Nuclear Strategy in the Modern Era*, 264; Chari, Iqbal, and Cohen, *Four Crises and a Peace Process*, 66–67.

7. Quoted in Khan, *Eating Grass*, 230.

8. Quoted in Khan, *Eating Grass*, 230. See also Narang, *Nuclear Strategy in the Modern Era*, 266.

9. Khan, *Eating Grass*, 229–232. See also Chari, Iqbal, and Cohen, *Four Crises and a Peace Process*, 101–103.

10. On the Kargil War, see Bruce Riedel, *American Diplomacy and the 1999 Kargil Summit at Blair House* (Philadelphia: University of Pennsylvania Center for the Advanced Study of India, 2002); Ashley J. Tellis, C. Christine Fair, and Jamison Jo Medby, *Limited Conflicts under the Nuclear Umbrella: Indian and Pakistani Lessons from the Kargil Crisis* (Santa Monica, CA: RAND Corporation, 2002); Ved Prakesh Malik, *Kargil: From Surprise to Victory* (Delhi: Harper Collins, 2006); Kapur, *Dangerous Deterrent*, chap. 6; Chari, Iqbal, and Cohen, *Four Crises and a Peace Process*, chap. 5; Peter Lavoy, ed., *Asymmetric Warfare in South Asia: The Causes and Consequences of the Kargil Conflict* (New York: Cambridge University Press, 2009).

11. Chari, Iqbal, and Cohen, *Four Crises and a Peace Process*, 139; Narang, *Nuclear Strategy in the Modern Era*, 270–272.

12. Quoted in Narang, *Nuclear Strategy in the Modern Era*, 270.

13. Narang, *Nuclear Strategy in the Modern Era*, 270.

14. Quoted in Narang, *Nuclear Strategy in the Modern Era*, 272.

15. Quoted in Narang, *Nuclear Strategy in the Modern Era*, 272.

16. Kargil Review Committee, *From Surprise to Reckoning: The Kargil Review Committee Report* (New Delhi: Sage, 2006), 225.

17. Narang, *Nuclear Strategy in the Modern Era*, 273–282.

18. C. Christine Fair, *Fighting to the End: The Pakistan Army's Way of War* (Oxford: Oxford University Press, 2014), 203.

19. Vipin Narang, "Posturing for Peace? Pakistan's Nuclear Postures and South Asian Stability," *International Security* 34, no. 3 (2009–2010): 39.

20. S. Paul Kapur, "Ten Years of Instability in a Nuclear South Asia," *International Security* 33, no. 2 (2008): 72.

21. See, for example, Tellis, Fair, and Medby, *Limited Conflicts under the Nuclear Umbrella*; S. Paul Kapur, "India and Pakistan's Unstable Peace: Why Nuclear South Asia Is Not Like Cold War Europe," *International Security* 30, no. 2 (2005): 127–152; Kapur, *Dangerous Deterrent*; Kapur, "Ten Years of Instability"; Narang, "Posturing for Peace?"; Fair, *Fighting to the End*.

22. Quoted in Kapur, "India and Pakistan's Unstable Peace," 145.

23. Quoted in Kapur, "India and Pakistan's Unstable Peace," 143.

24. Khan, *Eating Grass*, 207.

25. For discussions of the development of India's nuclear program, see Scott D. Sagan, "Why Do States Build Nuclear Weapons? Three Models in Search of a Bomb," *International Security* 21, no. 3 (1996/1997): 65–69; Itty Abraham, *The Making of the Indian Atomic Bomb: Science, Secrecy and*

the Postcolonial State (London: Zed Books, 1998); Sumit Ganguly, "India's Pathway to Pokhran II: The Prospects and Sources of New Delhi's Nuclear Weapons Program," *International Security* 23, no. 4 (1999): 148–177; George Perkovich, *India's Nuclear Bomb: The Impact on Global Proliferation* (Los Angeles: University of California Press, 2002); Jacques E. C. Hymans, *The Psychology of Nuclear Proliferation: Identity, Emotions and Foreign Policy* (Cambridge: Cambridge University Press, 2006), chap. 7; Gaurav Kampani, "New Delhi's Long Nuclear Journey: How Secrecy and Institutional Roadblocks Delayed India's Weaponization," *International Security* 38, no. 4 (2014): 79–114; Narang, *Nuclear Strategy in the Modern Era*, chap. 4; Vipin Narang, "Strategies of Nuclear Proliferation: How States Pursue the Bomb," *International Security* 41, no. 3 (2017): 110–150.

26. Narang, *Nuclear Strategy in the Modern Era*, 111–112.

27. Baldev Raj Nayar and T. V. Paul, *India in the World Order: Searching for Major-Power Status* (Cambridge: Cambridge University Press, 2003), 214.

28. Nayar and Paul, *India in the World Order*, 2–3.

29. Perkovich, *India's Nuclear Bomb*, 14, 59.

30. Narang, "Strategies of Nuclear Proliferation," 136. See also Abraham, *Making of the Indian Atomic Bomb*.

31. Hymans argues that it was only in 1998, with the coming to power of a leader with an "oppositional nationalist" NIC, that India decided to publicly test a nuclear weapon. But he argues that the development of India's nuclear technologies over the preceding decades and resistance to the US-led nonproliferation regime can be explained by the "sportsmanlike nationalism" of previous Indian prime ministers. Hymans, *Psychology of Nuclear Proliferation*, chap. 7.

32. Ross H. Munro, "The Loser: India in the Nineties," *National Interest*, no. 32 (1993): 62–63. See also James Chiriyankandath, "Realigning India: Indian Foreign Policy after the Cold War," *Round Table* 93, no. 374 (2004): 199; Ganguly, "India's Pathway to Pokhran II," 167.

33. Thongkholal Haokip, "India's Look East Policy: Its Evolution and Approach," *South Asian Survey* 18, no. 2 (2011): 239. See also G. V. C. Naidu, "Whither the Look East Policy: India and Southeast Asia," *Strategic Analysis* 28, no. 2 (2004): 331–346; Rajiv Sikri, "India's 'Look East' Policy," *Asia Pacific Review* 16, no. 1 (2009): 131–145.

34. Ashok Kapur, *India: From Regional to World Power* (New York: Routledge, 2006), 5.

35. Rohan Mukherjee and David M. Malone, "Indian Foreign Policy and Contemporary Security Challenges," *International Affairs* 87, no. 1 (2011): 89.

36. Sandy Gordon, *India's Rise to Power* (New York: St. Martin's Press, 1995), 121.

37. Haokip, "India's Look East Policy," 243.

38. Nayar and Paul, *India in the World Order*, 231.

39. For example, Michal Smetana, "(De-)stigmatising the Outsider: Nuclear-Armed India, United States, and the Global Nonproliferation Order," *Journal of International Relations and Development*, forthcoming.

40. Ashton B. Carter, "America's New Strategic Partner?," *Foreign Affairs* 85, no. 4 (2006): 33.

41. On the French nuclear program, see Lawrence Scheinman, *Atomic Energy Policy in France under the Fourth Republic* (Princeton, NJ: Princeton University Press, 1965); Wolf Mendl, *Deterrence and Persuasion: French Nuclear Armament in the Context of National Policy, 1945–1969* (London: Faber & Faber, 1970); Wilfrid L. Kohl, *French Nuclear Diplomacy* (Princeton, NJ: Princeton University Press, 1971); Pierre Gallois, "French Defense Planning: The Future in the Past," *International Security* 1, no. 2 (1976): 15–31; David S. Yost, "France's Deterrent Posture and Security in Europe, Part I: Capabilities and Doctrine," *Adelphi Papers* 194 (1985): 1–72; David S. Yost, "France's Deterrent Posture and Security in Europe, Part II: Strategic and Arms Control Implications," *Adelphi Papers* 195 (1985): 1–75; Philip H. Gordon, "Charles de Gaulle and the Nuclear Revolution," in *Cold War Statesmen Confront the Bomb: Nuclear Diplomacy since 1945*, ed. John Lewis Gaddis (Oxford: Oxford University Press, 1999); Bruno Tertrais, "'Destruction Assurée': The Origins and Development of French Nuclear Strategy, 1945–1981," in *Getting MAD: Nuclear Mutual Assured Destruction, Its Origins and Practices*, ed. Henry Sokolsi (Carlisle, PA: Strategic Studies Institute, 2004): 51–122; Avery Goldstein, *Deterrence and Security in the 21st Century: China, Britain, France, and the Enduring Legacy of the Nuclear Revolution* (Stanford, CA: Stanford University Press, 2000), chap. 6; Hymans, *Psychology of Nuclear Proliferation*, chap. 4; Narang, *Nuclear Strategy in the Modern Era*, chap. 6.

42. Gordon, "Charles de Gaulle and the Nuclear Revolution," 218; Gallois, "French Defense Planning," 17–18. On the capabilities and vulnerabilities of the Mirage bombers as a delivery vehicle, see Philip G. Cerny, *The Politics of Grandeur: Ideological Aspects of De Gaulle's Foreign Policy* (Cambridge: Cambridge University Press, 1980), 195.

43. For a different perspective that argues that the Soviet Union posed a proximate offensive threat to France, see Narang, *Nuclear Strategy in the Modern Era*, chap. 6.

44. Yost, "France's Deterrent Posture and Security in Europe, Part I," 1.

45. Mendl, *Deterrence and Persuasion*, 19.

46. Gallois, "French Defense Planning," 17.

47. Kohl, *French Nuclear Diplomacy*, 9.

48. Quoted in Kohl, *French Nuclear Diplomacy*, 234.

49. Quoted in Narang, *Nuclear Strategy in the Modern Era*, 168.

50. Quoted in Kohl, *French Nuclear Diplomacy*, 129.

51. Quoted in Timothy Andrew Sayle, *Enduring Alliance: A History of NATO and the Postwar Global Order* (Ithaca, NY: Cornell University Press, 2019), 47.

52. Quoted in Gallois, "French Defense Planning," 17.

53. Quoted in Narang, *Nuclear Strategy in the Modern Era*, 157. See also Gallois, "French Defense Planning," 17.

54. Alfred Grosser, *French Foreign Policy under De Gaulle* (Toronto: Little, Brown, 1967), 102–103; Hymans, *Psychology of Nuclear Proliferation*, 87–113.

55. Quoted in Mendl, *Deterrence and Persuasion*, 57.

56. Quoted in Yost, "France's Deterrent Posture and Security in Europe, Part I," 45.

57. Frank Costigliola, "The Failed Design: Kennedy, de Gaulle, and the Struggle for Europe," *Diplomatic History* 8, no. 3 (1984): 235–237; Goldstein, *Deterrence and Security in the 21st Century*, 193. For the argument that fears about Germany took priority over concerns about the United States in driving many of France's nuclear decisions, see Hymans, *Psychology of Nuclear Proliferation*, chap. 4.

58. Goldstein, *Deterrence and Security in the 21st Century*, 197.

59. Yost, "France's Deterrent Posture and Security in Europe, Part I," 5.

60. Gordon, "Charles de Gaulle and the Nuclear Revolution," 234; Kohl, *French Nuclear Diplomacy*.

61. Quoted in David S. Yost, *Strategic Stability in the Cold War: Lessons for Continuing Challenges* (Paris: Institut Français des Relations Internationales, 2011), 30.

62. On various aspects of Israel's nuclear program and doctrine, see Shai Feldman, *Israeli Nuclear Deterrence: A Strategy for the 1980s* (New York: Columbia University Press, 1982); Uri Bar-Joseph, "The Hidden Debate: The Formation of Nuclear Doctrines in the Middle East," *Journal of Strategic Studies* 5, no. 2 (1982): 205–227; Avner Cohen, "Stumbling into Opacity: The United States, Israel, and the Atom, 1960–63," *Security Studies* 4, no. 2 (1994): 195–241; Avner Cohen, "Cairo, Dimona, and the June 1967 War," *Middle East Journal* 50, no. 2 (1996): 190–210; Avner Cohen, *Israel and the Bomb* (New York: Columbia University Press, 1998); Avner Cohen, *The Worst-Kept Secret: Israel's Bargain with the Bomb* (New York: Columbia University Press, 2010); Zeev Maoz, "The Mixed Blessing of Israel's Nuclear Policy," *International Security* 28, no. 2 (2003): 44–77; Zaki Shalom, "Israel's Nuclear Option Revisited," *Journal of Israeli History* 24, no. 2 (2005): 267–277; Michael Karpin, *The Bomb in the Basement: How Israel Went Nuclear and What That Means for the World* (New York: Simon & Schuster, 2006); Narang, *Nuclear Strategy in the Modern Era*, chap. 7; Or Rabinowitz, *Bargaining on Nuclear Tests: Washington and Its Cold War Deals* (Oxford: Oxford University Press, 2014), chap. 5; Or Rabinowitz and Nicholas L. Miller, "Keeping the Bombs in the Basement: U.S. Nonproliferation Policy toward Israel, South Africa, and Pakistan," *International Security* 40, no. 1 (2015): 47–86.

63. Quoted in Cohen, "Stumbling into Opacity," 199.

64. Cohen, "Cairo, Dimona, and the June 1967 War."

65. On the 1967 war, see, for example, Martin Gilbert, *Israel: A History* (New York: William Morrow, 1998), chap. 22; Isabella Ginor and Gideon Remez, *Foxbats over Dimona: The Soviets' Nuclear Gamble in the Six-Day War* (New Haven, CT: Yale University Press, 2008); Guy Laron, *The Six-Day War: The Breaking of the Middle East* (New Haven, CT: Yale University Press, 2017); Cohen, "Cairo, Dimona, and the June 1967 War."

66. Cohen, *Israel and the Bomb*, 275.

67. For example, Elbridge Colby, Avner Cohen, William McCants, Bradley Morris, and William Rosenau, *The Israeli Nuclear Alert of 1973: Deterrence and Signaling in Crisis* (Washington, DC: Center for Naval Analyses, 2013); Narang, *Nuclear Strategy in the Modern Era*, 187–190.

68. Narang, *Nuclear Strategy in the Modern Era*, 189–190; Cohen, *Worst-Kept Secret*, 80–81; Martin Van Creveld, *The Sword and the Olive: A Critical History of the Israeli Defense Force* (New York: PublicAffairs, 1998), 231–232.

69. Narang, *Nuclear Strategy in the Modern Era*, 191.

70. Rabinowitz, *Bargaining on Nuclear Tests*, chap. 5.

71. On China's nuclear program and posture, see Alice Langley Hsieh, *Communist China's Strategy in the Nuclear Era* (Englewood Cliffs, NJ: Prentice-Hall, 1963); John Wilson Lewis and Litai Xue, *China Builds the Bomb* (Stanford, CA: Stanford University Press, 1991); John Wilson Lewis and Hua Di, "China's Ballistic Missile Programs: Technologies, Strategies, Goals," *International Security* 17, no. 2 (1992): 5–40; John Wilson Lewis and Litai Xue, *China's Strategic Seapower* (Stanford, CA: Stanford University Press, 1996); Alastair Iain Johnston, "China's 'New Old Thinking': The Concept of Limited Deterrence," *International Security* 20, no. 3 (1995/1996): 5–42; Alastair Lain Johnston, "Prospects for Chinese Nuclear Force Modernization: Limited Deterrence versus Multilateral Arms Control," *China Quarterly* 146 (1996): 548–576; Goldstein, *Deterrence and Security in the 21st Century*, chaps. 3–4; Jeffrey G. Lewis, *The Minimum Means of Reprisal: China's Search for Security in the Nuclear Age* (Cambridge, MA: MIT Press, 2007); Jingdong Yuan, "Effective, Reliable, and Credible: China's Nuclear Modernization," *Nonproliferation Review* 14, no. 2 (2007): 275–301; M. Taylor Fravel and Evan S. Medeiros, "China's Search for Assured Retaliation: The Evolution of Chinese Nuclear Strategy and Force Structure," *International Security* 35, no. 2 (2010): 48–87; Jacques E. C. Hymans, *Achieving Nuclear Ambitions: Scientists, Politicians, and Proliferation* (New York: Cambridge University Press, 2012), chap. 4; Narang, *Nuclear Strategy in the Modern Era*, chap. 5; Fiona S. Cunningham and M. Taylor Fravel, "Assuring Assured Retaliation: China's Nuclear Posture and US-China Strategic Stability," *International Security* 40, no. 2 (2015): 7–50; Baohui Zhang, *China's Assertive Nuclear Posture: State Security in an Anarchic International Order* (Abingdon: Routledge, 2015); Caitlin Talmadge, "Would China Go Nuclear? Assessing the Risk of Chinese Nuclear Escalation in a Conventional War with the United States," *International Security* 41, no. 4 (2017): 50–92; M. Taylor Fravel, *Active Defense: China's Military Strategy since 1949* (Princeton, NJ: Princeton University Press, 2019), chap. 8.

72. On the use of nuclear threats in the Korean War, see, for example, Richard K. Betts, *Nuclear Blackmail and Nuclear Balance* (Washington, DC: Brookings Institution Press, 1987), 31–47; Rosemary J. Foot, "Nuclear Coercion and the Ending of the Korean Conflict," *International Security* 13, no. 3 (1988): 92–112.

73. Fravel and Medeiros, "China's Search for Assured Retaliation," 48.

74. Lewis and Xue, *China's Strategic Seapower*; Fravel and Medeiros, "China's Search for Assured Retaliation"; Narang, *Nuclear Strategy in the Modern Era*, chap. 5; Fravel, *Active Defense*, chap. 8.

75. Narang, *Nuclear Strategy in the Modern Era*, 140–141.

76. Some scholars have argued that Chinese aggression in the Ussuri River clashes in 1969 may have been partly driven by China's nuclear acquisition. See, for example, Kapur, *Dangerous Deterrent*, 144–154. Nonetheless, the evidence for this proposition remains limited.

77. Fravel and Medeiros, "China's Search for Assured Retaliation," 51.

78. Quoted in Fravel and Medeiros, "China's Search for Assured Retaliation," 61.

79. Cunningham and Fravel, "Assuring Assured Retaliation."

80. In the language of social science, the theory tells us the treatment effect of nuclear weapons on the treated units (countries that have acquired nuclear weapons).

81. Narang, "Nuclear Strategies of Emerging Nuclear Powers," 86–87.

82. Steven R. Ward, *Immortal: A Military History of Iran and Its Armed Forces* (Washington, DC: Georgetown University Press, 2009), 3–4.

83. Whitney Raas and Austin Long, "Osirak Redux? Assessing Israeli Capabilities to Destroy Iranian Nuclear Facilities," *International Security* 31, no. 4 (2007): 7–33.

84. This prediction is in line with the expectations of Stephen Ward. See Ward, *Immortal*, 321. Of course, it is possible that Iran's threat environment could change in the future. For example, if the Islamic State were to regain its lost strength and acquire substantially more territory in Iraq and a greater ability to project power, or if the current Saudi Arabia–Iran proxy conflict escalated into a more conventional military rivalry, it is at least conceivable that Iran could face a severe territorial threat at some point in the future.

85. Narang, "Nuclear Strategies of Emerging Nuclear Powers," 86.

86. Jahangir Amuzegar, "Iran's 20-Year Economic Perspective: Promises and Pitfalls," *Middle East Policy* 16, no. 3 (2009): 41–57.

87. Joshua Rovner, "After America: The Flow of Persian Gulf Oil in the Absence of U.S. Military Force," in *Crude Strategy: Rethinking the U.S. Military Commitment to Defend Persian Gulf Oil*, ed. Charles L. Glaser and Rosemary A. Kelanic (Washington, DC: Georgetown University Press, 2016). For a broader discussion of the balance of power in the Middle East, see Joshua Rovner and Caitlin Talmadge, "Hegemony, Force Posture, and the Provision of Public Goods: The Once and Future Role of Outside Powers in Securing Persian Gulf Oil," *Security Studies* 23, no. 3 (2014): 548–581.

88. Erica D. Borghard and Mira Rapp-Hooper, "Hizbullah and the Iranian Nuclear Programme," *Survival* 55, no. 4 (2013): 86.

89. For an optimistic perspective, see Kenneth N. Waltz, "Why Iran Should Get the Bomb: Nuclear Balancing Would Mean Stability," *Foreign Affairs* 91, no. 4 (2012): 2–5. For a pessimistic perspective, see Matthew Kroenig, *A Time to Attack: The Looming Iranian Nuclear Threat* (New York: Palgrave Macmillan, 2014).

Conclusion

1. Jeffrey G. Lewis, *The Minimum Means of Reprisal: China's Search for Security in the Nuclear Age* (Cambridge, MA: MIT Press, 2007); M. Taylor Fravel and Evan S. Medeiros, "China's Search for Assured Retaliation: The Evolution of Chinese Nuclear Strategy and Force Structure," *International Security* 35, no. 2 (2010): 48–87.

2. For example, Nina Tannenwald, *The Nuclear Taboo: The United States and the Non-use of Nuclear Weapons since 1945* (Cambridge: Cambridge University Press, 2008).

3. For an argument along these lines about differences in the relative likelihood of nuclear testing between military- and civilian-controlled nuclear programs, see Jacques E. C. Hymans, "When Does a State Become a 'Nuclear Weapon State'? An Exercise in Measurement Validation," *Nonproliferation Review* 17, no. 1 (2010): 161–180.

4. On the merits of strategic approaches to studying international politics, see David A. Lake and Robert Powell, eds., *Strategic Choice and International Relations* (Princeton, NJ: Princeton University Press, 1999).

5. For examples, see Austin Long and Brendan Rittenhouse Green, "Stalking the Secure Second Strike: Intelligence, Counterforce, and Nuclear Strategy," *Journal of Strategic Studies* 38, nos. 1–2 (2015): 38–73; Keir A. Lieber and Daryl G. Press, "The New Era of Counterforce: Technological Change and the Future of Nuclear Deterrence," *International Security* 41, no. 4 (2017): 9–49; Brendan Rittenhouse Green and Austin Long, "The MAD Who Wasn't There: Soviet Reactions to the Late Cold War Strategic Balance," *Security Studies* 26, no. 4 (2017): 606–641; Matthew Kroenig, *The Logic of American Nuclear Strategy: Why Strategic Superiority Matters* (Oxford: Oxford University Press, 2018); Mark S. Bell, "Nuclear Opportunism: A Theory of How States Use Nuclear Weapons in International Politics," *Journal of Strategic Studies* 42, no. 1 (2019): 3–28; Brendan Rittenhouse Green, *The Revolution That Failed: Nuclear Competition, Arms Control, and the Cold War* (Cambridge: Cambridge University Press, 2020); Keir A. Lieber and Daryl G. Press, *The Myth of the Nuclear Revolution: Power Politics in the Atomic Age* (Ithaca, NY: Cornell University Press, 2020).

6. For similar points on the importance of incorporating heterogeneity into our understanding of nuclear proliferation and nuclear crises, see Mark S. Bell, "Examining Explanations for Nuclear Proliferation," *International Studies Quarterly* 60, no. 3 (2016): 520–529; Mark S. Bell

and Julia Macdonald, "How to Think about Nuclear Crises," *Texas National Security Review* 2, no. 2 (2019): 40–64.

7. Richard K. Betts, "The New Threat of Mass Destruction," *Foreign Affairs* 77, no. 1 (1998): 27; T. V. Paul, "Great Equalizers or Agents of Chaos? Weapons of Mass Destruction and the Emerging International Order," in *International Order and the Future of World Politics*, ed. T. V. Paul and John A. Hall (Cambridge: Cambridge University Press, 1999): 373–392. This view is also implicit in the work of S. Paul Kapur, since he argues that weak states are the ones that benefit from nuclear acquisition.

8. See, for example, Nicholas L. Miller, "Nuclear Dominoes: A Self-Defeating Prophecy?," *Security Studies* 23, no. 1 (2014): 33–73; Nicholas L. Miller, "The Secret Success of Nonproliferation Sanctions," *International Organization* 68, no. 4 (2014): 913–944; Nicholas L. Miller, *Stopping the Bomb: The Sources and Effectiveness of U.S. Nonproliferation Policy* (Ithaca, NY: Cornell University Press, 2018); Or Rabinowitz, *Bargaining on Nuclear Tests: Washington and Its Cold War Deals* (Oxford: Oxford University Press, 2014); Matthew Kroenig, "Force or Friendship? Explaining Great Power Nonproliferation Policy," *Security Studies* 23, no. 1 (2014): 1–32; Gene Gerzhoy, "Alliance Coercion and Nuclear Restraint: How the United States Thwarted West Germany's Nuclear Ambitions," *International Security* 39, no. 4 (2015): 91–129; Francis J. Gavin, "Strategies of Inhibition: U.S. Grand Strategy, the Nuclear Revolution, and Nonproliferation," *International Security* 40, no. 1 (2015): 9–46; Andrew Coe and Jane Vaynman, "Superpower Collusion and the Nuclear Nonproliferation Treaty," *Journal of Politics* 77, no. 4 (2015): 983–997.

9. For example, Kenneth N. Waltz, "The Spread of Nuclear Weapons: More May Be Better," *Adelphi Papers* 21, no. 171 (1981): 1–32.

10. Glenn H. Snyder, "The Balance of Power and the Balance of Terror," in *Balance of Power*, ed. Paul Seabury (San Francisco: Chandler, 1965): 184–201.

11. For example, Matthew Kroenig, "Nuclear Superiority and the Balance of Resolve: Explaining Nuclear Crisis Outcomes," *International Organization* 67, no. 1 (2013): 141–171; Todd S. Sechser and Matthew Fuhrmann, "Crisis Bargaining and Nuclear Blackmail," *International Organization* 67, no. 1 (2013): 173–195. See also Bell and Macdonald, "How to Think about Nuclear Crises."

12. For example, John Mueller, *Atomic Obsession: Nuclear Alarmism from Hiroshima to Al Qaeda* (Oxford: Oxford University Press, 2010); Sechser and Fuhrmann, "Crisis Bargaining and Nuclear Blackmail."

13. For example, Kyle Beardsley and Victor Asal, "Winning with the Bomb," *Journal of Conflict Resolution* 53, no. 2 (2009): 278–301; Kroenig, "Nuclear Superiority and the Balance of Resolve."

14. See, for example, Hymans, "When Does a State Become a 'Nuclear Weapon State'?" Many quantitative codings for when states acquire nuclear weapons also rely heavily on the date of a first nuclear test. See, for example, the codings used in Sonali Singh and Christopher R. Way, "The Correlates of Nuclear Proliferation: A Quantitative Test," *Journal of Conflict Resolution* 48, no. 6 (2004): 859–885; Dong-Joon Jo and Erik Gartzke, "Determinants of Nuclear Weapons Proliferation," *Journal of Conflict Resolution* 51, no. 1 (2007): 167–194.

15. For example, Mueller, *Atomic Obsession*, 95–99.

Index

Note: Page numbers in italics refer to figures.

Lightning Source UK Ltd.
Milton Keynes UK
UKHW012046110321
380188UK00001B/74